BLACK BRASS

BLACK GENERALS AND ADMIRALS IN THE
ARMED FORCES OF THE UNITED STATES

Second Edition

Henry E. Dabbs

HOWELL PRESS
Charlottesville, Virginia

Edited by Ross A. Howell, Jr., Katherine A. Neale, Jamie L. Bronner, and Natalie Gehl
Designed by
C. Mayapriya Long, Bookwrights

First published in 1984 by African-American Heritage House.
Second edition copyright ©1997 by Henry E. Dabbs.
All rights reserved.

Printed in Canada
Published by Howell Press, Inc., 1147 River Road, Suite 2,
Charlottesville, Virginia 22901.
Telephone (804) 977-4006
First Printing

Library of Congress Cataloging-in-Publication Data
Dabbs, Henry.
Black brass : black generals and admirals in the armed forces of the United States / Henry Dabbs. – 2nd ed.
     p.   cm.
Includes bibliographical references and index.
1st ed. Published as A first edition reference work on Black brass.
ISBN: 1-57427-047-8.
     1.   Afro-American generals—Biography. 2. Afro-American admirals—
           Biography. 3.
Generals—United States—Biography. 4. Admirals—United States—Biography. 5. United States—Armed forces—Biography. 6. United States—Armed forces—Afro Americans. I. Title.

U52.D33 1996   355'.0089'96073
                                                                    QBI96-20073

HOWELL PRESS

Dedicated to

Loretta and Lisa

CONTENTS

PHOTOGRAPHS

(listed in order of appearance)

PREFACE

The second edition of *Black Brass* is a follow-up to the precedent-setting first edition, which was the first of its genre in the history of print. Up to that time, there had been books which included Black General Officers within the context of a larger format, but none before *Black Brass* were dedicated exclusively to the study of the Black General Officer. The first edition of *Black Brass* was the most comprehensive study of the role of the Black General Officer in the history of American publishing. This second edition is no less formidable!

It is divided into four main sections. The first section is introductory in nature, encompassing an historical perspective of the Black commander tradition as well as an historical survey of Black Americans in the military in general, and Black Officers in particular. The second section is a dedication to officers who were pioneers in United States military history.

The third section, which is the main body of text, is sub-divided into four sections focusing on the Black General Officer in the Army, Navy, Air Force, and Marine Corps. It is a sequential listing, beginning with the highest ranking General Officer. Each sub-division is in alphabetical order according to rank. (In some cases, where there were not a photographs available, the biographies are placed at the end of that respective section in alphabetical order. This was done to maintain aesthetic continuity.) Retired officers follow each active officer section alphabetically according to rank.

At the end of the Air Force sub-division is a listing of General Officers whose status is other than regular/retired (i.e., National Guard, retired). For the Naval designation, the specific Admiralty rank precedes the name of each of the flag rank officers. Rear Admiral, Lower Half, has replaced the rank of Commodore (one star), and the designation Lower Half, Selectee, means that the said officer has been recommended for the rank of Admiral but is awaiting congressional approval. The rank of Rear Admiral, Lower Half, is one rank behind that of Rear Admiral (two stars).

The fourth section of this work consists of a chronology of major events in Black military history (1492-1995); Black Congressional Medal of Honor recipients (Civil War to present); and a selected bibliography.

As to the sociological implications of this work today, Black Americans and Americans at large can take pride in the fact that there has been progress made; Blacks have paid dearly, but there has been progress. Nowhere is it more evident than in the military. And that is what this book is all about, Black achievers. The men and women profiled in this book are people of great ability. They possess the talent that would have taken them to the top of any chosen profession, if it were not for the fact that they are Black.

The armed forces, America's largest corporation, at this point in time, has offered a better opportunity for Blacks to advance to the top of the corporate ladder than its civilian counterpart. Obviously, Black executives have the ability to run America's Fortune 500 corporations; they simply have not been given the opportunity.

That is not to say that there is no room for improvement in the military; obviously, past history indicates otherwise. However, since General Benjamin Oliver Davis, Sr., America's first Black general, received his star in 1940, until General Colin L. Powell was appointed the twelfth Chairman of the Joint Chiefs of Staff by President Bush, a great deal of progress has been made, as witnessed by the historical significance of this event. On October 1, 1989, at age fifty-three, General Powell became the youngest Chairman of the Joint Chiefs of Staff ever, and the first African-American ever to hold the most powerful and prestigious position in the American military, the most awesome force on the earth. Corporate America can boast no such record.

The policy of discrimination based on race is specious to begin with since it is a scientific fact that there is only one race—the human race! Attaching colors to people of different ethnic backgrounds is just another device to divide them—to perpetuate an artificial difference. Although the battle to eradicate discrimination from every aspect of this nation's life is far from over, the equal opportunity policies of the military are beginning to have a positive impact.

We are now at the dawn of the twenty-first century. Young African-Americans must rededicate themselves with personal pride, hard work, and commitment to excellence so that they are intellectually prepared to take advantage of the opportunities and promise that this, the greatest of all nations on earth has to offer in the coming century.

At this writing, all branches of the military have stated emphatically with words and deeds that they are continuing their commitment to full equality for all members of the armed forces of the United States of America.

Henry E. Dabbs
Orlando, Florida
1997

ACKNOWLEDGMENTS

The author and publisher wish to thank the following who have kindly given permission for the use of copyright material: The Loeb Classical Library (William Heinemann Ltd.: Harvard University Press) for extracts from the Foster translation of *Livy* and the Patton translation of *Polybius*; Penguin Books Ltd., for an extract from *Juvenal: The Sixteen Satires*, translated by Peter Green (Penguin Classics, revised edition, 1974). Copyright © Peter Green 1967, 1974; Tuesday Publications, Inc., for *Black Heroes in World History.* New York: Bantam Books, 1966; Beacon Press for an extract from *Army Life in a Black Regiment* (Appendix E, Farewell Address of Lt. Col. Throwbridge) by Thomas Wentworth Higginson; and Doubleday & Company, Inc., for an extract of a letter sent to *The New Era* by Cadet James W. Smith, taken from the *Black West* by William Loren Katz. Copyright 1971, © 1973 by William Loren Katz. Reprinted by permission of Doubleday & Company, Inc.

Just as in my first edition of *Black Brass*, this second edition could not have been possible without the help of many other wonderful people. It is an honor and a pleasure to express my appreciation to all those who assisted me in bringing this work to fruition. My thanks are extended to the Schomberg Collection of the New York Public Library; the Library of Congress Manuscript Division; National Archives of the United States, U.S. War Records Office; the offices of: VADM J. Paul Reason, RDML Edward Moore, Jr., RDML(S) David L. Brewer, RDML(S) Everett L. Greene, RDML Anthony J. Watson, VADM Walter J. Davis, Jr., RDML(S) Osie "V" Combs, Jr., RDML(S) Larry L. Poe, and RDMLM Eugene Fussell for their help in supplying me with photos.

I would also like to thank the following departments: Navy Department Bureau of Naval Personnel, Washington, DC; General Officer Management Office, Chief of Staff, 200 Army Pentagon, Washington, DC; Department of Navy, Headquarters, U.S. Marine Corps (PA), Washington, DC; AFGOMO, 1040 Air Force Pentagon; Department of the Navy, PO 70, Space and Naval Warfare Systems Command, Washington, DC; Department of the Navy, Commander, Navy Recruiting Command, Arlington, Virginia; Department of the Navy, Navy Media Center, Naval Station, Anacostia Building 168, Washington, DC; Geraldine K. Harcarik, Archivist, Historical Resources Branch; and Mary Haynes, U.S. Army Center of Military History, Washington, DC, is owed a special salute for her valuable comments and suggestions on how to cut through the red tape. And last but not least, I owe a special thanks to my wife Loretta who encouraged me to once again put my feet to the fire and write this second edition. Thank you, sweetheart!

INTRODUCTION

On February 26, 1982, seventy (seventy-six were invited) Black Flag and General Officers gathered in Washington, DC, to participate in activities honoring their accomplishments. Mayor Marion Barry declared that day, "Black Flag and General Officer Day." At a reception later that evening, Secretary of Defense Casper Weinberger and several other dignitaries spoke, singing the praises of these officers. It was a gala affair.

Over half of the officers who attended were retired. Among those not retired were Lieutenant General Robinson, U.S. Army (soon to be announced as the first Black four-star Army general), and Brigadier General Hazel W. Johnson, U.S. Army, Director of the Army Nurse Corps. Remembered, although deceased, were Brigadier General Benjamin O. Davis, U.S. Army, Brigadier General "Rock" Cartwright, U.S. Army, and General Daniel "Chappie" James, Jr., U.S. Air Force. Brigadier General Benjamin O. Davis would have represented the first Black U.S. General and General Daniel "Chappie" James, Jr., the first Black four-star U.S. General. When one thinks of all the military talent in that room, one can only wonder how this great country of ours could have willfully denied similar Black men in earlier generations the opportunity to rise to the top of their profession. The reason was obvious—the military was not a profession which encouraged or desired Black participation in officer ranks.

World War II changed this for all the services as the Navy and Marine Corps commissioned their first Black officers. The integration of the armed forces by presidential directive in 1948, had an even greater impact. The civilian unrest of the fifties and sixties, coupled with several incidents in the services, affected the military as much or more than any other sector of American life. The military took a new look at Black officers and quickly jumped on the integration "bandwagon." Similarly, the Black officers took a new look at the services. Their talents were being sought—they gained new respect, new opportunities, new responsibilities, and new rank. It was still an uphill battle, which they fought and won. Ultimately, through perseverance, performance, and untiring devotion, they reached the stars.

This book, *Black Brass*, is a compilation of the biographies of these officers. It also lists, in detail, a chronology of Black military history since the founding of this country. Mr. Dabbs has rendered a valuable service to the people of this country by compiling these biographies and historical facts under one cover.

S.L. Gravely, Jr.
Vice Admiral
U.S. Navy (Retired)

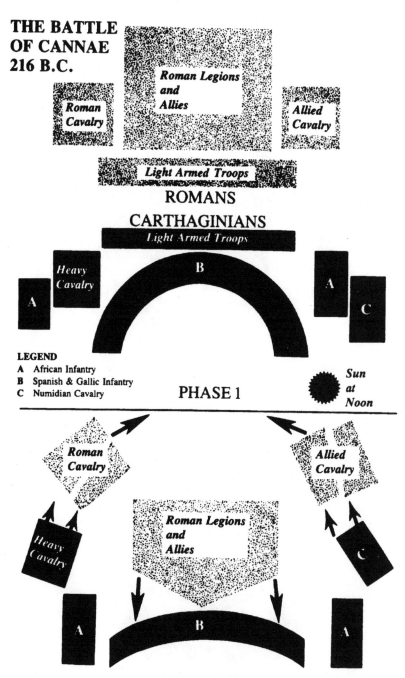

THE BATTLE OF CANNAE 216 B.C.

Roman Cavalry

Roman Legions and Allies

Allied Cavalry

Light Armed Troops

ROMANS

CARTHAGINIANS

Light Armed Troops

Heavy Cavalry

B

A

A

C

LEGEND
A   African Infantry
B   Spanish & Gallic Infantry
C   Numidian Cavalry

PHASE 1

Sun at Noon

Roman Cavalry

Allied Cavalry

Heavy Cavalry

Roman Legions and Allies

C

A

B

A

PHASE 2

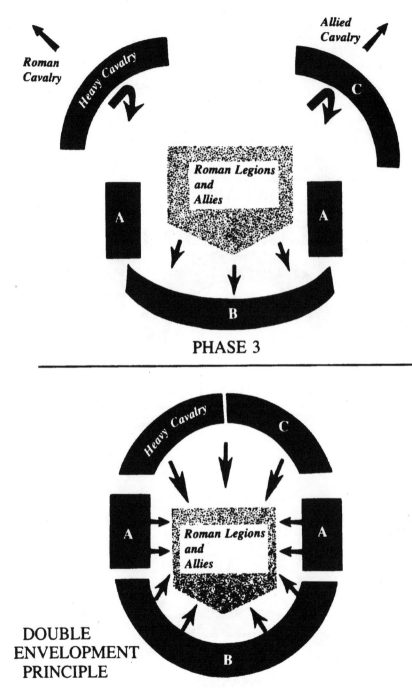

PHASE 3

DOUBLE
ENVELOPMENT
PRINCIPLE

PHASE 4

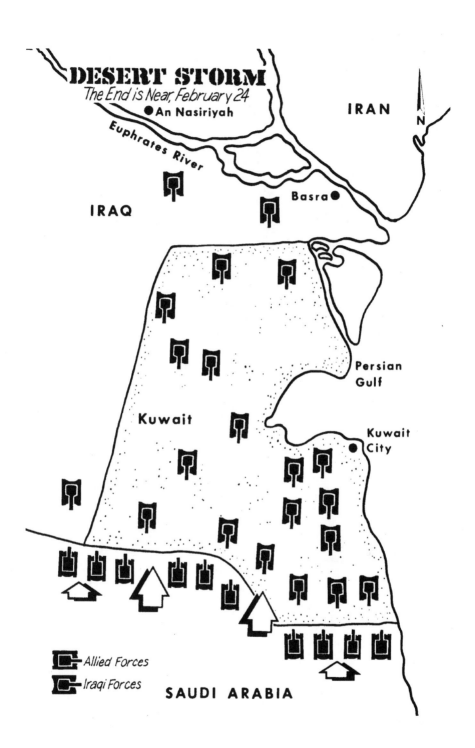

DESERT STORM
The End is Near, February 24

●An Nasiriyah

IRAN

N

Euphrates River

IRAQ

Basra●

Persian
Gulf

Kuwait

Kuwait
City

Allied Forces
Iraqi Forces

SAUDI ARABIA

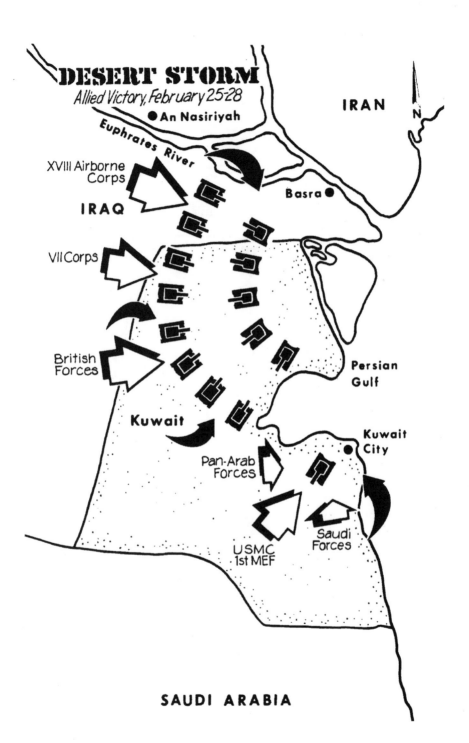

DESERT STORM
Allied Victory, February 25-28

● An Nasiriyah

Euphrates River

IRAN

N

XVIII Airborne Corps

IRAQ

Basra ●

VII Corps

British Forces

Persian Gulf

Kuwait

Kuwait City

Pan-Arab Forces

USMC 1st MEF

Saudi Forces

SAUDI ARABIA

PROLOGUE

The Black commander tradition did not begin with the Black generals and admirals presented in this work. Instead, it stretches back to the dawn of history. Back to Egypt, an African civilization, where Black Pharaohs ruled one of the greatest nations yet conceived by mankind: the civilization that gave birth to Greece and Rome. Dressed for battle, Black Pharaohs like Thotmes III and Seti poised upon swift chariots drawn by Hyksos horses, led their men into battle, hurling themselves at the enemy like armored vehicles. They formed a screen, behind which the infantry, armed with spears, bows, and axes, could advance and annihilate the enemy.

Down through the ages, the Black commander tradition persists. Again, the continent is Africa. The city: Carthage, in North Africa. From this city in Black Africa would rise the most brilliant military genius of all time. His name—Hannibal. The greatest of the great in the art of war, Hannibal is considered to be the father of military strategy. He annihilated several Roman armies, one of which was the largest Rome ever fielded—102,000 men. In battle after battle, wielding his weapon of strategic and tactical brilliance, he defeated Roman armies with almost contemptuous ease. For fifteen years, with the exception of Rome itself, Hannibal dominated Italy from Naples to the Alps. Livy,[1] the Roman historian, writing about Hannibal at the battle of Cannae, sums up the results in this manner:

> The year before, a Consul and his army had been lost at Trasimene, and now it was not merely one blow following another, but a calamity many times as great as before…. There was no longer any Roman camp or general, or soldier. Hannibal was master of Apulia, Samnium and well nigh the whole of Italy.

---

[1] Livy, born in Padua in 59 B.C., devoted himself to a history of Rome. His history is invaluable because of the details it has preserved. Livy's work survives in several manuscripts, the oldest of which dates from the tenth century. Livy frequently quoted Lucius Coelius Antipater, Polybius, and Timagenes of Alexandria (a historian-geographer who came to Rome in 54 B.C.)

Livy spent more than forty years writing his *Historia Ab Urbe Condita* (*History from the Founding of the City*). This master work originally consisted of 142 books, of which only thirty-five are extant. Livy, whose real name was Titus Livius, died in A.D. 17.

Born in 247 B.C., Hannibal was the son of General Hamiclar Barca. Livy wrote that Hannibal was fearless, indefatigable, utterly prudent in danger, able to endure heat or cold, controlled in eating habits, unpretentious in dress, and willing to sleep on the ground, wrapped only in his cloak. A superb horseman, he was always by far the first in the ranks of both cavalry and infantry—foremost to enter a battle, he was the last to leave once it had begun.

In May 218 B.C., Hannibal left Southern Spain (a Carthaginian colony) with an army of eighty-two thousand men, ten thousand horses, and thirty-seven mammoth elephants and their mahouts. This was a heterogeneous, multiracial army consisting of Africans, Arabs, Spaniards, Greeks, and Celts. They marched six abreast and stretched for more than twelve miles across the Iberian landscape. After several months of bloody fighting across Spain and France, Hannibal finally reached the Alps. He had traveled nearly fifteen hundred treacherous miles. With only sixty thousand of his original force remaining, he accomplished the astounding feat of traversing the Alps and descending on Rome.

According to Polybius[2], who had been at Lacinium, Hannibal's personal account of the crossing reveals that upon reaching Italian soil at the foot of the Alps, the leader had only thirty thousand men and not more than six thousand horses. The Pyrenees and the Alps had taken a heavy toll. Livy adds another interesting facet to the feat accomplished by Hannibal's descent into Italy. During the bone-wearing, bloody crossing, a rockslide barred the path of the army along a treacherous, narrow mountain pass. Hannibal ordered trees felled. His soldiers built a huge pile of logs over the rocks, set the logs on fire, and poured vinegar over the glowing rocks, causing them to crumble. Hannibal's army moved on.

At one point, before making the final descent, Hannibal paused with his weary army. Livy described it this way:

---

[2] Born in Arcadia in 202 B.C., Polybius was a contemporary of Hannibal. In fact, his life overlapped Hannibal's by twenty years. He also lived in the household of Consul Aemilius Paullus, one of the commanders of the Roman Army at the Battle of Cannae. Polybius was not only a military historian, he was also a soldier and served as a cavalry general in Greece. (It was he who had the honor of carrying the urn containing the ashes of Philopoemen, the last great soldier of classical Greece at his funeral in 183 B.C.) Considered by many as one of the greatest military historians of antiquity because of his balanced, critical approach, Polybius made the journey over the Alps in Hannibal's footsteps (about sixty years after the actual event) to satisfy himself about the details of the crossing. Other lesser-known historians include Sosilos, who tutored Hannibal in Greek and wrote about his life; Silenos, who accompanied the Carthenigian Army (translated by the Roman historian Lucius Coelius Antipater); and Lucius Cincius Alimentus, who was taken prisoner by Hannibal and learned the figures of the losses suffered crossing the Alps from Hannibal himself. Polybius died in 122 B.C.

The soldiers, worn with toil and fighting, were permitted to rest; a number of baggage animals, which had fallen among rocks, made their way to the camp by following the tracks of the army. Exhausted and discouraged as the soldiers were by many hardships, a snow-storm—for the Pleiades was now setting—threw them into a great fear. The ground was everywhere covered deep with snow when at dawn they began to march, and as the column moved slowly on, de-jection and despair were to be read on every countenance. Then Hannibal, who had gone on before the standards, made the army halt on a certain promontory which commanded an extensive pros-pect, and pointing out Italy to them, and just under the Alps the plains about the Po, he told them that they were not scaling the ramparts not only of Italy, but of Rome itself; the rest of the way would be level or downhill; and after one, or at least two battles, they would have in their hands and in their power the citadel and capital of Italy.

Once in Italy, courage and initiative were all that Hannibal had left. The mountains were behind him, and in front of him, the Romans. Hannibal knew his situation was desperate, but if he acknowledged how desperate, in fact ridiculous, his situation was, he might have been tempted to go back over the Alps. Here was his band of battle-weary, half-starved men, thousands of miles from home, in direct confrontation with the mightiest military power on earth. According to Polybius, Rome at that time had more than a million fighting men: 250,000 infantry; 25,000 cavalry; and auxiliaries of 770,000 infantry and cavalry.

The Romans, for their part, could not help but admire the Africans for their astounding feat, but they also knew how vulnerable they were to attack. No one knew it better than Publius Cornelius Scipio, the Roman commander, who said to his men:

These Africans are but the resemblances, nay, rather the shadows of men, being worn-out with hunger, cold, dirt, and filth, and bruised and enfeebled among stones and rocks. Their joints are frost-bitten; their sinews stiffened with the snow; their limbs withered by the frost; their armour battered and shivered; their horses, lame and power-less. With such cavalry, which such infantry you will have to fight; indeed you will not have enemies in reality, but rather their last re-mains.

Moreover, we have beaten these miserable Carthanigians by land and sea often before. Now they have had the temerity to cross the Alps. But they won't be strong enough to return over it. We have them in a trap. What I do fear is that victory is going to be so cheap that the world is not going to give us credit for it.

Thus spoke Scipio. Hannibal, always the great commander, assembled his men on the eve of battle and told them that he had fulfilled his promise to lead them to plunder such as no army had ever seen before and that it was now up to them to seize it or die in the attempt. He said, "Behind you are the Alps; before you, the Romans and the river. Your only hope is battle and victory. And victory will not be difficult. Think of the splendid and prosperous career before you. It will conduct you to Rome, second in wealth only to Carthage. There are great treasures to be divided amongst us, if we win. If we lose we are lost, for there is noplace of safety we can reach by flight. We must win!"

Hannibal, the master psychologist, never gave a greater performance. He had the capacity to make men believe in themselves, to reach down and find a hidden reserve of strength, that necessary edge. His army fought like beings possessed. They fought with a fury that only desperate men know.

Hannibal's army first met and defeated two consular armies consisting of forty thousand men, led by Publius Cornelius Scipio and Sempronius at the battle of Trebia in 218 B.C. The Second Punic War had begun. At Trebia, Hannibal utilized for one of the first times in the recorded history of warfare, the principle of calculated shock force. His elephants were used tactically to terrorize the Romans. Then his infantry and cavalry moved in and cut the Romans to pieces, taking thousands of prisoners and a huge cache of arms.

The next year at the battle of Trasimene, 217 B.C., Hannibal went up against Consul Flaminius, one of Rome's ablest generals. Again the Romans were outgeneraled by the incredible Hannibal. It was a triumph of strategy and tactical planning. Fifteen thousand Romans and their allies died in the battle, and a similar number were taken prisoner. Hannibal lost only fifteen hundred men. The road to Rome lay open. These battles, however, were only the preliminaries for the main event, which would take place the following year at Cannae.

To have some appreciation of the debt that the modern military world owes Hannibal, one must realize that the nine Principles of War—objective, offensive, simplicity, unit of command, mass, economy of force, maneuver, surprise, and security—which govern the prosecution of war by the United States Armed Forces, the most sophisticated war machine the world has ever seen, were used brilliantly by Hannibal at the Battle of Cannae more than two hundred years before the birth of Christ! The battle is worth a close look so that the reader can fully appreciate the measure of the man.

By the spring of 216 B.C., Hannibal had bypassed Rome and was encamped on the Adriatic, southeast of the capital. Plans were being laid to annihilate him. In June, the Romans moved eight legions into camp, facing Hannibal's army. Each legion carried as its standard the silver eagle with streamers. The day of the battle, eight silver eagles peered majestically over the field, their streamers fluttering gently on the hot June breeze. Beneath these eagles was assembled the most massive army Rome ever fielded. The battle was about to be joined. Hannibal's staff consisted of a small, brilliant, hardcore group of experienced professionals: General Gisgo, Hanno, Mago (Hannibal's youngest brother), Hasdrubal (his older brother), and Maharbal (the incomparable leader of the Numidian cavalry, the finest horsemen in the world). Hannibal's army consisted of forty thousand infantry and ten thousand cavalry. The Romans, terrible in battle, conquerors of the known world, were hard, steel-disciplined fighting men, weapons of the state. Each Roman soldier trained ten hours a day for five years to earn the title of soldier. These were machine-men with swords.

The legions were ably commanded by Consuls Servius, Paullus, and Varro, magnificently dressed in plumed helmets, splendidly molded breastplates, and rich, flowing capes. According to Polybius, each legion was made up of about six thousand men "apart from allies;" therefore, forty-eight thousand Romans were in the field. Each legion was divided into ten cohorts of six hundred men each. In every legion, the first cohort comprised the bravest and most experienced legionnaires, the cream of the legion. As was the custom in that age, the legions were accompanied by an equal number of allies. Hannibal's army of fifty thousand was going up against a Roman army of ninety-six thousand infantry and six thousand cavalry.

From the beginning, the Romans argued among themselves over which tactics to employ. Paullus argued that the terrain favored Hannibal's cavalry. Varro disagreed and overruled Paullus. This was to prove to be a tragic miscalculation. The Romans made the first move, line upon line, bristling with weapons. Slowly, majestically, they moved toward the Carthaginians. Hannibal elected to deploy his Numidian cavalry on his right flank and the heavy brigades on his left, next to the river. He placed half his main body of African infantry alongside the heavy brigade. In the center, which he commanded, he placed the largest body of his troops; the other half of his African infantry was deployed to the right, on the inside of the Numidian cavalry. Commanding in the center with him was his brother Mago, Hanno commanded the right flank, Hasdrubal led the left flank, and the dashing Maharbal commanded the Numidian cavalry.

Hannibal's cavalry was made up of two basic units which were still in use centuries later: the light brigade and the heavy brigade. The light brigade was made up of Numidians from North Africa; they were used to probe opposing lines and create situations that the heavy brigade and infantry could exploit.

The space between the armies now closed to several hundred yards. The Romans were advancing, machinelike, locked in their conventional formation that had brought them victory on so many battlefields before. But they were not up against a conventional general; they were up against Hannibal, a general who created a new tactic for each new battlefield he strode upon. Roman cavalry was also predictably deployed on each flank. In the center was the main body of the legions; the reluctant Paullus commanded the cavalry and Varro led the allied cavalry. As the armies closed on one another, the center of the Carthaginian army had formed a strange C shape with the cusp facing the enemy.

A detachment of Hannibal's light cavalry probed the front of the Roman lines, then retreated back to the safety of the main body. On the left, Hannibal's heavy cavalry opened with a ferocious attack upon the Roman cavalry and swept the enemy before them. Exploiting the successful onslaught, the heavy cavalry swept through the openings and wheeled right. Meanwhile, on the right, Maharbal's Numidians were making maximum use of the flat terrain, attacking in undulating waves, with lightning-like swiftness, systematically picking the Roman allied cavalry apart. In the center, the cusp of the C, imperceptibly at first, slowly gave way under the relentless force of the Roman infantry pressing at its center. Hannibal's heavy cavalry continued to close on the Roman main body.

The Numidians on the right flank had routed the allied cavalry and scattered it in confusion. In the center, the Hannibal-led main body was locked in a deathlike embrace with Rome's finest warriors. Both sides fought with ferocity and abandon. The gallant Romans continued to exploit their seeming success, slowly driving the Carthaginian C back into a U formation. The African infantry, now on both flanks of the Roman main body, waited. On a signal from Hannibal, trumpets sounded. The trap was about to be sprung. The daring stroke of genius which was the signature of this great commander was about to be written…in blood.

At the sound of the trumpets, the Carthaginian cavalry commanded by Hasdrubal and the Numidian Horse led by Maharbal wheeled about in unison and closed at a gallop on the Romans' rear flanks, left and right. The earth trembled under the hoofbeats of thousands of Carthaginian mounted cavalry as they made their terrible charge. Hannibal's masterful tactic of double envelopment, which had never been used in the history of warfare until this very moment, was about to change the tide of military history. Now was the time for the heavily armed veteran African troops on the left and right flanks, who up until this time had been no more than interested spectators, to make their move. And move they did. The terrified Romans found themselves surrounded by a moving wall of steel, closing in on all sides. The carnage was horrendous. It was complete. The Romans were decimated.

In one afternoon, Hannibal's army inflicted more casualties upon the Roman army than any other single battle in recorded history! Greek historian Polybius puts the total loss of Romans at seventy thousand. The total of seventy thousand men killed is just under a third of all American casualties in the four years of World War II. Yet the Battle of Cannae lasted only a few hours! Hannibal lost about four thousand Gauls, eighteen hundred Spaniards and Africans, and two hundred cavalry.

Hannibal was more than just a great commander. His influence upon later generations is as great as that of Alexander. His example of government by direct personal example demonstrated to the world the method of governing a polyglot nation efficiently. And it was Black Hannibal who taught the Romans the art of building and deploying an army. Today's modern U.S. Army owes its concept of leadership, officers' code of conduct, tactics, and strategy primarily to Hannibal. Is it any wonder that Hannibal's tactics are still taught in military academies throughout the world?

Juvenal's *Satires*, written in the first century, point out that even three hundred years after Hannibal's death, the specter of the great Black Carthaginian was stamped indelibly on the Roman consciousness:

Now Spain swells his empire, now he surmounts
The Pyrenees. Nature throws in his path
High Alpine passes, blizzard of snow; but he splits
The very rocks asunder, moves mountains with vinegar.
Now Italy is his, yet still he forces on:
"We have accomplished nothing, 'til we have stormed
The gates of Rome, till our Carthaginian standard
Is set in the city's heart."

Never in the history of warfare has one individual possessed in such abundant quantities the originality of thought, the skill, the daring, the intellect, and the faculty of command as did Hannibal. Above the vast, mystic expanse of the receding plains of the centuries looms the imposing image of Hannibal, the greatest of the great at the art of war.

Napoleon, after selecting the seven supreme military geniuses of all time, ranked Hannibal first. He said:

And this Hannibal, the most audacious of all; the most astonishing, perhaps; so bold, so sure, so great in everything; who at twenty-six conceived what is hardly conceivable, executed what one may truly call the impossible.

During Napoleon's reign, there were at least a dozen West Indian and Black generals serving on his staff. One of them, Gen. Thomas Alexandre Dumas (1762-1806), was at one time Napoleon's superior. Gen. Dumas was the son of a French nobleman, the Marquis de la Pailleterie, who settled in St. Domingue, now Haiti, and married a Black woman Marie Dumas, who later became Madame la Marquise.

General Dumas rose through the ranks from sergeant to general in chief. Anatole France was so fascinated by the story of the dashing commander of Napoleon's cavalry that he dubbed him "Alexandre the Greatest."

General Dumas fought under Napoleon in Italy. During the Mantua Campaign, he commanded the First Division. For his heroic efforts at the bridge of Clausen in the Tyrol, where he single-handedly held off an entire squadron of Austrians, Napoleon named him "Horaticus Cocles of the Tyrol." (Horaticus

Cocles was a legendary Roman hero celebrated for his defense of the bridge over the Tiber against the Etruscans.) General Dumas's strength and courage were legendary. While he was with the Army of the Alps, he scaled the heights of Mont-Cenis with three thousand men and captured that crucial point. His combat record against the Austrians was so awesome that Napoleon had a national medal struck in his honor, sent him a brace of pistols made in Versailles as a souvenir, and appointed him Governor of Treviso, Italy.

In the Egyptian campaign, General Dumas was commander of Napoleon's cavalry. Among those serving under him were two of Napoleon's brothers-in-law, Joachim Murat and Charles Victor Emmanuel Leclerc. General Dumas distinguished himself at the Battle of the Pyramids and in the taking of the Grand Mosque. In 1793, he was Commander in Chief of Napoleon's Republican Armies.

The General's son was the famed French novelist, Alexandre Dumas, author of such classics as *The Three Musketeers* and *The Count of Monte Cristo*. His grandson was Alexandre Dumas, the foremost French dramatist of the nineteenth century, whose works include the masterpiece *Camille*, a role that has been played by world-famous actresses such as Sarah Bernhardt and Greta Garbo.

General Dumas's statue stands in the Place Malsherbes in Paris, close to those of his son and grandson. The French nation also honored General Dumas by enshrining his name on the Arc de Triomphe, an honor she reserves for her immortals.

Gen. Joachim Murat (1771-1815) was recognized as one of the most spectacular handlers of cavalry in the history of warfare. He was born in Lot, in the Auvergne, France, an area settled by the descendants of the Moors after they were driven out of Spain. General Murat himself claimed descent from a Moorish king, and historian Fredrick Mason, an authority on Napoleon's cavalry, stated that it is commonly held that Murat was of that ancestry. His intimate acquaintance, Laura, Duchess d'Abrantes, described him as *metis*, meaning mulatto.

So great was his gift of leadership, which was displayed in a hundred or so battles, that his men vested him with invincibility. Murat always led in battle, conspicuous in his dashing uniform of velvet and gold, with a flowing white plume mounted on his helmet. He was said to use only two words in a battle—"Forward!" and "Charge!" Napoleon made him General in 1799, as a reward for defeating the Turks in Egypt. The Emperor's great victories at Austerlitz, Jena, and Friedland were due in large part to General Murat's superb deployment of cavalry. He became the second most powerful man in France. Napoleon's youngest sister, Marie Caroline, became his bride. For his many victories in battle, Napoleon named him, successively, Grand Duke of Berg and Cleves, Prince and Grand Admiral of France, and Marshal of France. Finally, Napoleon made General Murat King of Naples, after the ouster of the Bourbons. Naples, at the time, was one of the richest principalities in Europe.

Napoleon's other Black generals include: Gen. Jean Brillat Belly, adjutant general in Napoleon's army and delegate to the French Convention from Haiti; Gen. Andre Rigaud; Gen. Alexandre Petion; Gen. Magliore Pelage; Gen. Antoine Moline Chanlatte; Gen. François Henri Barthelmy; Gen. Vincent Anatole Mentor; Gen. Pierre Michel; Gen. Pierre Montaigne Villate; and Gen. Charles Louis Etienne.

Haiti's immortal nation builder, Gen. Toussaint L'Ouverture (1743-1803), was a master of guerrilla warfare and a brilliant tactician who transformed a disorganized mob of rebel slaves into a well-disciplined army that defeated the finest armies that England, France, and Spain could send against them. Born a slave in 1743 on the plantation of Count de Breda on the island of St. Domingue, he taught himself the rudiments of education, and forged the most powerful army in the West Indies during the eighteenth century. Because of General L'Ouverture's domination of Napoleon's armed expeditions, the power of France in the New World was broken. Napoleon did not have the men or materiel to constantly resupply his forces, who were defeated at every turn by General L'Ouverture's army. While his armed expeditions were in Haiti, Napoleon was thousands of miles away, commanding his army against the Austrians, who had occupied part of Northern Italy (1796-1797). After Italy, Napoleon invaded Egypt in 1798, moving even further from the New World. Napoleon did not return to France until 1799; by then, his forces in Haiti were decimated. This hastened the 1803 sale by France of the Louisiana Territory, which would comprise nearly half the area of the continental United States, for a meager financial consideration.

Wendell Phillips paid General L'Ouverture his ultimate tribute when he said:

> You think me a fanatic tonight, for you read history not with your eyes but with your prejudices. But fifty years hence when Truth gets a hearing the Muse of History will put Phocion for the Greeks, and Brutus for the Romans, Hampden for England, Fayette for France, choose Washington as the bright, consummate flower of our earliest civilization and John Brown, the ripe flower of our noon-day, then dipping her pen in the sunlight, will write in the clear blue above them all, the name of the soldier, the statesman, the martyr, Toussaint L'Ouverture!

"Conquer or die" was the inscription on each warrior's shield of Shaka the Great, King of the Zulus. Born in South Africa in 1786, he created the most formidable military nation on the African continent in the nineteenth century. Founder of the Zulu military system, Shaka built an army of more than seven hundred thousand men, about 150,000 of whom were warriors in constant readiness for battle. On an hour's notice, his troops could march fifty miles in a single day without a halt and "eat up" a town at the end of the march.

The army was divided into divisions and corps. Each division had a field marshal. Shaka's field marshals were Mziligazi, Manukuza, Qnetu, Mdlaka, and Mgobozi, chief of staff. Shaka, in less than three years, was able to conquer and unite an area three times the size of Europe. He was the military ruler of a nation of two million people.

The monolithic military entity Shaka the Great created was so powerful that it survived for years after his death. When his warriors came face-to-face with the imperial power of England in the late 1870s, they inflicted upon the British the worst defeat a modern army has ever suffered at the hands of a third world nation. Sir Henry Rider Haggard (1856-1925), writing about events in Africa in the nineteenth century, said of Shaka, "he was one of the most remarkable men who ever filled a throne since the days of the Pharaohs."

Gen. A. A. Dodds, a Senegalese, was one of France's best-known military men prior to World War I. The *New York Tribune*, dated April 17, 1910, stated that Dodds was so popular that he could easily have seized power in France:

> The entire nation irrespective of party or politics turned out to welcome him and to such an extent did he become an object of popular enthusiasm that there is no doubt that he might easily have established himself in the role of military dictator had it not been for his loyalty to the Republic.

Such was the praise for France's greatest colonial soldier of the twentieth century; Gen. A. A. Dodds, conqueror of Dahomey.

Capt. Sosthene H. Mortenol, commander of the Air Defense of Paris 1916-1918, was the military strategist who located and destroyed the German "Big Berthas" that bombarded Paris from a distance of sixty-eighty miles during World War I. His brilliant efforts at defending Paris led to Captain Sosthene being honored by the French government as commander of the Legion of Honor. The citation read:

> Superior officer of the highest merit. At his post day and night to watch over Paris. Performed with rare devotion and enlightened competence the function of the D.C.A. The Cross of Commander is the just recompense for a well-filled career and for excellent services rendered.

Other outstanding military commanders who held the same rank were Marshals Ferdinand Foch and Douglas Haig, and General John J. Pershing.

The Hour is at Hand

So nigh is grandeur to our dust
So near is God to man,
When duty whispers low, Thou must
The youth replies, I can.

— Ralph Waldo Emerson

In order to get the proper perspective on the accomplishments of today's Black general officers, one must have an understanding of the Black man's role in American military history. At this point, a brief historical survey is in order.

American Blacks fought in most major battles of the Revolutionary War including Lexington, Concord, Bunker Hill, Trenton, Long Island, Savannah, Valley Forge, and Yorktown. In the most serious prewar clash between Americans and the British, the Boston Massacre of 1770, the first to die for the cause of American independence was Crispus Attucks, a Black patriot. Black Americans served in a variety of capacities: as spies, pilots, infantrymen, laborers, cooks, and teamsters. Some were with the minutemen at Lexington and Concord; others wintered with Washington at Valley Forge and crossed the Delaware en route to surprising the Hessians quartered at Trenton. All told, between eight and ten thousand Blacks served in the colonial armies of the Revolution.

Black sailors fought in every sea engagement of the War of 1812. When Oliver Perry complained to his immediate superior, Commodore Isaac Chauncey, that he had been sent Black sailors as reinforcements before the Battle of Lake Erie in 1813, Chauncey replied: "I have yet to learn that the color of the skin or the cut and trimmings of the coat can affect a man's qualifications or usefulness. I have fifty Blacks on board this ship and many of them are my best men...."

The most famous battle of the war found "Old Hickory," Andrew Jackson, so hard pressed for troops that he was forced to issue a call for Black recruits. These Black recruits played an important role in Jackson's victory at the Battle of New Orleans.

After the battle, Jackson addressed the courageous Black soldiers. He said:

> To the men of color. Soldiers! From the shores of Mobile I collected you to arms—I invited you to share the perils and to divide the glory of your white countrymen. I expected much from you; for I was uninformed of those qualities which must render you so formidable to an invading foe. I knew that you could endure hunger and thirst and all the hardships of war. I knew that you loved the land of your nativity, and that, like ourselves, you had to defend all that is most dear to man. But you have surpassed my hopes. I have found in you, united to these qualities that noble enthusiasm which impels to great deeds.

It was not until July 17, 1862, that Congress authorized President Lincoln to employ "persons of African descent" in the military service of the United States. Besides the 187,000 combat troops, there were more than 202,000 members of the so-called service units (laborers, cooks, and teamsters). Organizationally, Black units were subdivided into 121 combat infantry regiments (close to one hundred thousand men), 7 cavalry regiments (over seven thousand men), 12 heavy artillery regiments (over twelve thousand men), and 10 companies of light artillery with over fourteen hundred men. These Black troops saw combat in more than two hundred battles.

How well the Black Soldier performed in the Civil War can be summed up in the farewell address of Lt. Col. Throwbridge of the Thirty-third United States Colored troops (formerly First South Carolina Volunteers), General Order, No. 1, dated February 9, 1866:

> Comrades—the hour is at hand when we must separate forever, and nothing can take from us the pride we feel, when we look back upon the history of the First South Carolina Volunteers—the first black regiment that ever bore arms in defense of freedom on the continent of America.
>
> On the ninth day of May, 1862, at which time there were nearly four million of your race in a bondage sanctioned by the laws of the land, and protected by our flag—on that day, in the face of floods of prejudice, that wellnigh deluged every avenue of manhood and liberty, you came forth to do battle for your country and your kindred. For long and weary months without pay, or even the privilege of being recognized as soldiers, you labored on, only to be disbanded and sent to your homes, without even a hope of reward. And when our country, necessitated by the deadly struggle with armed traitors, finally granted you the opportunity again to come forth in defense of the nation's life, the alacrity with which you responded to the call gave abundant evidence of your readiness to strike a manly blow for the liberty of your race. And from that little band of hopeful, trusting, and brave men, who gathered at Camp Saxton, on Port Royal Island, in the fall of 1862, amidst the terrible prejudices that then surrounded us, has grown an army of a hundred and forty thousand black soldiers, whose valor and heroism has won for your race a name which will live as long as the undying pages of history shall endure; and by whose efforts, united with those of the white man, armed rebellion has been conquered, the millions of bondmen have been emancipated, and the fundamental law of the land has been so altered as to remove forever the possibility of human slavery being re-established within the borders of redeemed America. The flag of our fathers, restored to its rightful significance, now floats over every foot of our territory, from Maine to California, and beholds only freemen! The prejudices which formerly existed against you are wellnigh rooted out.
>
> Soldiers, you have done your duty, and acquitted yourselves like men, who, actuated by such ennobling motives, could not fail; and as the result of your fidelity and obedience, you have won your freedom. And O, how great the reward!
>
> It seems fitting to me that the last hours of our existence as a regiment should be passed amidst the unmarked graves of your comrades—at Fort Wagner. Near you rest the bones of Colonel Shaw, bur-

ied by an enemy's hand, in the same grave with his black soldiers, who fell at his side; where, in the future, your children's children will come on pilgrimages to do homage to the ashes of those that fell in this glorious struggle.

The flag which was presented to us by the Rev. George B. Cheever and his congregation of New York City, on the first of January, 1863—the day when Lincoln's immortal proclamation of freedom was given to the world—and which you have borne so nobly through the war, is now to be rolled up forever, and deposited in our nation's capital. And while there it shall rest, with the battles in which you have participated inscribed upon its folds, it will be a source of pride to us all to remember that it has never been disgraced by a cowardly faltering in the hour of danger or polluted by a traitor's touch.

Now that you are to lay aside your arms, and return to the peaceful avocations of life, I adjure you, by the associations and history of the past, and the love you bear for your liberties, to harbor no feelings of hatred towards your former masters, but to seeking the paths of honesty, virtue, sobriety, and industry, and by a willing obedience of the laws of the land, to grow up to the full stature of American citizens. The church, the school-house, and the right forever to be free are now secured to you, and every prospect before you is full of hope and encouragement. The nation guarantees to you full protection and justice, and will require from you in return that respect for the laws and orderly deportment which will prove to every one your rights to all the privileges of freemen.

To the officers of the regiment I would say, your toils are ended, your mission is fulfilled, and we separate forever. The fidelity, patience, and patriotism with which you have discharged your duties, to your men and to your country, entitle you to a far higher tribute than any words of thankfulness which I can give you from the bottom of my heart. You will find your reward in the proud conviction that the cause for which you have battled so nobly has been crowned with abundant success.

Officers and soldiers of the Thirty-Third United States Colored Troops, once the First South Carolina Volunteers, I bid you all farewell!

By order of Lt. Col. C.T. Trowbridge, commanding Regiment.

E.W. HYDE
Lieutenant and Acting Adjutant

On the frontier, the Ninth and Tenth Cavalry, and the Twenty-fourth and Twenty-fifth Infantry were known to the Indians as "Buffalo Soldiers." They served in Texas and the Southwest. They fought in campaigns against the

Cheyennes and Arapahos and in subduing the Apache uprising of the Southwest, led by Victorio, Mangus, Colorado, and Geronimo. Frederick Remington, author/illustrator and one of the foremost experts on the American West, said of the Black cavalry, "The soldiers in the colored regiments were all veterans with several years of frontier life behind them, men who could never be replaced, men whose like would never come again."

Despite humiliation and harassment, Black soldiers fought with valor during the Spanish-American War. One White southerner who saw them in action, commented, "Of all the men I saw fighting, there were none to beat the Tenth Cavalry and the colored infantry, and I don't mind saying so." Black soldiers of the Ninth and Tenth Cavalry and Twenty-fourth and Twenty-fifth Infantry distinguished themselves in combat at El Caney, Santiago, and San Juan Hill. They won seven medals of honor during the conflict. Officer promotions during the war were scanty, although some Black troops were advanced on the basis of combat heroism. In most cases, few command positions were meted out to Black officers at the head of the regimental-sized units.

During World War I, Blacks were only allowed to volunteer as laborers in the Army and servants in the Navy. They were assigned to the American Expeditionary Force, serving as stevedores, road builders, wood choppers, railroad hands, mechanics, and gravediggers. Black combat troops were organized into two divisions (the Ninety-second and Ninety-third), each composed of four regiments. The Ninety-second consisted of the 365th-368th regiments, and the Ninety-third was made up of the 369th and 372d regiments.

The most famous of the Black regiments was unquestionably the Fighting 369th, or "The Hell Fighters," as they were called by the Germans. The unit went into action in the Champagne sector, and remained on the front lines for 191 consecutive days without losing a trench, retreating an inch, or surrendering a prisoner. The entire unit was awarded the croix de guerre by the government of France.

In World War II, three million Black Americans registered for military service. Seven hundred thousand served in the Army; 165,000 in the Navy; 5,000 in the Coast Guard; 17,000 in the Marines; and 4,000 in the WAVES and WAACS. Gen. Dwight D. Eisenhower, watching a Black battalion charge a beach at Normandy, commended the troops for carrying out their mission "with courage and determination." Gen. George S. Patton found the all-Black 761st Tank Battalion worthy of fighting in his select unit. At the Battle of the Bulge—Germany's last ditch attempt to drive a wedge into Allied lines—Black troops were called into action on an emergency basis to help withstand a ferocious Nazi assault. General Lanham commented that he had "never seen soldiers who have performed better in combat."

The Ninety-ninth Pursuit Squadron remains the most glamorous Black unit of World War II. Commanded by Colonel Benjamin O. Davis, Jr., this unit flew more than five hundred combat missions, and more than three thousand sorties against the Germans by the summer of 1944. After being attached to the 332d Fighter Group, again commanded by Colonel Davis, the record grew even more impressive. By the spring of 1945, the unit boasted nearly sixteen hundred combat missions and more than fifteen thousand sorties.

Despite records like these, recognition was not forthcoming until pressure was applied. In 1948, A. Philip Randolph urged Blacks to resist induction into segregated armed forces. After studying the situation carefully, President Harry Truman decided not only to issue Executive Order 9981, barring segregation of the armed forces, but to appoint a Blue Ribbon panel to study equality of treatment and opportunity throughout the armed forces of the United States.

The treatment accorded Black servicemen in the past was a contributing factor to the sense of disillusionment gripping many elements of the Black community with the announcement of war. Dr. DuBois, for example, sensed instantly that Blacks would continue to face the double burden of defending a nation abroad even as that nation, by virtue of its domestic policies, had not yet assured all of its citizens equal protection under the constitution. Still, most Black civilians endorsed the war effort. Some even went to court to earn the right to enter the service of their choice. Such was the case of air cadet Yancy Williams, who fearlessly insisted that prospective Black airmen be allowed to join the Air Force as fighter pilots, not merely ground jockeys or maintenance personnel. Williams, a Howard University graduate, threatened a lawsuit, whereupon the Air Force quickly succumbed to the pressure of adverse publicity and opened its Jim Crow training facility at Tuskegee Institute in Alabama. Pressure mounted in the wake of World War II to continue to break down patterns of racial segregation and assure Blacks—both in and out of the service—the opportunity to make professional progress commensurate with their ability.

The *New York Daily News* headlined: "Negroes Gain 1st Korea Victory." The unit was the Twenty-fourth Infantry Regiment. By the end of the Korean War, all Black infantry units were discontinued; their men redistributed elsewhere. Still, racially motivated incidents continued to occur with great regularity. The situation became so severe that the NAACP counsel Thurgood Marshall was dispatched to Japan and Korea to interview Black troops. His findings offered convincing proof that many Blacks were being accused by, and tried before, officers who held them in the kind of prejudicial contempt that made justice a virtual impossibility. The same kind of racially charged tension reared its ugly head during the Vietnam conflict. The primary cause of the difficulty was the unwillingness of the biased White GI to accept Black troops; the more obvious manifestation of the problems was reflected in the Black GI's contempt for his intransigent counterpart.

By the late 1960s, numerous racially motivated outbreaks led the Department of Defense to offer concrete proposals to improve the racial climate within the military establishment, such as special indoctrination courses, mandatory biracial councils on housing, recreation, officer-soldier relationships, and promotion opportunities. The same problem existed in the 1970s. With the advent of the 1980s and 1990s, the armed forces have made a concerted effort to make sure that equal opportunity is available to all our citizens, not just the Whites, as it had been in the past. Today, the military brass of all branches of the armed forces are actively seeking to recruit the brightest and the best young African-Americans available. While no one can claim that discrimination has been totally wiped out; today, opportunities are available on a much larger scale and on a much broader range of career choices for young African-American than at any time in the past. The future looks bright and shining.

A Curious Bit of History

The history of the Black American officer begins with the Civil War. During that war, most of the Black units were commanded by Whites; there were only seventy-five Black officers, including eight physicians. There was no possibility of advancement for enlisted men into the ranks of commissioned officers. Despite the progress made at organizing all-Black units during the war, and despite the bravery displayed by so many Black soldiers during the conflict, very few breakthroughs were achieved for Black officers at the command level.

The highest ranking Black officer to serve the Union forces was Lieutenant Colonel Alexander T. Agusta, a surgeon. Altogether, from seventy-five to one hundred Black men reached officer rank, most of them chaplains or surgeons. Combat ratings rarely extended beyond captain. The highest ranking Black field officer during the Civil War was Major Martin R. Delaney of Wilberforce, Ohio. Major Delaney, a graduate of Harvard Medical School, and co-editor, along with Fredrick Douglass, of the abolitionist newspaper *North Star*, was appointed to his rank on February 26, 1865, some two months before the Confederate surrender at Appomattox. While serving as commander of the 104th U.S. Colored Troops, Major Delaney hoped to organize an all-Black army to fight the Confederates, but peace intervened, and put a halt to his plans.

Although Blacks fought in large numbers in both the Revolution and the War of 1812, there is no instance of any Black attaining the rank of commissioned officer. It is a curious bit of history, however, that in the Civil War, those who were fighting to keep Black men enslaved were the first to commission Black officers. In Louisiana, only a few days after the outbreak of war, the free Black population of New Orleans organized a military organization, called the Native Guard, which was accepted into the service of the state and its officers were duly commissioned by Thomas O. Moore, governor and commander in chief of the militia of the state of Louisiana. The date: August 22, 1862. These Black soldiers were the first to welcome General Butler when he entered New Orleans. In fact, General Butler used this organization as the basis for the organization of three Black regiments of Native Guards. All the line officers were Black. Governor Pinchback, America's first Black Governor, a captain in one of these regiments, tells the fate of these early Black officers. According to Governor Pinchback:

> General Butler, then in command of the Department of the Gulf, organized three regiments of colored soldiers; the First, Second and Third Regiments of Native Guards.

The First Regiment of Louisiana Native Guards, Colonel Stafford commanding, with all the field officers, white, and a full compliment of line officers (30) colored, was mustered into service at New Orleans, September 27, 1862, for three years. Soon after General Banks took command of the department and changed the designation of the regiment to First Infantry Corps d'Afrique. On April 4, 1864, it was changed again to 73d United States Colored Infantry.

The Second Louisiana Native Guards, with Colonel N.W. Daniels and Lt. Colonel Hall, white, and Major Francis E. Dumas, colored, and all the line officers colored except one Second Lieutenant, who was mustered into service for three years, October 12, 1862. General Banks changed its designation to 2d Infantry Corps d'Afrique, June 6, 1863, and April 6, 1964, it was changed to Second United States Colored Troops. Finally, it was consolidated with the 91st and 74th Colored Infantry, and mustered out October 11, 1865.

The Third Regiment of Louisiana Native Guards, with Colonel Nelson and all field officers white, and all line officers (30) colored, was mustered into service at New Orleans for three years, November 24, 1862. Its designation went through the same changes as the others at the same dates, and it was mustered out November 25, 1865, as the 75th Colored Infantry.

Soon after the organization of the Third Regiment, trouble for the colored officers began, and the department began a systematic effort to get rid of them. A board of Examiners was appointed and all colored officers of the Third Regiment were ordered before it. They refused to obey the order and tendered their resignations in a body. The resignations were accepted and that was the beginning of the end. Like action, with the same results followed in the First and Second Regiments, and officers were soon no more. All were driven out of the service except three or four who were never ordered to appear before the examination board. Among them was your humble servant, I was then a Captain of Company A, Second Regiment, but I soon tired of my isolation and resigned.

Later on in the war, with the general enlistment of Black soldiers, a number of Black chaplains and some surgeons were commissioned.

Toward the close of the war, several Black line officers and two field officers were appointed. The state of Massachusetts was foremost in according recognition to Black soldiers. But these later appointments came, in most cases, after the fighting was over, and gave few opportunities to command. At the close of the war, with the muster out of troops, the Black officers disappeared and upon reorganization of the Army, despite the brilliant record of the Black troops, no Black was given a commission of any sort.

With the outbreak of the Spanish-American War, the question of Black officers again came to the fore. Black Americans again demanded that Black officers be commissioned to command Black volunteers. They were not to be deluded by any extravagant praise of their past heroic services, which veiled a determination to ignore their just claims. Nothing had really changed. In 1863, a regiment of Black troops with Black officers was practically impossible. In 1898, a regiment of Black soldiers with Black field grade commanding officers was equally impossible. At the outbreak of the Spanish-American War, there was only one Black graduate of the United States Military Academy still on active duty. In fact, during the entire period of the nineteenth century, only three Black Americans graduated from the United States Military Academy at West Point. It would be forty-seven years before another Black American would graduate from the Academy. Therefore, as Black officers were not being promoted within the service and none were being allowed to attend service academies, is it any wonder that in 1940, at the beginning of the peacetime draft, there were only five thousand Blacks in the regular Army and less than a dozen Black officers?

With the advent of World War II, Blacks had deep trepidation about the continued double standards of defending a nation abroad while at home being denied their basic Constitutional rights as American citizens. During the entire war, there was only one Black general, B.O. Davis, Sr., America's first Black General. In the Air Force, Colonel B.O. Davis, Jr., was the highest ranking Black officer and leader of the Ninety-ninth Fighter Squadron. Officer promotions in the Navy and Marine Corps were at their lowest ebb. Pressure mounted from the Black community at large for all branches to make opportunities available commensurate with ability.

During the 1960s, progress and promotion for Black officers at the General Officer level continued at an abysmally slow pace. When General B.O. Davis, Jr., retired in the late sixties, of the 1,342 admirals and generals in the armed forces of the United States, only one was Black. He was General Fredric E. Davison, appointed brigadier general in July 1968, and named deputy commanding officer of the 199th Infantry Brigade in Vietnam. In May 1971, three more Blacks were among the eighty colonels promoted to brigadier general. That raised the number of Black generals to four. The Air Force, at that time, had one Black general, and on June 2, Navy Captain Samuel Lee Gravely was named the first Black admiral. In 1973, Daniel "Chappie" James, Jr., was named lieutenant general and became the highest ranking Black in the armed forces.

In the late 1970s, Clifford Alexander, Jr., the first Black secretary of the Army, promoted five Black colonels to the rank of general, the highest one-time total in American history. In 1979, Colonel Frank E. Petersen became the first Black general in Marine Corps history. In 1980, Colonel Hazel W. Johnson was promoted to the rank of brigadier general, the first Black woman ever.

The pace of the Black General Officer promotion began to accelerate in the late 1970s, reached a plateau in the 1980s, and began to decline in the 1990s with the reduction of military manpower requirements due to the end of the Cold War and the collapse of the Soviet Union.

The '90s witnessed the appointment of four Black women to the rank of brigadier general. They are: Colonel R. P. Hickerson, Colonel Nancy R. Adams, Colonel Claudia Kennedy, and Colonel Mary E. Morgan. Additionally, there were nine African-American male colonels promoted to brigadier general, nine promoted to major general, and one Black major general promoted to lieutenant general. The most historical moment of the 1990s saw the promotion of General Colin L. Powell to the prestigious and most powerful position in the armed forces of the United States, that of Chairman, Joint Chiefs of Staff. The first African-American ever.

THE ADVANCE GUARD

This section is dedicated to a very special breed of soldier. The men and women profiled here are officers, who, because of their courage and dedication to duty, have made a unique contribution not only to Black Americans, but to all Americans. These officers have rightfully been singled out and honored as the pioneers who made the way easier for all the other Black officers who followed. They are Lt. Henry O. Flipper; Col. Charles Young; Brig. Gen. Benjamin O. Davis, Sr.; Lt. Gen. Benjamin O. Davis, Jr.; Maj. Gen. Fredric E. Davison; Vice Adm. Samuel Lee Gravely, Jr.; Gen. Daniel "Chappie" James, Jr.; Brig. Gen. Hazel Winfred Johnson; Gen. Roscoe Robinson; Lt. Gen. Frank E. Petersen; and Gen. Colin L. Powell.

LIEUTENANT HENRY O. FLIPPER

(1856-1940)
First Black American Graduate of the United States Military
Academy at West Point

The year is 1873. High on its majestic perch, atop a plateau overlooking the curved channel of New York's Hudson River, stands the United States Military Academy at West Point, like a monolithic Promethean sentry. To this bastion of military history and tradition came a young Black man from Georgia. The United States Military Academy was no ordinary school, but then, this was no ordinary young man. This was an extraordinary man. Just how extraordinary, he and the rest of America were soon to discover. The young man's name was Henry Flipper. He would make American history, but he would pay dearly.

From 1873 until his graduation in 1877, Cadet Flipper was subjected to every overt and covert type of harassment and racial discrimination imaginable. Even those few cadets who were sympathetic dared not associate with him for fear of reprisal from the White student body. Of the twenty Black candidates admitted to the United States Military Academy in the nineteenth century, only three would graduate. Henry Flipper was to be the first.

He was not the first Black to attend the Military Academy, however. That honor belongs to James W. Smith of South Carolina, who entered the academy in 1870. Cadet Smith was so tormented by the White cadets that finally, unable to bear the hostility any longer, he struck back at his assailants and was expelled.

The following excerpt from a letter written to the *New Era* by Cadet James W. Smith on July 14, 1870, describing his first few days at the Academy offers firsthand insight into the racial environment of the academy:

> Your kind letter should have been answered long ere this, but really I have been too harassed with examinations and insults and ill treatment of these cadets that I could not write or do anything else scarcely.... We went into camp yesterday, and not a moment had passed since then but some of them has been cursing and abusing me.... It is just the same at the table, and what I get to eat I must snatch for like a dog. I don't wish to resign if I can get along at all; but I don't think it will be best for me to stay and take all the abuses and insults that are heaped upon me.

This was West Point in the nineteenth century.

In spite of this hostile, charged atmosphere, Henry Flipper graduated fiftieth in a class of seventy-six in June 1877. He was commissioned a second lieutenant in the Tenth U.S. Cavalry, an all-Black unit, except for the officers. From 1878 to 1882, Lieutenant Flipper received the same kind of social isolation from his fellow White officers that he experienced at the academy. Again, he prevailed.

It was while serving at Fort Concho, Texas, that an event took place that had a profound impact on his career. He was seen out riding with a pretty White woman. The fact that a Black man had the temerity to be seen in a public social situation with a White woman outraged his fellow officers. They planned to get rid of him at the first opportunity.

A short while later, in 1882, while serving as commissary officer at Fort Davis, Texas, Flipper was charged with "embezzling Army funds and conduct unbecoming an officer." At his trial, Lieutenant Flipper pleaded innocent. He was acquitted on the first charge but found guilty of the second. He was dismissed from the service.

Lieutenant Flipper continued the fight to vindicate his name for years after his Army career was over. He fought all the way to the halls of Congress with a bill asking that he be restored to the duty, grade, rank, pay, and station that he would have attained if he had remained in the Army. His efforts met with failure. Despite this, Lieutenant Flipper used the superior training he had received at West Point, America's first engineering school. He was not only America's first Black graduate of the United States Military Academy, but America's first Black graduate in the field of engineering.

Henry Flipper went on to become nationally known in his chosen field. He spent thirty-seven years as a civil and mining engineer on the frontier of the Southwest and in Mexico. Federal, state, and municipal governments sought his services as one of a handful of qualified consultants and civil engineers. Flipper also served as a consulting engineer to the builders of one of the first railroads in the Alaskan territory. The erudite Flipper also served as a translator for the United States Senate Committee on Foreign Relations, and was an assistant to Secretary of the Interior A.B. Fall.

Born in Thomasville, Georgia, on March 21, 1856, Flipper went to his grave trying to clear his name. He never did. Flipper died in Atlanta, Georgia, in 1940. That same year, Benjamin O. Davis, Sr., became the first Black general in United States military history.

Three years after Lieutenant Flipper had graduated from West Point, another Black cadet, Johnson C. Whittaker, who had completed two successful years at the academy, was found tied to his bed, his ears slashed, on April 6, 1880. He was accused of inflicting the wounds himself and was court-martialed. President Chester Arthur reviewed his case in 1882, and found the evidence inconclusive. The academy's board, which had originally convicted Whittaker, did not agree with President Arthur's conclusion. Cadet Johnson W. Whittaker was dismissed.

COLONEL CHARLES YOUNG

(1864-1922)
Highest Ranking Black Officer During World War I

At the outbreak of the Spanish-American War, there was only one Black graduate of the United States Military Academy still on active duty: Lieutenant Charles Young, the last Black of the nineteenth century to graduate from West Point.

A soldier, diplomat, poet, and composer, Charles Young was born March 12, 1864, in Mays Lick, Kentucky. At a very young age, he moved with his family to Ripley, Ohio. Shortly after graduating from high school, he won an appointment to West Point. The year was 1885. Nine other Black cadets had been admitted, but because of racial harassment of the most vicious sort, most of them did not graduate. In 1889, Charles Young became the third Black to graduate from the United States Military Academy at West Point. He was commissioned a second lieutenant in the all-Black Tenth U.S. Cavalry on August 31, 1889. Lieutenant Young was subsequently assigned to the Twenty-fifth U.S. Infantry and the Ninth U.S. Cavalry, where he was promoted to first lieutenant and assigned on detached service as a professor of military science and tactics at Wilberforce University in Ohio.

Lieutenant Young was a man of considerable intellectual ability. He was proficient in six languages; he wrote music and mastered the piano and violin; he wrote poetry and authored two books: *The Military Morale of Races* and a book about the life of the great Haitian liberator, Toussaint L'Ouverture.

When the Spanish American-War was ignited with the sinking of the battleship *Maine* in Havana Harbor, Lieutenant Young was reassigned to the Ninth Ohio Regiment, promoted to the temporary rank of major, and sent to Cuba, where he took part in the famed charge of San Juan Hill. He was subsequently promoted to the permanent rank of captain, and served in the Philippines from 1901 to 1903. Following this, he was assigned as military attaché to Haiti; staff officer in Washington, DC; and military attaché to Liberia with the field grade of major. His next assignment was with the Ninth Cavalry. The brilliant leadership he displayed while serving as commander of a squadron with this unit under General John J. "Blackjack" Pershing (so nicknamed because he considered it an honor to lead Black troops) during the border warfare in Mexico, led to his promotion to lieutenant colonel in 1916. One of his daring exploits involved the rescue of a detachment of White soldiers from the jaws of death at the hands of Pancho Villa's men near Parral, Mexico.

When World War I broke out, Colonel Young was the highest ranking Black in U.S. military

Promotion	Date
Second Lieutenant	August 31, 1889
First Lieutenant	December 22, 1896
Captain	February 2, 1901
Major	August 28, 1904
Lieutenant Colonel	July 1, 1916
Colonel	March 9, 1917

history. He was ready to do his duty, but he was in for an unpleasant surprise. The official explanation was that U.S. Army doctors had found him unfit for active duty because of his high blood pressure. Colonel Young was forced to retire from active duty. Colonel Young and Black American officials protested the decision by the War Department. The colonel set out to prove that he was physically fit. He mounted his horse in Xenia, Ohio, and rode all the way to Washington, DC, and back again to prove his physical fitness. The decision was not reversed.

At age forty-nine, Colonel Young was in his prime, highly experienced both at home and abroad. He was the highest ranking Black officer in America, the logical choice to command the all-Black division to be sent to France. But it was not to be. Despite his protest, and the protest of Black America, the star of a brigadier general that had once been within his grasp faded forever. From this point onward, Colonel Young was a broken man. There followed some ceremonial but meaningless assignments, including his recall in 1918, just days before the Armistice, making him—ceremonially at least—the highest ranking Black American officer in World War I. Four days before the Armistice, Colonel Young was assigned to Camp Grant in Illinois to take charge of trainees, an assignment that is traditionally handled by a company grade officer of lower rank. In 1919, he was again sent to Liberia as a military attaché to reorganize that country's military forces in keeping with the recommendations made by an earlier commission of inquiry by the Taft Administration.

After a career spanning more than three decades of frustration, the third and final Black West Point graduate of the nineteenth century died while on a research expedition to Monrovia, Liberia, on January 8, 1922. Colonel Charles Young was laid to rest with full military honors in Arlington National Cemetery. For forty-seven years after his graduation, no other Black man would graduate from the United States Military Academy.

BRIGADIER GENERAL BENJAMIN O. DAVIS, SR.
(1877-1970)
First Black American General

After a distinguished military career spanning fifty years, beginning with the Spanish-American War and ending in 1948, General Davis retired from the United States Army. He was born in the nation's capital, and graduated from Howard University. Davis enlisted in the Ninth United States Volunteers as a second lieutenant in 1898, during the Spanish-American War. After the war, he was promoted to first lieutenant in the Eighth U.S. Infantry. However, on March 6, 1899, he retired from the Army. Soon thereafter, he changed his mind, and on June 14, 1899, he reenlisted as a private in the famed all-Black U.S. Cavalry, Troop I. Two years later, he took a competitive officer candidate examination, passed, and was once again commissioned a second lieutenant in the regular Army.

During the next decade, Davis served in various capacities in the United States until he was sent to Monrovia, Liberia, as a military attaché, a post he held until 1912. He was promoted to captain in 1915, temporary major in 1917, lieutenant colonel in 1920, and full colonel in 1930. Subsequently, Colonel Davis served as a professor of military science and tactics at Tuskegee Institute and Wilberforce University. He also served as instructor of the 372d Infantry of the Ohio National Guard.

During World War II, Colonel Davis was promoted to brigadier general, becoming the first Black general in U.S. military history. The year was 1940.

In 1941, General Davis retired, but was recalled to active duty to supervise the integration of U.S. Armed Forces in the European theater of war. From 1945 to 1947, General Davis was assistant to the inspector general of the United States Army. He was appointed special assistant to the secretary of the Army before his retirement in 1948.

During his military career, General Davis was the recipient of numerous citations, awards, and honors, including the Bronze Star; the croix de guerre with Palm; the Distinguished Service Medal; and the Star of Africa Medal.

Promotion	Date
Second Lieutenant	September 4, 1898
First Lieutenant	January 3, 1899
Second Lieutenant	February 2, 1901
First Lieutenant	March 30, 1905
Captain	December 24, 1915
Major	August 5, 1917
Lieutenant Colonel	July 1, 1920
Colonel	February 18, 1930
Brigadier General	October 25, 1940

Perhaps the high point in General Davis's lonely, painstakingly difficult career came in 1944, when he, with fatherly pride, pinned the Silver Star on the lapel of his son, Col. Benjamin O. Davis, Jr., of the 332d Fighter Group. His son was later to become the highest ranking Black man in the armed forces of the United States. Gen. Benjamin O. Davis, Sr., died on November 26, 1970, and is buried at Arlington National Cemetery.

LIEUTENANT GENERAL BENJAMIN O. DAVIS, JR.
(1912-)
First Black American Air Force General

June 1936. The strains of "Army Blue" drift softly across the parade field at the United States Military Academy. It's graduation day. Finally, the last cadet has received his diploma, the Long Corps Yell reverberates between the classes and echoes across the field. And then the first captain commands, "Class dismissed!" The white caps of the graduating class, like so much confetti, fill a steel blue morning sky. The days of cadet gray are over.

Among the cadets that graduated that day was young Benjamin O. Davis, Jr., the son of the first Black general in American military history. Cadet Davis was also the first Black to graduate from the United States Military Academy since Charles Young had graduated forty-seven years earlier.

Born in Washington, DC, General Davis entered West Point in 1932 with the recommendation of Congressman Oscar DePriest of Chicago. Like the other Black cadets who came before him, Davis was harassed by White cadets who tried to force him to quit. Davis lived alone. Everyone else shared double-occupancy rooms. In spite of the torment, Davis ranked thirty-fifth in his graduating class of 276 cadets.

Davis's first assignment was as commander of the all-Black Twenty-fourth Infantry at Fort Benning, Georgia. In 1940, the then-captain was a professor of military science at Tuskegee Institute in Alabama when he received the news that his father had been promoted to brigadier general. It was a proud moment in the young Davis's life.

In keeping with the pioneering role his father played, the younger Davis established a precedent by transferring from the Infantry to the Army Air Corps, breaking the color barrier. Up until that time, Blacks were not accepted into the pilot training program because the military establishment claimed Blacks did not have the technical ability to master flying. Captain Davis and twelve other Black cadets reported as class 42C for their preflight training at the Tuskegee, Alabama, school; they were known as the Sixty-sixth Air Force Training Detachment. They were indeed detached; it was a segregated, all-Black unit. At the time, Captain Davis and his father were the only Black line officers in the United States Army; the remaining Black officers were chaplains! On September 2, 1941, Captain Davis completed his flight training and became the first Black man to officially fly solo as an officer of the U.S. Army Air Corps. The Sixty-sixth Air Force Training Detachment, headed by Captain Davis, was to become the most famous Black flying unit of World War II—the Ninety-ninth Pursuit Squadron.

By graduation in 1942, Class 42C had been reduced to Captain Davis and four other students. At this point in Davis's career, the U.S. Army Air Corps Promotion Board determined that it was necessary to bring him up to speed with his White contemporaries with similar time in grade. His promotions were so rapid that no sooner than he had received the gold oak leaves of a major, they were replaced by the silver leaves of lieutenant colonel. Soon thereafter, he succeeded Capt. George S. Roberts as commander of the newly formed Ninety-ninth Pursuit Squadron. In April 1943, Colonel Davis and the Ninety-ninth departed Tuskegee for combat duty overseas.

Swift and certain, the Ninety-ninth went on to compile a brilliant record in North Africa, Sicily, and Northern Italy during World War II. The Ninety-ninth was, in the words of the ancient Greek Ammianus, "Like a thunderbolt which strikes on a mountaintop and dashes away all that stands in their path."

In August 1943, Davis was relieved of his command to return to the United States to assume command of the newly formed all-Black 332d Fighter Group.

D-Day was January 22, 1944. The Anglo-American amphibian assault force of almost fifty thousand men and more than five thousand vehicles landed at Anzio and sought to strike inland with the purpose of forcing the Germans on the southern front to withdraw. But the Allied force was contained by several fierce German air and ground counterattacks, forcing the Allies to occupy a strategically exposed position on the beachhead. The Luftwaffe had been bombing and strafing the Allied position since 8:50 A.M. on January 23. On the morning of the January 27, sixteen German planes were pulling out of a bomb run over the Anzio beachhead when the Ninety-ninth Pursuit Squadron intercepted them. The Davis-trained Black fighter pilots in their P-40 Warhawks poised like glistening silver arrows in Saracen archers' bows, suddenly flew thick and swift, like a snowstorm. When the storm had subsided, six Messerschmitt Bf 109s and Focke-Wulf FW-190s were destroyed, and four others were damaged. On the afternoon of that same day, the Black Eagles of the Ninety-ninth took on twelve more German fighter planes, destroying four more. The next day, they destroyed another four.

A *Time* magazine article dated February 14, 1944, said:

> Any outfit would be proud of the record. These victories stamped the final seal of combat excellence on one of the most controversial outfits in the Army, the all-Negro fighter squadron.

In two hundred escort missions, the Ninety-ninth never lost a bomber to German aircraft fire.

By February 1944, the 332d Fighter Group arrived at Taranto, Italy. Colonel Davis had fully utilized his combat experience to mold this unit into one of the finest fighter groups in the U.S. Army Air Corps. Several months later, Davis was promoted to full colonel.

One incident that occurred on a mission flown on June 9, 1944, underscores what a truly remarkable pilot and leader Colonel Davis had become. The colonel had lead his 332d Fighter Group of P-47 and P-47D Thunderbolts on a penetration escort attack on an industrial target in Germany. On the way home, the bomber formation was attacked by more than one hundred German fighters over Udine, Italy. Colonel Davis led his men in such a brilliant fashion that he was cited for his exemplary leadership and courage. The unit citation read:

For: Extraordinary Achievement. Faced with the problem of protecting the large bomber formation with comparatively few fighters under his control, Colonel Davis so skillfully disposed his squadron that
in spite of the large number of enemy fighters, the bomber formation suffered only a few losses.

The 332d Fighter Group reached the zenith of its performance when, on
March 24, 1945—with Colonel Davis leading in his favorite P-51 Mustang—
the group flew
fighter cover for the B-17s of the Fifteenth Air Force. The mission was a
1,600-mile round trip to strike at the heart of the Vaterland: Berlin, Germany.
This was the longest mission in the history of the Fifteenth Air Corps.

Over the target, the 332d fought like the light cavalry of Alexander the
Great against the mighty Persians at the River Granicus. The Ebony-winged
warriors shot down attacking German fighters with cool, professional detachment. They cleared the way so that the phalanx of B-17s could make its terrible movement forward. For this outstanding airmanship, extraordinary heroism in action, and aggressive combat technique, Colonel Davis's entire group
was awarded the Presidential Unit Citation.

The 332d Fighter Group left Europe in June 1945. Colonel Davis had been
awarded the Air Medal with four Oak Leaf Clusters; the Legion of Merit with
one Oak Leaf Cluster; and the Silver Star. He earned the Silver Star for gallantry in action while leading a squadron of P-51 fighters on a hazardous mission against German airfields. His father, Brig. Gen. Benjamin O. Davis, Sr.,
pinned the Silver Star on his son. Colonel Davis also won the Distinguished
Flying Cross for leading the 332d on a successful bombing raid against a German installation deep in the heart of occupied France. The colonel flew sixty
missions against the enemy in Europe; the Black pilots he trained and lead in
the Ninety-ninth and 332d Fighter Group were cited for heroism eight hundred times during the war; they flew 1,579 missions, destroying 260 enemy
planes, and damaging 148 others. Ninety-five pilots in the 332d won the Distinguished Flying Cross, the Army Air Corps' highest award.

In June 1945, Colonel Davis assumed command of the all-Black 477th
Composite Group at Freeman Field, Seymour, Indiana. A month later, when
he took command of Godman Field in Kentucky, he became the first Black to
command an air base in U.S. military history. In March of 1946, the 477th
moved to Lockbourne Field, Columbus, Ohio. Several months later the group
became the 332d Fighter Wing, flying P-47N Thunderbolts exclusively. The
unit continued until June 1, 1949, when the United States Congress, led by
President Truman, integrated the armed forces throughout the world.

In May 1949, Colonel Davis served on a board of select officers to enact
an integration policy approved by Secretary of Defense Louis Johnson. The
board screened the records of three thousand Black officers and airmen at
the Lockbourne Air Base. As a result, the men were moved from segregated
barracks and reassigned to new quarters according to alphabetic order of their
last names, regardless of ethnic or racial background.

With the advent of the Korean War, Colonel Davis was appointed commander of the Fifty-first Fighter Interceptor Wing in 1952, and later served as director of operations and training of the Far East Air Forces (FEAF). A year later, he was promoted to the rank of brigadier general. Davis, like his father before him, became the highest ranking active-duty Black officer in the armed forces of the United States of America, and the first Black general in U.S. Air Force history. General Davis's subsequent assignments included commander, Air Task Force Thirteen (Provisional), a surface-to-air missile unit on Formosa in Taiwan; chief of staff, Operations, Headquarters, United States Air Force Europe, Wiesbaden, Germany. In 1959, General Davis was promoted to major general. From 1961 to 1965, General Davis served as director of manpower and organization and deputy chief of staff for programs and requirements for the U.S. Air Force. On April 30, 1965, he was promoted to lieutenant general and was assigned to Korea as chief of staff of the United Nations Command to coordinate all activities of the U.N. Force from 1965 to 1967. He also served as commander of the Thirteenth Air Force at Clark Air Base in the Philippines. General Davis brought his brilliant military career to a close as deputy commander in chief of the U.S. Strike Command at MacDill Air Force Base in Tampa, Florida, and commander in chief, U.S. Air Forces, Middle East, Southern Asia, and Africa.

A command pilot, General Davis's military decorations and awards include the Air Force Distinguished Service Medal; the Army Distinguished Service Medal; the Silver Star; the Legion of Merit with two Oak Leaf Clusters; the Distinguished Flying Cross; the Air Medal with four Oak Leaf Clusters; the Air Force Commendation Medal with two Oak Leaf Clusters; the Philippine Legion of Honor; the croix de guerre with Palm; the Star of Africa Medal; the Republic of China Cloud and Banner Medal with one Oak Leaf Cluster; the Republic of Korea Order of National Security Medal; the Kingdom of Thailand Knight of the Grand Cross First Class Most Noble Order Crown Medal; and the Republic of Vietnam Campaign Medal.

After retiring from the military, General Davis was appointed to several major civilian assignments. In 1970, during the Nixon administration, General Davis was appointed director of civil aviation security for the United States Department of Transportation. His job was to eliminate the risk of hijackings of commercial flights to Cuba and to eliminate the threat of Arab terrorists, who had seized and destroyed four commercial aircraft in 1970. As a deterrent against hijacking, General Davis developed the sky marshal program. His program required that armed federal marshals fly on United States commercial flights in an undercover capacity. Hijacking declined dramatically after this program was implemented.

Soon thereafter, President Richard Nixon promoted Davis

Promotion	Date
Second Lieutenant	June 12, 1936
First Lieutenant	June 12, 1939
Captain	September 9, 1940
Major	March 1, 1942
Lieutenant Colonel	May 29, 1942
Colonel	May 29, 1944
Brigadier General	October 12, 1954
Major General	June 30, 1959
Lieutenant General	April 30, 1965

Lt. Gen. Benjamin O. Davis, Jr.

to an even higher position in the Department of Transportation, that of assistant secretary in charge of civil aviation security. In this capacity General Davis was the spokesperson for the Department of Transportation for all matters pertaining to the security of the United States airline industry. Then, in 1971, he was appointed to an even more challenging position by Nixon: assistant secretary for safety and consumer affairs. In his new assignment, General Davis was still responsible for civil aviation security, and, in addition, he was the national coordinator of policy for handling hazardous materials and other transportation security programs.

General Davis resigned from the Department of Transportation in 1975. From 1975 to 1985, he was a member of more than thirty-five different boards, including the Domestic Council Committee on Drug Abuse, the Air Force Historical Foundation, the Air Force Academy Foundation, the National Defense Transportation Association, the Institute of Aerospace Safety and Management, the National Education Institute, the National Safety Council, the Association of Graduates of the United States Military Academy, the Cabinet Committee to Combat Terrorism, the Retired Officers Association, and many others.

General Davis also continued to serve as a consultant for the Department of Transportation and traveled nationwide, lecturing on issues of safety. In 1975, he was elected to the board of the Manhattan Life Insurance Company, for which he served until his retirement in 1985.

General Davis's many other awards and honors include the Order of the Sword Award from the Air Force Sergeants Association and the Distinguished Achievement Award from the Tuskegee Airmen, Incorporated. Also, the Benjamin O. Davis, Jr., Vocational Technical Center High School for Aerospace Studies in Detroit, Michigan, and the Fort Benjamin O. Davis, Sr., and Fort Benjamin O. Davis, Jr., National Guard Armory, in Tuskegee, Alabama, are both named after him.

MAJOR GENERAL FREDRIC E. DAVISON
(1917-)
First Black Army Combat General

The first Black Army combat general was a cum laude graduate of Howard University who earned his bachelor's degree in 1938, and his master's degree in 1940. He also earned a master's degree in international affairs from George Washington University and attended the Army War College.

Davison began his career when he received his commission as a second lieutenant through Army ROTC at Howard University. In March 1941, he was assigned to the 366th Infantry Regiment at Fort Devens, Massachusetts. His next assignment was as a student at the Infantry School in Fort Benning, Georgia. Upon graduating, he served as platoon leader, Company H, 366th Infantry Regiment, Fort Devens, Massachusetts, from 1942 until 1944, when the then captain was sent to the European theater of war where he served as the commanding officer of an antitank company in the 366th Infantry Regiment and as a munitions officer for a service company, also in the 366th Infantry Regiment. He also served as battalion S-3 (Operations) for the First Battalion of the 366th Infantry. In this capacity, Davison had staff responsibility for planning, organizing, and training for all combat operations as directed by the commanding officer. Davison also prepared estimates and recommendations for the commander concerning the appropriate action to be taken to accomplish the battalion's mission. He also commanded Company B of the 371st Infantry Regiment during the battle for Northern Italy in 1945. He led his men alongside the 442d Regimental Combat team in the bloody hand-to-hand fighting that occurred along the rugged coastline of the Ligurian Sea on the west coast. His unit also saw combat action from the inland village of Aulla, where his troops had to fight their way through well-defended fortifications bristling with German troops and heavy weapons to the city of Genoa and Turin, where the Allies found both cities already under control of friendly Italian partisans who had captured thousands of German prisoners.

By April 1945, the Fifth and Eighth Armies had joined forces north of Bologna and the Germans were in full retreat to the north across the Po Valley while Allied armed forces raced ahead to seal their escape into the Alps. The German armies were in chaos. Their beaten, exhausted soldiers surrendered by the tens of thousands. The Italian Campaign, the longest sustained Allied drive of World War II, was finally nearing an end. For his outstanding actions in this campaign, Captain Davison was awarded the Bronze Star Medal. He remained in Europe as part of the occupational forces until March 30, 1946.

Upon his return to the United States in 1946, Davison was assigned as commanding officer, Company D, First Battalion, 365th Infantry Regiment, Fort Dix, New Jersey, where he was stationed until 1947. From 1947 until 1959, Davison served in a number of capacities, including executive officer and assistant professor of military science and tactics, 3245th Army Service Unit, and later 3330th Army Service Unit, ROTC, State A & M College, Orangeburg, South Carolina; student, the Infantry School, Fort Benning Georgia; battalion S-3, 370th Armored Infantry Battalion, United States Army Europe, Germany; acting administration officer, Command and General Staff College, Fort Leavenworth, Kansas; student, Command and General Staff College, Fort Leavenworth Kansas; personnel actions officer, Infantry Branch, Career Management Division, Office of the Adjutant General, Washington, DC; action officer, Education Infantry Branch, Career Management Division, Office of the Adjutant General, Washington, DC; and plans and gyroscope officer, Assignment Section, Infantry Branch, Officers Assignment Division, Office of the Adjutant General, United States Army, Washington, DC.

In 1959, Lieutenant Colonel Davison was assigned to Korea as chief, Personnel Services Division, G-1 (Personnel) Section, Headquarters, Eighth United States Army, Pacific-Korea. As the G-1, Davison was responsible for personnel management pertaining to unit strength, moral, and discipline. He was also responsible for all correspondence of the executive officer and the commanding officer. He returned to the continental United States in July 1960, and served as chief, Reserve Component Branch, Military Personnel Division, G-1, Office, Second United States Army, Fort Meade, Maryland; chief, Manpower Division, G-1, Office, Second United States Army, Fort Meade, Maryland; student, United States Army War College, Carlisle Barracks, Pennsylvania; chief, Reserve Forces Division, Office, Deputy Under Secretary of the Army (Manpower and Reserve Forces), Office of the Under Secretary of the Army, Washington, DC; commanding officer, Third Training Brigade, United States Army Training Center, Air Defense, Fort Bliss, Texas; and member, the Williams Board, Office of Personnel Operations, United States Army, Washington, DC.

In November 1967, Colonel Davison served as deputy commander, 199th Infantry Brigade, United States Army, Vietnam. He was station at the Long Binh Base, which was the site of a series of furious North Vietnamese armored infantry and mortar attacks. The Long Binh Base was an important industrial area and was strategically located in the vital southeastern approaches to Saigon. It also contained a large United States Air Force base and was the headquarters of the Third Corps, United States Army. During the Tet Offensive in 1968, which occurred on the most sacred holiday on the Asian calendar (Lunar New Year), North Vietnamese forces surrounded the Long Binh Base and launched a ferocious attack beginning with heavy artillery and mortars that rained death from the skies. The artillery fire was followed with attacks by heavy tanks and infantry while sapper squads, which were laden with explosives, searched for weak spots in the base's defenses.

Promotion	Date
Second Lieutenant	March 17, 1939
First Lieutenant	May 29, 1942
Captain	November 3, 1943
Major	November 16, 1950
Lieutenant Colonel	April 4, 1957
Colonel	November 27, 1964
Brigadier General	October 1, 1969
Major General	April 1, 1971

The 199th Brigade was charged with the defense of the base. The commander of the brigade was absent, so the duty of commander fell to Colonel Davison, deputy brigade commander. Davison was up to the task. His skillful maneuvering of his troops was outstanding. He had at his disposal a state of the art armored and mechanized light infantry brigade that was swift and accurate with tremendous firepower. Davison also called in additional firepower support from tactical aircraft and gunships that laid down a withering fire that lit up the sky with a blinding light. And, all the while, Colonel Davison was seemingly everywhere, directing his men, giving orders and directions, and shouting encouragement as the din of battle raged on throughout the day. Near evening, the enemy had not breached the walls of the base. As darkness descended, the North Vietnamese fell back, beaten. The force returned to normal operation. For Davison's heroic action and the action of the 199th Infantry in defense of Long Binh Base, the entire unit was honored with the Valorous Unit Award Streamer embroidered "Saigon-Long Binh, 199th Infantry Brigade," and the Meritorious Unit Commendation Streamer embroidered "Vietnam 1968-1969, 199th Infantry Brigade."

When Colonel Davison assumed command of the defense of the base at Long Binh, he became the first African-American to command a combat unit in the history of the United States Army.

A month later at air command headquarters in Binh Chanh, South Vietnam, under the glare of flashing lights and television cameras, anxious newspaper reporters crowded around a husky, graying colonel described as tough and fondly called, "the Old Man" by his troops. Nearby, the brigade's staff officers and battalion commander looked on as Gen. Creighton Abrams, United States military commander in Vietnam, pinned the silver star of a brigadier general on the shoulders of Fredric Ellison Davison. After he had pinned the star on General Davison, Abrams said, "In my judgment, I know of no officer more deserving." And with that, Fredric Davison became only the third African-American in American military history to be promoted to general.

Returning to the United States in 1969, Davison was assigned as inspector general of the United States Army for a year; then as deputy chief of staff for Army personnel in Europe; and commanding general of the Military District of Washington, Washington, DC.

General Davison's decorations and awards include the Distinguished Service Medal; the Legion of Merit with one Oak Leaf Cluster; the Bronze Star Medal; the Air Medal (nineteen awards); the Army Commendation Medal with two Oak Leaf Clusters; and the Combat Infantryman Badge (second award).

VICE ADMIRAL SAMUEL LEE GRAVELY, JR.
(Retired, 1980)
First Black American Admiral

It has not always been smooth sailing for America's first Black Admiral, Samuel Lee Gravely, Jr. Yet, he has gone on to establish an unprecedented record in the annuals of U.S. Naval history. Admiral Gravely was the first Black graduate from a midshipman school; the first Black officer to be assigned shipboard duty; the first Black American to command a U.S. Navy ship; the first Black American to command an American warship under combat conditions since the Civil War (USS *Taussig*); the first Black to command a major Naval Warship (USS *Souett*); and the first to command a U.S. Navy Fleet.

Vice Admiral Gravely's impressive career began on September 15, 1942, when he enlisted in the U.S. Naval Reserve and reported for recruit training at the Naval Training Center, Great Lakes, Illinois. In January 1943, he reported as a student at the Service School, Hampton (Virginia) Institute, and in May, was assigned to the Second Base, San Diego, California. During the period of November 1943 to June 1944, he was a member of the V-12 Unit at the University of California (Los Angeles) and then attended Pre-Midshipmen School, Asbury Park, New Jersey.

Appointed midshipman in the U.S. Naval Reserve in August 1944, he attended the Midshipmen School, Columbia University, New York, and graduated in December of that year. Commissioned as an Ensign in the Naval Reserve to date from December 14, 1944, he subsequently advanced to the rank of Vice Admiral, having transferred to the U.S. Navy on August 16, 1955.

Following his commissioning, he reported in December 1944, as assistant battalion commander at the Naval Training Center, Great Lakes, where he remained until February 1945. For two months, he received instruction at the Sub-Chaser Training Center, Miami, Florida, and, in May 1945, joined the PC-1264. He served during the latter months of World War II, through February 1946, as communications officer, electronics officer, and later as executive officer and personnel officer of this submarine chaser. After brief duty as communications watch officer with the Fleet Training Group, Norfolk, Virginia, he was released from active duty, effective April 16, 1946. Prior to returning to active duty, he was employed as a railway postal clerk in Richmond, Virginia.

Called again into active service, he reported on August 30, 1949, as assistant to the officer in charge of recruiting at the Naval Recruiting Station and Officer Procurement, Washington, DC. From October 1951 to January 1952, he had instruction in the Communications Officers Short Course at the Naval Postgraduate School, Monterey, California, after which he served as radio officer on board the USS *Iowa* (BB-61). In June 1953, he transferred to the USS *Toledo* (CA-133), on which he served as communications officer and in various other capacities, including that of assistant operations officer. On both

DEPARTMENT OF THE NAVY

Vice Adm. Samuel L. Gravely, Jr.

vessels, he participated in action against North Korean and Chinese Communist forces in the Korean area, and wears the ribbon of the Korean Presidential Unit Citation awarded those ships.

Detached from the USS *Toledo* in July 1955, he was assigned to Headquarters, Third Naval District, New York, where he served two years as assistant district security officer. Between September and November 1957, he had instruction in amphibious warfare, attached to the Amphibious Training Command, Pacific Fleet, headquartered at Coronado, California, and then joined the USS *Seminole* (AKA-104) as operations officer. He had temporary duty under training for executive officer for a destroyer on the staff of Commander Destroyer Squadrons Seven and Five during the period August 1959 to January 1960, when he became the executive officer of the USS *Theodore E. Chandler* (DD-717). On January 15, 1961, he became commanding officer and remained in command of that destroyer until November 21, 1961, when he again became executive officer.

On January 31, 1962, he assumed command of the Radar Pickett Destroyer Escort, USS *Falgout* (DER-324) at Pearl Harbor, Hawaii. Under command of Lieutenant Commander Gravely, the USS *Falgout* patrolled the Pacific Early Warning Barrier. From August 1963 to June 1964, he attended the senior course in naval warfare at the Naval War College, Newport, Rhode Island, after which he served as program manager for the National Military Command Center and the National Emergency Airborne Command Post at the Defense Communications Agency, Arlington, Virginia. In January 1966, he became commanding officer of the USS *Taussig* (DD-746). On June 6, 1968, Captain Gravely was then detached from the USS *Taussig* to report to the Office of the Chief of Naval Operations. He was assigned as coordinator, Navy Satellite Communications Program in the Office of the Chief of Naval Operations (Communications and Cryptology) with additional duty in the Navy Space Program Division.

On May 22, 1970, Captain Gravely assumed command of the USS *Jouett* (DLG-29), one of the Navy's most modern guided missile frigates home-ported in San Diego. Captain Gravely was relieved on June 2, 1971, and donned two stars that day. On July 16, 1971, he assumed duty as commander, Naval Communications Command, and director, Naval Communications Divisions under the Chief of Naval Operations. After serving in those positions for two years, he moved to duty as commander, Cruiser-Destroyer Group Two, assuming command on August 1, 1973.

On August 29, 1975, Rear Admiral Gravely assumed duties as commandant of the Eleventh Naval District unit. On August 28, 1976, he donned three stars on board the USS *Jouett* (CG-29). He assumed command of the Third Fleet on September 10, 1976. After serving as commander of the Third Fleet for two years, he assumed duties as director, Defense Communications Agency from September 15, 1978, through August 1, 1980.

Vice Admiral Gravely retired from the U.S. Navy on August 1, 1980, and now resides in Haymarket, Virginia. On March 30, 1981, he joined an Industrial firm from McLean, Virginia, as director, Naval Programs and was subsequently assigned as director, Planning, and promoted to vice-president. On January 10, 1983, he joined the firm of Automated Business Systems and Services, Inc., of Hyattsville, Maryland, as director, Command Support Division. Vice Admiral Gravely is currently president, Gainsville Puritan Club; vice-president, Northern Virginia Council of the Navy League; and a member of the Board of Directors, Draper Laboratory. On May 15, 1981, a Sea Cadet unit was chartered in his name in Irvington, New Jersey. Earlier, a street was named in his honor in his hometown, Richmond, Virginia.

Vice Admiral Gravely has been awarded the Defense Distinguished Service Medal; the Legion of Merit with gold star; Bronze Star Medal and the

Navy Commendation Medal with gold Reserve Medal (for ten years service in the U.S. Naval Reserve); the American Campaign Medal; the Korean Presidential Unit Citation; the National Defense Medal with one bronze star; the China Service Medal (extended); the Korean Service Medal with two bronze stars; the United States Service Medal; the Armed Forces Expeditionary Medal; the Vietnam Service Medal with six bronze stars; the Vietnamese Campaign Medal; the Antarctic Service Medal; and the Venezuelan Order of Merit Second Class.

His civic awards include: Golden Hills United Presbyterian Church (1967) Military Service Award; Alpha Phi Alpha Fraternity (1971) Alpha Award of Merit; Distinguished Virginian (1972) by Governor Holton; Los Angeles Chapter, National Association of Media Women, Inc. (1972) Communications Award; The Scottish Rite Prince Hall Masonic Bodies of Maryland, Prince Hall Founding Fathers Military Commanders Award (1974); Savannah State College (1974) Major Richard R. Wright Award of Excellence; San Diego Press Club (1975) Military Headliner of the Year; Virginian of the Year (1979), Virginia Press Association; and Doctor of Laws (Hon.), (1979), Virginia Union University.

GENERAL DANIEL "CHAPPIE" JAMES, JR.
1920-1978
First Black Four-Star General

Early dawn. Somewhere in Thailand. The blue-gray mist hangs like a shroud over the airfield. A group of dark figures is silhouetted against this backdrop as they move in precision toward a waiting aircraft. One of the pilots, the leader, pours his powerful 6'4", 235-pound frame into the cockpit of the F-4 Phantom jet fighter, poised like some monstrous twenty-first-century technological killer insect. The leader reaches up and adjusts his helmet, resplendent with a sleek Black Panther insignia snarling menacingly at the gray dawn.

This is Black air warrior, Col. Daniel "Chappie" James, Jr., deputy commander, Eighth Tactical Fighter Wing, leader of the Wolf Pack, the most celebrated group of pilots in the United States Air Force. The engines scream awake with a terrifying roar. In a matter of seconds, the Wolf Pack knifes into the dawn sky and disappears. The date: January 2, 1967. Colonel James and his men have a rendezvous with destiny: the Bolo MiG Sweep, the fiercest air duel of the Vietnam War, between U.S. fighters and Communist MiG 21s. When the macabre aerial ballet is over, seven MiGs will have been shot down, the highest total for any mission flown during the entire war. Colonel James was to lead seventy-eight such missions over North Vietnam.

But wait, the Chappie James story does not begin here. It begins instead in Pensacola, Florida, in a Black ghetto, where the youngest boy in a family of seventeen children has a remarkable athletic gift and uses it to claw his way out of the morass of poverty.

He compiles an outstanding high school football record. The athletic scholarships from colleges across the nation pour in. He seizes the opportunity. One more escapee from oblivion. It's an old story. It will be repeated again. The young Black athlete goes off to college and becomes the campus football hero and marries his college sweetheart. There the fantasy ends. From this storybook beginning, Daniel James fought his way to the top of the toughest institution in existence—the military—where, under combat conditions, a mistake can cost you your life.

General James graduated from Tuskegee Institute in 1942. In June 1943, he entered the Aviation Cadet Program established by Congress in 1939, to build a reserve of civilian pilots who could be quickly converted to combat pilots in the event of a national emergency. (General James was one of the twenty civilian primary instructors at Tuskegee who helped train a young student officer and West Point graduate, Capt. Benjamin O. Davis, Jr., who later became the first Black general in U.S. Air Force history.)

James was commissioned a second lieutenant in the U.S. Air Force later that same year. He began his combat training at Selfridge Field, Michigan, where he was a member of the 617th Bombardment Squadron and the 477th Bombard-

Gen. Daniel "Chappie" James, Jr.

ment Group for several years. In 1947, he served as operations officer of the Thirty-second Composite Group and became the first Black to qualify as an advanced instrument pilot at the Lockbourne Air Base in Columbus, Ohio.

By the fall of 1949, General James had become the flight leader of the Twelfth Fighter Bomber Squadron, Eighteenth Fighter Wing in the Philippines. There followed a tour of duty in Korea, starting in July 1950, where he flew 101 combat missions in F-51s and F-80s.

After Korea, he was assigned to Otis Air Force Base in Massachusetts where he became the operations officer for the Fifty-eighth All-Weather Fighter Squadron. In 1953, General James became commander of the 437th Fighter Interceptor Squadron, and in 1955, he assumed command of the Sixtieth Fighter Interceptor Squadron. Upon graduation from the Air Command and Staff College in 1957, General James was named air staff officer, Office of the Deputy Chief of Staff for Operations, Air Defense Division, Washington, DC. And in 1961, he was assigned to the Royal Air Force in England, where he became the assistant director of operations of the Eighty-first Fighter Wing; director of operations, Eighty-first Tactical Fighter Wing; commander, Ninety-second Tactical Fighter Squadron; and deputy wing commander for operations, Eighty-first Fighter Wing.

Upon his return to the United States in the fall of 1964, General James was assigned to several command positions, including director of operational training and deputy commander for operations training of the 4453d Combat Crew Training Wing, Davis-Monthan Air Force Base, Arizona. General James's next assignment, in 1966, was at Ubon Royal Thai Air Base in Thailand, where he was deputy commander for operations, and, later, vice commander, Eighth Tactical Fighter Wing. This group of elite fighter pilots, led by General James, became known as the Wolf Pack because of their legendary skill at shooting down MiG fighter planes.

Upon his return from Vietnam, General James was assigned to the Thirty-third Tactical Fighter Wing at Eglin Air Force Base. In 1969, while stationed at Eglin Air Force Base, General James was named Florida's Outstanding American of the Year. He also received the Jaycee Distinguished Service Award. Following this, he assumed command of the 7272d Fighter Training Wing at Wheelus Air Base in the Libyan Arab Republic.

On March 31, 1970, General James was sworn in as principal deputy assistant of defense for public affairs by Secretary of Defense Melvin R. Laird. That same day, James was promoted to the rank of brigadier general. He later assumed the duty of vice commander, Military Airlift Command, Headquarters, Scott Air Force Base, Illinois. General James was promoted to major general in 1972, and to lieutenant general in 1973. And in August 1975, Gen. Daniel James, Jr., received his fourth star, becoming the first Black ever to hold this rank. On that same day, General James was appointed commander in chief of North American Air Defense Command (NORAD), a bi-national military command consisting of United States and Canadian strategic aerospace defense forces. He also served as commander in chief of the United States Air Force Aerospace Defense Command (ADCOM), the United States' element of NORAD.

General James, a legendary command pilot, was the recipient of numerous awards, both civilian and military. Known internationally as an eloquent advocate of the American way of life, excerpts from some of his speeches have been read into the *Congressional Record*. The general was twice awarded the George Washington Freedom Foundation Medal; the Arnold Air Society Eugene M. Zuckert Award for outstanding contributions to Air Force professionalism; the Builder of a Greater Arizona Award; the Phoenix Urban League Man of the Year Award; the Distinguished Service Achievement Award from Kappa

Alpha Psi Fraternity; the American Legion National Commander's Public Relations Award; the Veterans of Foreign Wars Commander in Chief's Gold Medal Award and Citation; the Capital Press Club, Doolittle Chapter's Man of the Year Award; the Florida Association of Broadcasters Gold Medal Award; the American Veterans of World War II Silver Helmet Award; the United Service Excellence Award; the American Academy of Achievement Golden Plate Award; the United Negro College Fund's Distinguished Service Award; the Horatio Alger Award; the Veterans of Foreign Wars Americanism Medal; the Bishop Wright Air Industry Award; and the Kitty Hawk Award. General James was also awarded honorary degrees from the University of West Florida in 1971, the University of Akron in 1973, Virginia State College in 1974, Delaware State College in 1975, and St. Louis University in 1976, and was named honorary national commander of the Arnold Air Society in 1971.

As a distinguished command pilot, General James was one of the most decorated war heroes in the history of the armed forces of the United States. His numerous decorations and awards include the Distinguished Service Medal with one Oak Leaf Cluster; the Legion of Merit with one Oak Leaf Cluster; the Distinguished Flying Cross with two Oak Leaf Clusters; the Meritorious Service Medal; the Air Medal with thirteen Oak Leaf Clusters; the Army Commendation Medal; the Distinguished Unit Citation Emblem with one Oak Leaf Cluster (for service prior to 1965); the Presidential Unit Citation Emblem with three Oak Leaf Clusters (for service after 1965); the Air Force Outstanding Unit Award Ribbon with three Oak Leaf Clusters; the Combat Readiness Medal; the Good Conduct Medal; the American Defense Service Medal; the American Campaign Medal; the World War II Victory Medal; the National Defense Service Medal with one Service Star; the Korean Service Medal with four Service Stars; the Air Force Longevity Service Award Ribbon with seven Oak Leaf Clusters; the Vietnam Service Medal with four Service Stars; the Armed Forces Reserve Medal; the Small Arms Expert Marksmanship Ribbon; the Republic of Korea Presidential Unit Citation Ribbon; the United Nations Service Medal; and the Republic of Vietnam Campaign Medal.

The fierce, lion-hunting Assyrian warrior-kings, who were addressed as "The Sun," were always first in battle. So was General James. He led his men with dedication, skill, and courage. He felt a deep personal commitment, not only to his fellow pilots, but also to the ground troops who depended on fighter support for survival. He did everything in his power to never let them down.

Concerning patriotism, James was often quoted as saying, "My motto is build a nation, not tear it down!"

On February 25, 1978, at the age of fifty-eight, the highest ranking Black officer in the history of America died of a massive heart attack in Colorado Springs. The man is dead. Long live his legend.

In General James's office, neatly framed, hung the words that could serve as this Black warrior's epitaph: "Yea, though I fly thru/the valley of death,/I shall fear no evil,/For I am the 'meanest muthah' in the valley!"

BRIGADIER GENERAL HAZEL W. JOHNSON
(1930-)
First Black American Female General

Ever since she was a little girl growing up on a farm in West Chester, Pennsylvania, Hazel Johnson dreamed of someday becoming a nurse. Her dream came true. After she received her diploma in nursing from Harlem Hospital in New York City in 1950, Johnson went on to earn her bachelor's degree in nursing from Villanova University in 1959, a master's degree in nursing education from the Teacher's College at Colombia University in 1963, and a doctorate in education administration from Catholic University in 1978. General Johnson also holds an honorary doctorate in the humanities from Morgan State University, an honorary doctorate in social sciences from Villanova University, and an honorary doctorate in public service from the University of Maryland.

In 1955, Hazel Johnson entered the Army Nurse Corps. Her first assignments were general duty, obstetrics, and staff nurse positions, initially at Walter Reed Army Medical Center in Washington, DC, and then at the 8169 United States Army Evacuation Hospital in Camp Zama, Japan. Returning to the United States, she served at Madigan General Hospital in Tacoma, Washington. She returned to Walter Reed Army Medical Center as a staff and operating room nurse in 1960. From 1963 to 1967, she served as an operating room instructor and supervisor at Letterman General Hospital in San Francisco, California, the Forty-fifth Surgical Hospital in Fort Sam Houston, Texas, and the Valley Forge General Hospital in Valley Forge, Pennsylvania.

From 1967 to 1973, Johnson was assigned to the staff of the United States Army Medical Research and Development Command. In this capacity, she served as project director of the equipment development for the operating room and central sterilizing area of the Army Medical Department's Field Hospital Systems. This was a multi-million dollar project. And, as a result of her efforts, the design of the new sterilizers for use by United States military hospitals worldwide was greatly improved.

After the completion of her doctoral studies, Johnson was appointed director of the Walter Reed Army Institute of Nursing. This undergraduate nursing program is located at Walter Reed Army Medical Center and was an extension of the University of Maryland's nursing school. Hazel Johnson was a colonel at this time and served as both a teaching professional and as an active member of the curriculum committee and the

Promotion	Date
Second Lieutenant	June 1, 1955
First Lieutenant	May 11, 1960
Captain	January 19, 1961
Major	November 5, 1965
Lieutenant Colonel	March 19, 1969
Colonel	December 2, 1974
Brigadier General	September 1, 1979

Brigadier General Hazel W. Johnson

search committee for the dean of the undergraduate nursing program. Colonel Johnson participated fully in all academic and university responsibilities. Following this duty assignment, she was transferred to Korea in June of 1978, as assistant for nursing, Office of the Surgeon, Eighth Army Command; and chief, Department of Nursing, United States Army Hospital 121, Evacuation Hospital, Seoul, Korea. In the latter assignment, she was the senior ranking United States military nurse in South Korea and chief consultant for nursing matters to the Eighth Army Command. In addition, Colonel Johnson was chief of the department of nursing at the largest United States Army hospital in Korea.

Upon completion of her tour in May 1979, Johnson was selected to the position of chief of the Army Nurse Corps. In an impressive ceremony held at the Pentagon, the U.S. Army Surgeon General Lt. Gen. Charles C. Pixley pinned the star of brigadier general on Hazel Johnson. The new general was sworn in as the sixteenth chief of the Army Nurse Corps and the first Black female general officer in the history of the United States Army.

In his remarks, General Pixley praised General Johnson for her pioneering efforts in the research and development of sanitation equipment for use by mobile field units as well as her talents as a truly outstanding officer with a genius for administration and operations. General Johnson's response was, in part, "I hold my own and the Corps' future reputation in my hands and pray that I will be given wisdom, foresight, knowledge, and an understanding heart as we accomplish the tasks before us." She went on to say, "With deep humility, professional pride, and a sense of this moment in history, I accept the challenge and responsibilities inherent in the position and the role of chief of the Army Nurse Corps." She then went on to outline her objectives for the future, which included the promotion and support of the highest nursing standards, continued support of recruiting efforts for professional nurses for both the active and reserve components of the Army Nurse Corps, and the support of nursing research at all levels of clinical and nursing administration.

General Johnson retired in 1983, after twenty-eight years of outstanding service to her country and her profession.

Since retirement, she has been active in a number of organizations, including the Association of Operation Room Nurses Committee for Education, the American Nurses' Association, the County Pennsylvania Nurses Association, the National League for Nursing, and the Association of the United States Army and Sigma Theta Tau Sorority. She also served as the military consultant to the surgeon general for infection control and educational matters in nursing. She currently holds a teaching appointment at Georgetown University as an adjunct professor of nursing and is a guest lecturer at the University of Maryland.

General Johnson's decoration and awards include the Legion of Merit; the Meritorious Service Medal; and the Army Commendation Medal with one Oak Leaf Cluster.

Among General Johnson's significant civilian awards are the Evangeline B. Bovard Army Nurse of the Year Award, which she received at Letterman General Hospital; the Army Nurse of the Year Dr. Anita Newcomb McGee Award awarded by the Daughters of the American Revolution; the Chapel of Four Chaplains Golden Heart Award; the Roy Wilkins Meritorious Service Award given by the National Association for the Advancement of Colored People; the Bethune Tubman Truth Award given by the Black Women Hall of Fame Foundation; the American Black Achievement Award in Business; the Professions given by *Ebony* magazine; and the Community Service Award given by the Tuskegee Airmen, Incorporated.

GENERAL ROSCOE ROBINSON, JR.
1928-1993
First Black American Four-Star General in the United States Army

Roscoe Robinson was born in St. Louis, Missouri. He received a bachelor's degree in military engineering from West Point, and a master's degree in international affairs from the University of Pittsburgh. He also attended the United States Army Command and General Staff College and the National War College.

During his more than thirty-one years in the Army, General Robinson's distinguished career assignments included combat duty as rifle company commander, battalion S-2 (Intelligence), Thirty-first Infantry Regiment, Seventh Infantry Division, United States Army, Korea. As a young lieutenant, Robinson saw action during the furious battle for Pork Chop Hill, and fought through white-hot phosphorous mortar barrages and exploding shells that sent razor-sharp shrapnel in every direction at the Chosin Reservoir. His division performed valiantly and, for their efforts, the entire unit was honored with the Republic of Korea Presidential Unit Citation Streamer embroidered with the words: "Korea, 1950-1953, Seventh Infantry Division." And for his outstanding valor, Lt. Robinson was awarded the Bronze Star.

As battalion S-2, Robinson was responsible for the production and dissemination of combat intelligence and counterintelligence matters. He served as advisor to the commanding officer and other staff officers in security matters. His duties also included collecting, collating, evaluating, and interpreting information about the enemy, weather, terrain, and any other factors that might have a bearing on the successful achievement of the unit's mission.

Upon returning to the continental United States, he served with several airborne units, attended a variety of service schools, and was handpicked for a tour with the United States military mission to Liberia in the late 1950s. The group included outstanding staff officers and civilian experts in various industrial areas.

In 1968, Lieutenant Colonel Robinson served in Vietnam as the deputy chief of staff for logistics of the First Air Cavalry Division. As the S-4 (Logistics), he was responsible for the logistics services and facilities available to the battalion. Most importantly, these are supply, transportation, maintenance, logistics plans, and records. The S-4 prepares logistical plans and relevant portions of published plans and orders. In many units, depending on the mission, the S-4 is also a commander of a service supporting unit, such as supply.

Colonel Robinson also saw action as the first African-American to command the Second Battalion, Seventh Cavalry, First Air Cavalry Division. During his tour of duty as commander, he led his troops in a joint forces attack on an area called Fishook, about fifty miles from Saigon, across the board in Cambodia. Fishook was the home of numerous enemy bases as well as the Communist headquarters that directed the war effort in the southern area of South Vietnam. In 1968, while the elite forces of the South Vietnamese attacked surrounding areas in Cambodia, the Second Battalion, Seventh Cavalry, led by Robinson, and other elements of both the South Vietnamese and the First Cavalry Division, made a highly mechanized, lightning strike in Fishook. The operation was highly successful. Upon completion, the task force had killed more than a thousand Communist soldiers and captured more than two hundred prisoners along with vital supplies.

A short time later, Colonel Robinson led his troops in one of the longest joint combat operations of the Vietnam War. The operation called for a devastating attack by B-52 bombers, tactical air and artillery strikes, followed by helicopter drops of the First Air Cavalry Division, Armored Infantry Brigade, which would be used to cut off the enemy's escape routes. The attack opened with a dozen B-52 bombers pounding Fishook during the dawn hours of May 1, 1968, with more than five hundred thousand pounds of explosives. This was followed by a murderous artillery barrage to clear the way for the air brigade drop. The Seventh Cavalry, led by Colonel Robinson, was among the invasion troops. Again, their performance during this Cambodian operation caused massive losses to the North Vietnamese. More than twenty-two thousand rifles and more than two thousand men were captured. In addition, thousands of other weapons, guns, and ammunition were destroyed. The enemy lost more than eleven hundred troops. The Allies lost only a fraction of that number. The combined forces in this operation numbered more than fifty thousand South Vietnamese and United States Army troops.

For their outstanding combat performance, the entire First Cavalry Division was decorated with the Republic of Vietnam Cross of Gallantry with Palm. Colonel Robinson received the Silver Star for his heroic service in Vietnam.

In 1969, he returned to the United States and studied at the National War College and then served as Southeast Asia special actions officer, J-5 (Management), General Staff Administration, United States Pacific Command, Hawaii; and executive to the chief of staff, United States Pacific Command, Hawaii, until his promotion to full colonel.

Returning to the continental United States from Hawaii in May 1972, Colonel Robinson assumed command of the Second Brigade, Eighty-second Airborne Division, Fort Bragg, North Carolina. In December of 1975, he again left the United States to serve as deputy commander, United States Army Garrison, Okinawa. Colonel Robinson was promoted to general and remained in Okinawa to become commanding general of the United States Army Garrison,

Promotion	Date
Second Lieutenant	June 1, 1951
First Lieutenant	June 12, 1954
Captain	December 16, 1957
Major	June 1, 1965
Lieutenant Colonel	June 1, 1972
Colonel	March 16, 1976
Brigadier General	July 28, 1977
Major General	June 1, 1980
Lieutenant General	June 1, 1981
General	August 30, 1982

Gen. Roscoe Robinson, Jr.

Okinawa. This command was followed by assignments as commanding general, Eighty-second Airborne Division, Fort Bragg, North Carolina; deputy chief of staff for operations, United States Army Europe and Seventh Army, Germany; and commanding general, United States Army, Japan IX Corps.

The brilliant career of General Robinson reached its zenith in August 1982, when he became the first African-American in the U.S. Army to achieve the rank of four-star general and the second Black to achieve that rank in the U.S.

military. (General Daniel "Chappie" James, Jr., USAF, was the first.) In his last duty assignment, General Robinson served as United States representative, NATO Military Committee, United States Army Element, International Military Activities. General Robinson retired on November 30, 1985.

After his retirement, General Robinson served on several corporate boards, including Northwest Airlines, Comsat Corporation, Giant Food Corporation, Metropolitan Life, Washington Mutual Fund, Alliant Tech Corporation, Wackenhut Incorporated, Armed Forces Benefit Association, and the McDonnell-Douglas Corporation. He was also instrumental in the development of minority studies for the United States Army. General Robinson also received numerous honors, including the most recent in May 1993, the Distinguished Graduate Award from the West Point Association of Graduates.

General Roscoe Robinson, Jr., a distinguished combat commander, died of leukemia at the Walter Reed Army Medical Center in Washington, DC. He was sixty-four years old. The date: July 22, 1993.

General Robinson's decorations and awards include the Silver Star with one Oak Leaf Cluster; the Legion of Merit with two Oak Leaf Clusters; the Distinguished Flying Cross; the Bronze Star Medal; Air Medals; the Army Commendation Medal; the Combat Infantryman Badge (second award); and the Master Parachutist Badge.

LIEUTENANT GENERAL FRANK E. PETERSEN
First Black American General in the United States Marine Corps

A Native of Topeka, Kansas, General Petersen has the distinction of being the first Black Marine Corps General in the history of the United States. He enlisted in the United States Navy in 1950, as an electronics technician and then enrolled in the Naval Aviation Cadet Program. General Petersen won his wings and accepted a commission as a second lieutenant in the Marine Corps.

A graduate of Topeka High School in 1949, he attended Washburn University in Topeka for one year prior to joining the Marine Corps in June 1950. The General subsequently continued his education in the Corps and earned his bachelor's degree in 1967. He earned his master's degree in 1973, from George Washington University, Washington, DC. Additionally, General Petersen attended the Amphibious Warfare School, Quantico, Virginia; the Aviation Safety Officer's Course, University of Southern California; and the National War College, Washington, DC.

His command and staff assignments have included: squadron commander, VMF314; tactical air planner and programmer for the deputy chief of staff for Aviation; special assistant for Minority Affairs to the commandant of the Marine Corps; commanding officer of Marine Aircraft Group Thirty-two; executive assistant to the assistant commandant of the Marine Corps; chief of staff for Ninth Marine Amphibious Brigade; deputy director for Operations, National Military Command Center; director, Facilities and Services Division, Installations and Logistics Department, Headquarters Marine Corps; assistant wing commander for First Marine Aircraft Wing; and commanding general for the Ninth Marine Amphibious Brigade.

A superlative fighter pilot, General Petersen has flown in excess of four thousand hours in various fighter/attack aircraft, including the AV8 Harrier. He served two combat tours, Korea in 1953, and Vietnam in 1968. The General has flown more than 350 combat missions.

General Petersen's history-making promotion to brigadier general occurred in February 1979, and in May 1983, he again made history when he was promoted to the rank of major general.

Early in General Petersen's career he decided that he would become a pilot. He was motivated by the story of America's first African-American aviator, Jesse Brown, who had been shot down in North Korea and perished in the cockpit of his aircraft from injuries. Deeply moved, the then seaman apprentice enlisted in the Naval Aviation Program and as they say, the rest is history.

When General Petersen received his third star from Marine Commandant P.X. Kelley, he became not only the first African-American but one of only 8 three-star generals in the United States Marine Corps. General Petersen has also been honored with the prestigious Silver Hawk Award. It was presented to him in a special ceremony by assistant commandant of the Marine Corps, General J.K. Davis. It

UNITED STATES MARINE CORPS

Lt. Gen. Frank E. Petersen

represents the singular honor that General Petersen retired as the senior ranking aviator in the United States Marine Corps and the United States Navy.

General Petersen's last duty assignment was commanding general of the Marine Corps Development and Education Command in Quantico, Virginia. The trailblazing, superlative African-American flight warrior retired in 1988, "Semper Fi."

His numerous decorations and awards include: the Defense Superior Service Medal; the Defense Distinguished Service Medal; Legion of Merit with Combat V; Distinguished Flying Cross; Meritorious Service Medal; Air Medal; Navy Commendation Medal with Combat V; Air Force Commendation Medal; and Purple Heart.

GENERAL COLIN L. POWELL
First Black Chairman of the Joint Chiefs of Staff

Born in New York City, Colin Powell earned his bachelor's degree in geology from the City University of New York (CUNY) and a master's degree in business administration from George Washington University. He is also a graduate of the United States Army Command and General Staff College and the National War College.

After completing the Infantry Officer Basic Course, the Ranger Course, and the Airborne Course at Fort Benning, Georgia, Lieutenant Powell was stationed in Germany. Subsequent operational assignments took him to Fort Devens, Massachusetts; Fort Campbell, Kentucky; Fort Leavenworth, Kansas; and Fort Carson, Colorado. General Powell served two tours of duty in Vietnam. During his first tour, from 1962 to 1963, he served as advisor and later assistant operations officer, Self Defense Corps Training Center, Second Infantry Division, I Corps, Military Assistance Advisory Group, United States Army, Vietnam. As the assistant operations officer, then Captain Powell was responsible for planning combat operations, organization, and training as required by the commanding officer. Additionally, he wrote operations directives, plans and orders, command post exercises (PX's), and field training exercises (FTX's), and developed training aids, ammunition requirements, and a host of related duties that enable the commander to make an informed decision regarding the successful completion of the unit's mission. Powell returned to Vietnam from 1968 to 1969 after serving as task officer, United States Army Infantry Board, Fort Benning, Georgia; student, Infantry Officer Advanced Course, United States Army Infantry School, Fort Benning, Georgia; test officer, Supporting Weapons Test Division, United States Army Infantry Board, Fort Benning, Georgia; and student, United States Army Command and General Staff College, Fort Leavenworth, Kansas.

During his second tour in Vietnam, Major Powell served as executive officer, Third Battalion, First Infantry, Eleventh Infantry Brigade, Americal Division (Mechanized Infantry), United States Army, Vietnam. He also served as assistant chief of staff, G-3 (Operations), and later deputy G-3, Americal Division (Mechanized Infantry), United States Army, Vietnam.

Returning to the United States in 1969, Powell served as assistant chief of staff, Operations, and later deputy analyst, Planning and Programming, Analysis Directorate, Office of the Assistant Vice Chief of Staff, United States Army, Washington, DC; commander, First Battalion, Thirty-second Infantry, Second Infantry Division, Korea; operations research analyst, Office of the Deputy Assistant Secretary of Defense (Manpower, Requirements, and Analysis), Office of the Assistant Secretary of Defense (Manpower and Reserve Affairs), Washington, DC; commander, Second Brigade, 101st Airborne Division (Air Assault), Fort Campbell, Kentucky; executive to the special assistant to the secretary and deputy secretary of defense, Office of the Deputy Secretary of Defense, Washington, DC.

In 1982, then Brigadier General Powell became the assistant division commander, Fourth Infantry Division (Mechanized), Fort Carson, Colorado. In this command capacity, General Powell was responsible for the training and operations of a force of more than eighteen thousand mechanized troops. The general next served a year at Fort Leavenworth, Kansas, as deputy commanding general of Combined Arms Development. This was followed by another tour of duty at the Pentagon in Washington, DC, as the military assistant to Secretary of Defense Casper Weinberger from 1983 to 1986. There followed a series of command and staff positions. By this time, General Powell had been promoted to lieutenant general. His assignments included commanding general, Fifth U.S. Corps, Frankfurt, West Germany. Six months later, Powell was called to the White House by President Ronald Reagan to serve as deputy to National Security Advisor Frank Carlucci. Powell subsequently succeeded Carlucci as national security advisor, becoming the first African-American to hold that position. In that capacity, the general was the president's number one advisor on matters relating to the coordination of major government agencies dealing with the security of the nation, including the Central Intelligence Agency, the State Department, and the Department of Defense.

General Powell, rapidly ascending the command ladder, was promoted to four-star general in April 1989, and again returned to command duties as head of the Forces Command headquartered at Fort McPherson, Georgia, where he commanded a group of active duty and reservists that totaled nearly one million soldiers.

Then, on October 1, 1989, General Powell made military history when he was sworn in by Defense Secretary Dick Cheney as the twelfth chairman of the Joint Chiefs of Staff (JCS) and the first African-American ever to hold that position. General Powell was appointed by President George Bush. He was only fifty-three at the time, which made him the youngest chairman of the JCS ever. With this appointment, the general was now the most powerful military man on earth and the principal military advisor to the president on all matters of national defense and security. His wife Alma, looked on proudly as she held the bible during the impressive ceremony. This was followed by a full-dress military ceremony in which General Powell, accompanied by Secretary Cheney, reviewed an impressive array of troops that included high ranking representatives from all branches of the armed forces of the United States.

Only a year later, in 1990, General Powell masterminded the tactical deployment of multinational forces in the highly

Promotion	Date
Second Lieutenant	June 30, 1958
First Lieutenant	June 30, 1961
Captain	June 30, 1965
Major	June 30, 1966
Lieutenant Colonel	June 30, 1970
Colonel	February 1, 1976
Brigadier General	June 1, 1979
Major General	August 1, 1983
Lieutenant General	July 1, 1986
General	April 4, 1989

Gen. Colin L. Powell

efficient execution of operations Desert Shield and Desert Storm, the most complex and technologically sophisticated war in the history of our nation. By the time what has come to be known as the Gulf War was over, Chairman Powell had commanded more than eight hundred thousand troops and a coalition of air, naval, and ground forces that pulverized Saddam Hussein's enormous army of nearly a million troops.[1]

On September 30, 1993, the son of honest, hard-working Jamaican immigrants from the South Bronx, retired. Gen. Colin L. Powell, chairman of the Joint Chiefs of Staff, was a man who not only pursued excellence, but achieved it.

---

[1] see maps pages xiii–xiv

Through hard work and equal dedication, the general retired from an exceptionally brilliant career in the service of his country.

General Powell served as the twelfth chairman of the Joint Chiefs of Staff from October 1, 1989, to September 30, 1993, under both President George Bush and President Bill Clinton. General Powell's decorations and awards include the Defense Distinguished Service Medal with three Oak Leaf Clusters; the Defense Superior Service Medal; the Distinguished Service Medal; the Legion of Merit with one Oak Leaf Cluster; the Soldier's Medal; the Bronze Star Medal; the Air Medal; the Joint Service Commendation Medal; the Expert Infantryman Badge; the Combat Infantryman Badge; the Parachutist Badge; the Pathfinder Badge; the Ranger Tab; the Air Assault Badge; the Army Commendation Medal with two Oak Leaf Clusters; the Presidential Service Badge; the Secretary of Defense Identification Badge; the Army Staff Identification Badge; the Joint Chiefs of Staff Identification Badge; and the Purple Heart. The general has also been decorated by the governments of Argentina, Behrain, Brazil, Canada, France, Germany, Greece, Jamaica, Japan, Korea, Kuwait, Saudi Arabia, Senegal, and Venezuela.

General Powell's civilian awards honoring his public service include two awards of the Presidential Medal of Freedom; the President's Citizen Medal; the Congressional Gold Medal; the Secretary of State Distinguished Service Medal; and the Secretary of Energy Distinguished Service Medal. Additionally, he received an honorary knighthood (Knight Commander of the Bath) from the Queen of England in December of 1993.

Gen. Colin Powell published his memoirs, *My American Journey*, in 1995 and the book instantly vaulted to number one on the *New York Times'* best seller list. Shortly before the publication of his book, Colin Powell had announced that he was considering running for the office of president of the United States.

After a triumphant book tour of America and Europe, Powell was faced with the decision of whether or not to declare his candidacy. He had many powerful supports in his camp, including George Bush, Jack Kemp, Mary Matalin, Frank Carlucci, Tom Kean, and Casper Weinberger. A short time later, however, Powell ended weeks of speculation about his presidential aspirations by announcing that he would not be a candidate for the office.

On the last page of *My American Journey*, there is an omen to his decision not to run. He cautions, in the words of the old saying, "Be careful of what you choose. You may get it."

BLACK UNITED STATES ARMY GENERAL OFFICERS

LIEUTENANT GENERAL SAMUEL E. EBBESEN

Deputy Assistant Secretary of Defense for Military Manpower and Personnel Policy, Office of the Secretary of Defense, Washington, DC

A native of Saint Croix, Virgin Islands, General Ebbesen received his bachelor's degree in political science from the City College of New York and his master's degree in public administration from Auburn University. The general is also a graduate of several military schools, including the Infantry School Basic and Advanced Courses, the United States Army Command and General Staff College, and the Air War College.

During his thirty-four years in the United States Army, the general has had the following staff and command assignments: commander, Company F, First Training Regiment, Fort Dix, New Jersey; battalion communications officer, First Battalion, Fifteenth Infantry, Third Infantry Division, United States Army, Europe, Germany; infantry training advisor, School and Training Detachment, Training Directorate, United States Military Assistance Command, Vietnam; and chief, Operations Branch, Plans and Operations Division, Directorate of Operations and Training, United States Army Infantry Center, Fort Benning, Georgia.

General Ebbesen left the United States in July 1969, and held various assignments, including headquarters commandant, Fourth Infantry Division, United States Army, Vietnam; battalion S-3 (Operations), First Battalion, Eighth Infantry, Fourth Infantry Division, United States Army, Vietnam; and district senior advisor, Advisor Team 15, XXIV Corps, United States Military Assistance Command, Vietnam.

Over the next decade, General Ebbesen's various duty assignments included staff officer, Office of the Study Coordinator, Office of the Deputy Chief of Staff for Operations and Plans, United States Army Combat Development Command, Fort Belvoir, Virginia; personnel management officer, Infantry Branch, Officer Personnel Management Directorate, United States Army Military Personnel Center, Alexandria, Virginia; special assistant to the executive officer, Officer Personnel Management Directorate, United States Army Military Personnel Center, Alexandria, Virginia; battalion executive officer, Second Battalion, Thirty-first Infantry, Seventh Infantry Division, Fort Ord, California; deputy G-3 (Operations) and later G-3, Seventh Infantry Division, Fort Ord, California; executive officer, Second Brigade, Seventh Infantry Division, Fort Ord, California; commander, Second Battalion, Thirty-second Infantry, Seventh Infantry Division, Fort Ord, California; special assistant to the chief of staff, Seventh Infantry Division, Fort Ord, California; deputy chief, Plans and Operations Division, and later executive officer, Office of the Chief, Legislative Liaison, Office of the Secretary of the Army,

Promotion	Date
Second Lieutenant	October 15, 1962
First Lieutenant	September 5, 1964
Captain	September 5, 1968
Major	September 5, 1975
Lieutenant Colonel	June 3, 1976
Colonel	September 1, 1982
Brigadier General	January 1, 1988
Major General	January 1, 1991
Lieutenant General	August 3, 1992

Lt. Gen. Samuel E. Ebbesen

Washington, DC; commander, First Brigade, 101st Airborne Division (Air Assault), Fort Campbell, Kentucky; chief of staff, I Corps, Fort Lewis, Washington; deputy chief, Legislative Liaison, Office of the Chief of Legislative Liaison, United States Army, Washington, DC; assistant division commander, Sixth Infantry Division, Fort Wainwright, Alaska; commanding general, Sixth Infantry Division (Light), Fort Wainwright, Alaska; and commanding general, Second United States Army, Fort Gillem, Georgia.

During his illustrious career, General Ebbesen has been awarded the Distinguished Service Medal; the Legion of Merit with three Oak Leaf Clusters; the Bronze Star Medal with "V" device and two Oak Leaf Clusters; the Bronze Star Medal with one Oak Leaf Cluster; the Air Medal; the Army Commendation Medal with two Oak Leaf Clusters; the Combat Infantryman Badge; the Parachutist Badge; the Air Assault Badge; and the Army Staff Identification Badge.

LIEUTENANT GENERAL ROBERT E. GRAY
Deputy Commander in Chief, United States Army, Europe and Seventh Army, Heidelberg, Germany

Born in Algoma, West Virginia, General Gray is a graduate of Ohio State University, where he earned his bachelor's degree in computer science. The general is also a graduate of the United States Army War College and the United States Army Command and General Staff College, where he earned a master of military science.

General Gray's major duty assignments have included communications officer, Fifty-sixth Artillery Group, United States Army, Europe, Germany; commander, Company C, Ninety-seventh Signal Battalion, Seventh United States Army Communications Command, United States Army, Europe, Germany; S-4 (Logistics), 501st Signal Battalion, 101st Airborne Division (Airmobile), United States Army, Vietnam; and commander, Company A, 501st Signal Battalion, 101st Airborne Division (Airmobile), United States Army, Vietnam.

Upon his return from Vietnam, he was assigned as automatic data processing officer, Computer Security Element, Counterintelligence and Security Division, Defense Intelligence Agency, Washington, DC; communications-electronics staff officer, Plans and Policy Branch, Systems Management Division, Information Systems Directorate, Defense Intelligence Agency, Washington, DC; executive officer, Fiftieth Signal Battalion, Thirty-fifth Signal Group, XVIII Airborne Corps, Fort Bragg, North Carolina; tactical plans officer, G-3 (Operations), Contingency Plans Division, XVIII Airborne Corps, Fort Bragg, North Carolina; and commander, Eighty-second Signal Battalion, Eighty-second Airborne Division, Fort Bragg, North Carolina.

General Gray received his first star in November 1984, and was later assigned as chief, Command, Control, and Communications Division, United States Army Combined Arms Combat Development Activity, Fort Leavenworth, Kansas; commander, Thirty-fifth Signal Brigade, XVIII Airborne Corps, Fort Bragg, North Carolina; special assistant to the commanding general, XVIII Airborne Corps, Fort Bragg, North Carolina; deputy commanding general, United States Army Signal Center and Fort Gordon, and assistant commandant, United States Army Signal School, Fort Gordon, Georgia; deputy director for plans, Programs and Systems, Office of the Director of Information Systems for Command, Control, Communication, and Computers, Office of the Secretary of the Army, Washington, DC; commanding general, United States Army Signal Center and Fort Gordon, and commandant, United States Army Signal School, Fort Gordon, Georgia; and chief of staff, United States Army, Europe and Seventh Army, Germany.

General Gray's numerous awards and decorations include

Promotion	Date
Second Lieutenant	May 26, 1966
First Lieutenant	May 26, 1969
Captain	May 26, 1973
Major	May 26, 1980
Lieutenant Colonel	August 13, 1982
Colonel	November 1, 1984
Brigadier General	April 1, 1990
Major General	January 1, 1993
Lieutenant General	May 25, 1995

Lt. Gen. Robert E. Gray

the Distinguished Service Medal; the Legion of Merit with one Oak Leaf Cluster; the Bronze Star Medal; the Meritorious Service Medal with two Oak Leaf Clusters; the Air Medal; the Army Commendation Medal with one Oak Leaf Cluster; the Army Good Conduct Medal; and the Master Parachutist Badge.

LIEUTENANT GENERAL JOHNNIE E. WILSON
Deputy Chief of Staff for Logistics, United States Army,
Washington, DC

Born in Baton Rouge, Louisiana, General Wilson received his bachelor's degree in business administration from the University of Nebraska at Omaha, and his master's degree in logistics management from the Florida Institute of Technology. The general is also a graduate of the United States Command and General Staff College and the Industrial College of the Armed Forces. General Wilson began his career as a second lieutenant after graduating from Officers Candidate School.

His major duty assignments have been mechanical maintenance officer and later commander, Company A, 782d Maintenance Battalion, Eighty-second Airborne Division, Fort Bragg, North Carolina; assistant brigade supply officer and later commander, Company C, 173d Support Battalion (Airborne), 173d Airborne Brigade, United States Army, Vietnam; student, Ordnance Office Advanced Course, United States Army Ordnance, Aberdeen Proving Ground, Maryland; student, University of Nebraska, Omaha, Nebraska; commander and later technical supply officer, Company B, 123d Maintenance Battalion, First Armored Division, United States Army, Europe.

The general returned to the continental United States from Europe in 1976 and was assigned as student, United States Army Command and General Staff College, Fort Leavenworth, Kansas; student, Florida Institute of Technology, Melbourne, Florida; professional development officer and later personnel management officer and chief, Ordnance Assignment Branch, Combat Service Support Division, United States Army Military Personnel Center, Alexandria, Virginia; commander, 709th Maintenance Battalion, Ninth Infantry Division, Fort Lewis, Washington; student, Industrial College of the Armed Forces, Fort McNair, Washington, DC; commander, Division Support Command, First Armored Division, United States Army, Europe; commander, Thirteenth Support Command, Fort Hood, Texas; deputy commanding general, Twenty-first Theater Army Area Command, United States Army, Europe and Seventh Army, Germany; commanding general, United States Army Ordnance Center, and commandant, United States Army Ordnance School, Aberdeen Proving Ground, Maryland; and chief of staff, United States Army Materiel Command, Alexandria, Virginia.

General Wilson's decorations and awards include the Distinguished Service Medal with one Oak Leaf Cluster; the Legion of Merit; the Bronze Star Medal with two Oak Leaf Clusters; the Meritorious Service Medal with two Oak Leaf Clusters; the Army Commendation Medal; the Good Conduct Medal; and the Master Parachutist Badge.

Promotion	Date
Second Lieutenant	May 31, 1967
First Lieutenant	May 31, 1970
Captain	May 31, 1974
Major	May 31, 1981
Lieutenant Colonel	July 13, 1980
Colonel	November 1, 1984
Brigadier General	September 1, 1989
Major General	July 1, 1992
Lieutenant General	February 9, 1994

Lt. Gen. Johnnie E. Wilson

MAJOR GENERAL JOE N. BALLARD
Chief of Staff, United States Army Training and Doctrine
Command, Fort Monroe, Virginia

General Ballard was born in Meeker, Louisiana, and is a graduate of Southern University A & M College with a bachelor's degree in electrical engineering. He also earned a master's degree in engineering management at the University of Missouri and attended the Engineer Officer Basic and Advanced Courses, the United States Army Command and General Staff College, and the United States Army War College.

During his more than thirty-one years in the Army, General Ballard's assignments have included commander, Company C, Second Battalion, Second Training Brigade, United States Army Training Center, Fort Polk, Louisiana; commander, C Company, 864th Engineer Battalion, United States Army, Vietnam; chief, Lines of Communications Section Operations, Eighteenth Engineer Brigade, United States Army, Vietnam; engineer construction planning officer, Planning and Real Estate Branch, Engineer Division, Fifth United States Army, Fort Sheridan, Illinois; test and evaluation officer, United States Army Combat Developments Command Engineer Agency, Fort Belvoir, Virginia; area commander, United States Army District Recruiting Command, Detroit, Michigan; and operations officer and later executive officer, 326th Engineer Battalion, 101st Airborne Division (Air Assault), Fort Campbell, Kentucky.

Ballard left the United States in 1979 for Korea, where he served as chief, Mapping and Intelligence Sections, Engineer Division, and executive officer, United States Forces Korea/Eighth Army Engineer, Eighth United States Army, Korea.

Returning to the United States in 1982, General Ballard served as facility energy manager, Office of the Deputy Chief of Staff for Logistics, United States Army, Washington, DC; commander, Eighty-second Engineer Battalion, Seventh Engineer Brigade, VII Corps, United States Army, Europe, Germany; assignment officer, Engineer Branch, United States Army Military Personnel Center, Alexandria, Virginia; chief, Assignments Branch, Colonels Division, Officer Personnel Management Directorate, United States Army Military Personnel Center, Alexandria, Virginia; commander, Eighteenth Engineer Brigade, United States Army, Europe, Germany; and assistant deputy chief of staff, Engineer, United States Army, Europe and Seventh Army, Germany.

These duties were followed by a variety of assignments that included deputy commanding general, United States Army Engineer Center and Fort Leonard Wood, and assistant commandant, United States Army Engineer School, Fort Leonard Wood, Mis-

Promotion	Date
Second Lieutenant	January 28, 1965
First Lieutenant	January 27, 1967
Captain	July 15, 1972
Major	July 15, 1979
Lieutenant Colonel	October 13, 1980
Colonel	August 1, 1987
Brigadier General	October 1, 1991
Major General	August 1, 1994

Maj. Gen. Joe N. Ballard

souri; special assistant to director of management, Total Army Basing Study, Office of the Chief of Staff, United States Army, Washington, DC; and commanding general, United States Army Engineer Center and Fort Leonard Wood, Fort Leonard Wood, Missouri.

General Ballard's decorations and awards include the Legion of Merit with two Oak Leaf Clusters; the Bronze Star Medal with one Oak Leaf Cluster; the Defense Meritorious Service Medal; the Meritorious Service Medal with three Oak Leaf Clusters; the Army Commendation Medal with one Oak Leaf Cluster; and the Army Staff Identification Badge.

MAJOR GENERAL JOHN S. COWINGS
Commandant, Industrial College of the Armed Forces, National Defense University, Fort McNair, Washington, DC

A Reserve Officer Training Corps (ROTC) graduate, General Cowings graduated from New York University with a bachelor's degree in civil government and from Golden Gate University with a bachelor's degree in management. He is also a graduate of the Ordnance Officer Basic and Advanced Courses, the United States Army Command and General Staff College, and the Industrial College of the Armed Forces.

During his more than thirty-one years of military service, General Cowings's major assignments have included duty both stateside and abroad. He has served as shop officer and later acting commander, Company C, 701st Maintenance Battalion, First Infantry Division, United States Army, Vietnam; commander, Company D, 701st Maintenance Battalion, First Infantry Division, United States Army, Vietnam; commander, Maintenance Company, General Support Group, Fort Ord, California; special assistant to the commanding general, United States Army Combat Development Experimentation Command, Fort Ord, California; historical officer and later student, United States Army Command and General Staff College, Fort Leavenworth, Kansas; and research and development coordinator, United States Army Institute for the Behavioral and Social Sciences, Far East Field Unit, United States Army, Korea.

General Cowings returned to the United States in June 1977 and served as staff officer, Manpower Coordination Branch, Allocation and Documents Division, Office of the Deputy Chief of Staff for Personnel, United States Army, Washington, DC; executive officer, Office of the Director of Manpower, Plans and Budget, Office of the Deputy Chief of Staff for Personnel, United States Army, Washington, DC; commander, 708th Maintenance Battalion, Eighth Infantry Division (Mechanized), United States Army, Europe, Germany; logistics staff officer and North Atlantic Treaty Organization (NATO) team chief, Office of the Deputy Chief of Staff for Logistics, United States Army, Washington, DC; student, Industrial College of the Armed Forces, Fort McNair, Washington, DC; director, Maintenance Directorate, and commander, Rock Island Arsenal, United States Army Munitions and Chemical Command, Rock Island, Illinois; and chief of staff, Tank-Automotive Command, Warren, Michigan.

Cowings was promoted to brigadier general in 1990 and was assigned as commanding general, Third Support Command (Corps), United States Army, Europe and Seventh Army, Germany; deputy director for plans, Analysis and Resources, J-4 (Logistics), the Joint Chiefs of Staff, Washington, DC; and command-

Promotion	Date
Second Lieutenant	November 7, 1965
First Lieutenant	November 7, 1968
Captain	November 7, 1972
Major	November 7, 1979
Lieutenant Colonel	August 12, 1982
Colonel	October 1, 1985
Brigadier General	July 1, 1990
Major General	July 1, 1993

Maj. Gen. John S. Cowings

ing general, United States Army Aviation and Troop Command, St. Louis, Missouri.

General Cowings's decorations and awards include the Distinguished Service Medal; the Defense Superior Service Medal; the Legion of Merit with one Oak Leaf Cluster; the Bronze Star Medal with one Oak Leaf Cluster; the Meritorious Service Medal with six Oak Leaf Clusters; the Army Commendation Medal with two Oak Leaf Clusters; the Joint Chiefs of Staff Identification Badge; and the Army Staff Identification Badge.

MAJOR GENERAL ARTHUR T. DEAN
Deputy Chief of Staff for Personnel and Installation
Management, Forces Command, Fort McPherson, Georgia

On August 15, 1967, Arthur Dean was commissioned a second lieutenant through Army ROTC. A native of Wadesboro, North Carolina, the general earned a bachelor's degree in history from Morgan State University and a master's degree in personnel management from Central Michigan University. General Dean also graduated from the Field Artillery Officer Basic Course, the Adjutant General Officer Advanced Course, the United States Army Command and General Staff College, and the United States Army War College.

General Dean's major duty assignments have included forward observer, Battery A, 320th Artillery, Eighty-second Airborne Division, Fort Bragg, North Carolina; assistant personnel management officer, Adjutant General Section, Eighty-second Airborne Division, Fort Bragg, North Carolina; chief, Administrative Services Branch, and later chief, Classified Control, Publications, Supply and Records Branch, United States Military Assistance Command, Vietnam.

After returning home from Vietnam in 1971, his duty assignments included student, Adjutant General School, Fort Benjamin Harrison, Indiana; instructor, Communicative Arts Division, United States Army Adjutant General School, Fort Benjamin Harrison, Indiana; commander, Company B, United States Army Administration Center and Fort Benjamin Harrison, Fort Benjamin Harrison, Indiana; commander, United States Army Manhattan Recruiting Area, Newburgh District Recruiting Command, Newburgh, New York; assistant executive officer, Adjutant General Office, and assistant chief of staff, Adjutant General Center, Washington, DC; personnel management officer, Majors Division, United States Army Military Personnel Center, Alexandria, Virginia; military assistant, Office of the Assistant Secretary of the Army (Manpower and Reserve Affairs), Washington, DC; assistant chief of staff, Personnel, First Corps Support Command, Fort Bragg, North Carolina; commander, Eighteenth Personnel and Administration Battalion, Fort Bragg, North Carolina; commander, Task Force Victory, First Corps Support Command, XVIII Airborne Corps, Fort Bragg, North Carolina, with duty in Honduras; adjutant general, V Corps, United States Army, Europe and Seventh Army, Germany; commander, United States Army Postal Group, First Personnel Command, Europe; commander, United States Army First Recruiting Brigade (Northeast), Fort Meade, Maryland; assistant to the commanding general, Postal Operations, Desert Storm, Saudi Arabia; commander, First Recruiting Brigade (Northeast), Fort Meade, Maryland; and director, Enlisted Personnel Management Director-

Promotion	Date
Second Lieutenant	August 15, 1967
First Lieutenant	August 15, 1970
Captain	August 15, 1974
Major	July 14, 1980
Lieutenant Colonel	August 15, 1981
Colonel	May 1, 1987
Brigadier General	April 1, 1992
Major General	July 1, 1995

Maj. Gen. Arthur T. Dean

ate, United States Total Army Personnel Command, Alexandria, Virginia.

His decorations and awards include the Legion of Merit with two Oak Leaf Clusters; the Bronze Star Medal; the Meritorious Service Medal with four Oak Leaf Clusters; the Joint Service Commendation Medal; the Army Commendation Medal with two Oak Leaf Clusters; the Army Achievement Medal with one Oak Leaf Cluster; the Senior Parachutist Badge; the Ranger Tab; and the Army Staff Identification Badge.

MAJOR GENERAL LARRY R. ELLIS
Assistant Chief of Staff, C-3/J-3/G-3 (Operations), United Nations Command/Combined Forces Command, United States Forces Korea/Eighth United States Army APO AP

Larry Ellis attended Morgan State University, where he earned his bachelor's degree in physical education, and Indiana University, where he received his master's degree in physical education. General Ellis is also a graduate of the Armed Forces Staff College and the United States Army War College.

General Ellis has served as executive officer, Company B, Second Battalion (Airborne), 325th Infantry, Eighty-second Airborne Division, Fort Bragg, North Carolina; platoon leader, Headquarters Company, First Battalion (Airmobile), 502d Infantry, 101st Airborne Division, United States Army, Vietnam; reconnaissance platoon leader, Company E, First Battalion (Airmobile), 502d Infantry, 101st Airborne Division, United States Army, Vietnam; commander, Company C, First Battalion (Airmobile), 502d Infantry, 101st Airborne Division, United States Army, Vietnam; and S-4 (Logistics), First Battalion (Airmobile), 502d Infantry, 101st Airborne Division, United States Army, Vietnam.

Returning to the United States from Vietnam in 1970, Ellis was assigned as commander, Company C, Second Battalion (Airborne), 508th Infantry, Eighty-second Airborne Division, Fort Bragg, North Carolina; S-3 (Operations), Headquarters and Headquarters Company, Second Battalion (Airborne), 508th Infantry, Eighty-second Airborne Division, Fort Bragg, North Carolina; aide-de-camp to the commanding general, Eighty-second Airborne Division, Fort Bragg, North Carolina; and physical training officer, Department of Physical Education, United States Military Academy, West Point, New York.

Leaving the United States for another tour of duty in Europe in 1979, Ellis's duty assignments were supply policy officer, Office of the Deputy Chief of Staff for Operations and Plans, United States Army, Europe and Seventh Army, Germany; assistant secretary, General Staff, Command Group, United States Army, Europe and Seventh Army, Germany; and executive officer, Second Battalion, Thirteenth Infantry (Mechanized), Eighth Infantry Division, United States Army, Europe and Seventh Army, Germany.

Back in the United States in May 1983, General Ellis's command and staff duties included manpower analyst, Program Analysis and Evaluation Division, Office of the Chief of Staff, United States Army, Washington, DC; chief, Manpower and Force Analysis Division, Program Analysis and Evaluation Directorate, Office of the Chief of Staff, United States Army, Washington, DC; commander, First Brigade, Third Infantry Division, United States Army, Europe and Seventh Army, Germany; deputy director, Military Personnel Management, Office of the Deputy

Promotion	Date
Second Lieutenant	February 5, 1969
First Lieutenant	February 5, 1972
Captain	February 5, 1976
Major	June 6, 1978
Lieutenant Colonel	November 1, 1982
Colonel	June 1, 1988
Brigadier General	July 1, 1992
Major General	July 1, 1995

Maj. Gen. Larry R. Ellis

Chief of Staff for Personnel, United States Army, Washington, DC; deputy director, Strategic Planning and Policy J-5 (Management), United States Pacific Command, Camp H.M. Smith, Hawaii; and assistant division commander, Second Infantry Division, Eighth United States Army, Korea.

General Ellis has been awarded the Defense Superior Service Medal; the Legion of Merit with two Oak Leaf Clusters; the Bronze Star Medal; the Meritorious Service Medal with two Oak Leaf Clusters; the Air Medal; the Army Commendation Medal with one Oak Leaf Cluster; the Combat Infantryman Badge; the Senior Parachutist Badge; and the Army Staff Identification Badge.

MAJOR GENERAL FRED A. GORDEN
Chief of Public Affairs, Office of the Secretary of the Army, the Pentagon, Washington, DC

General Gorden was born in Anniston, Alabama. He is a graduate of the United States Military Academy at West Point. The general also has a master's degree in foreign language literature from Middlebury College. He is also a graduate of several military schools, including the Field Artillery School Basic and Advanced Courses, the Armed Forces Staff College, and the National War College.

General Gorden has been a member of the United States Army for more than thirty-four years. His numerous staff and command assignments include forward observer and later liaison officer, assistant executive officer, and executive officer, Battery B, Twenty-second Artillery, 193d Infantry Brigade, Fort Kobbe, Canal Zone, Panama; assistant S-3 (Operations), 193d Infantry Brigade, Fort Kobbe, Canal Zone, Panama; assistant S-3 and later liaison officer, Second Battalion, 320th Artillery, First Brigade, 101st Airborne Division, United States Army, Vietnam; commander, Battery C, Second Battalion, 320th Artillery, First Brigade, 101st Airborne Division, United States Army, Vietnam; and assistant S-3, Second Howitzer Battalion, 320th Artillery, First Brigade, 101st Airborne Division, United States Army, Vietnam.

After returning from Vietnam in 1968, General Gorden was assigned as student, Defense Language Institute (East Coast Branch), Washington, DC; Spanish instructor and later assistant professor, Department of Foreign Languages, United States Military Academy, West Point, New York; assignment officer and later personnel management officer, Field Artillery Branch, United States Army Military Personnel Center, Alexandria, Virginia; executive officer, First Battalion, Fifteenth Field Artillery, Second Infantry Division, Korea; special assistant to the commander and later S-3, Division Artillery, Twenty-fifth Infantry Division, Schofield Barracks, Hawaii; commander, First Battalion, Eighth Field Artillery, Twenty-fifth Infantry Division, Schofield Barracks, Hawaii; and inspector general, 25th Infantry Division, Schofield Barracks, Hawaii.

General Gorden's other duty assignments were executive officer, Office of the Chief of Legislative Liaison, United States Army, Washington, DC; commander, Division Artillery, Seventh Infantry Division, Fort Ord, California; director, Inter-American Region, Office of the Assistant Secretary of Defense (International Security Affairs), Washington, DC; assistant division commander, Seventh Infantry Division, Fort Ord, California; commandant of cadets, United States Military Academy, West Point, New York; commanding general, Twenty-fifth

Promotion	Date
Second Lieutenant	June 6, 1962
First Lieutenant	June 6, 1965
Captain	June 6, 1969
Major	June 6, 1976
Lieutenant Colonel	June 6, 1980
Colonel	March 15, 1982
Brigadier General	October 1, 1985
Major General	July 1, 1989

DEPARTMENT OF THE ARMY

Maj. Gen. Fred A. Gorden

Infantry Division (Light), Schofield Barracks, Hawaii; acting director of military personnel management, Office of the Deputy Chief of Staff for Personnel, United States Army, Washington, DC; assistant deputy chief of staff for personnel, Office of the Deputy Chief of Staff for Personnel, United States Army, Washington, DC; and commanding general, United States Army Military District of Washington, Washington, DC.

General Gorden's decorations and awards include the Defense Distinguished Service Medal; the Distinguished Service Medal; the Legion of Merit; the Bronze Star Medal with "V" device and one Oak Leaf Cluster; the Meritorious Service Medal with one Oak Leaf Cluster; the Air Medal; the Army Commendation Medal with one Oak Leaf Cluster; the Parachutist Badge; the Ranger Tab; and the Office of the Secretary of Defense Identification Badge.

MAJOR GENERAL KENNETH D. GRAY
Assistant Judge Advocate General, Office of the Judge
Advocate General, United States Army, Washington, DC

Born in Excelsior, West Virginia, Gray received his commission as a second lieutenant through Army ROTC. He received his bachelor's degree in political science from West Virginia State College and his law degree from West Virginia University.

He served as legal officer, First United States Army Student Detachment, Fort Meade, Maryland; student, the Judge Advocate General's Officer Basic Course, The Judge Advocate General's School, Charlottesville, Virginia; defense counsel, United States Army Training Center, Fort Ord, California; staff judge advocate and later defense counsel, United States Army Support Command, United States Army, Vietnam; assistant military affairs officer, First United States Army, Fort Meade, Maryland; personnel procurement officer and later personnel management officer, Office of the Judge Advocate General, United States Army, Washington, DC; student, the Judge Advocate General's Officer Graduate Course; and later criminal law instructor and later senior instructor, the Judge Advocate General's School, Charlottesville, Virginia.

In 1978, Gray was assigned to Europe as deputy staff judge advocate, First Armored Division, VII Corps, United States Army, Europe and Seventh Army, Germany.

He returned to the United States in 1980 and assumed various staff and command duties as follows: student, United States Army Command and General Staff College, Fort Leavenworth, Kansas; staff judge advocate, Second Armored Division, Fort Hood, Texas; chief, Personnel, Plans and Training Office, Office of the Judge Advocate General, Washington, DC; student, The Industrial College of the Armed Forces, Fort McNair, Washington, DC; staff judge advocate, III Corps and Fort Hood, Fort Hood, Texas; special assistant, Office of the Judge Advocate General, United States Army, Washington, DC; acting commander, United States Army Legal Services Agency, and associate judge, Army Court of Military Review, Falls Church, Virginia; commander, United States Army Legal Services Agency, and chief judge, United States Army Court of Military Review, Falls Church, Virginia.

General Gray's decorations and awards include the Legion of Merit; the Bronze Star Medal; the Meritorious Service Medal with two Oak Leaf Clusters; the Army Commendation Medal; the Army Achievement Medal; and the Army Staff Identification Badge.

Promotion	Date
Second Lieutenant	July 30, 1966
First Lieutenant	July 30, 1969
Captain	July 30, 1973
Major	July 30, 1980
Lieutenant Colonel	July 5, 1981
Colonel	March 1, 1986
Brigadier General	April 1, 1991
Major General	October 1, 1993

Maj. Gen. Kenneth D. Gray

MAJOR GENERAL LARRY R. JORDAN
Deputy, the Inspector General, Office of the Secretary of the Army, the Pentagon, Washington, DC

General Jordan, born in Kansas City, Kansas, received his bachelor's degree from the United States Military Academy, and his master's degree in history from Indiana University. The general is also a graduate of the United States Marine Corps Warfare School, the United States Army Command and General Staff College, and the National War College.

An outstanding officer with more than twenty-eight years of service, his major duty assignments have included student, Ranger Course, United States Army Infantry School, Fort Benning, Georgia; student, Armor Officer Basic Course, Fort Knox, Kentucky; platoon leader, Company C, Second Battalion, Sixty-sixth Armor, Second Armored Division, Fort Hood, Texas; platoon leader, Company B, Second Battalion, Twenty-first Infantry Division, United States Army, Vietnam; executive officer, Troop A, Second Squadron, First Cavalry, First Cavalry Division, United States Army, Vietnam; commander, Company C, and later Headquarters Company, First Battalion, Sixty-third Armor, First Infantry Division (Mechanized), Fort Riley, Kansas; student, Marine Corps Amphibious Warfare Course, Amphibious Warfare School, Marine Corps Development and Education Command, Quantico, Virginia; project officer, United States Army Combat Arms Training Board, Fort Benning, Georgia; student, University of Indiana, Bloomington, Indiana; and assistant professor, United States Army Command and General Staff College, Fort Leavenworth, Kansas.

Leaving the United States again in 1979, the general was assigned as S-5 (Management), Civil-Military Operations, First Brigade, Third Armored Division, V Corps, United States Army, Europe and Seventh Army, Germany; war plans officer, Office of the Deputy Chief of Staff for Logistics, United States Army, Europe, Germany; staff action officer, Office of the Deputy Chief of Staff for Operations and Plans, United States Army, Washington, DC; commander, First Battalion, Sixty-seventh Armored Regiment, Second Armored Division, Fort Hood, Texas; student, National War College, Fort McNair, Washington, DC; senior exercise planner J-7 (Planning), the Joint Chiefs of Staff, Washington, DC; chief of staff, First Armored Division, United States Army, Europe, Germany; commander Second Brigade, Third Infantry Division, United States Army, Europe and Seventh Army, Germany; assistant division commander, Third Armored Division, United States Army, Europe and Seventh Army, Germany; and assistant division commander, Eighth Infantry Division (Mechanized), United States Army, Europe and Seventh Army, Germany.

Returning to the continental United States in 1992, the general

Promotion	Date
Second Lieutenant	June 5, 1968
First Lieutenant	June 5, 1971
Captain	June 5, 1975
Major	June 13, 1978
Lieutenant Colonel	April 1, 1984
Colonel	June 1, 1988
Brigadier General	February 1, 1992
Major General	January 1, 1995

Maj. Gen. Larry R. Jordan

served as deputy commanding general and later commanding general, United States Army Armor Center and Fort Knox, and commandant, United States Army Armor School, Fort Knox, Kentucky; and assistant deputy chief of staff for personnel, Office of the Deputy Chief of Staff for Personnel, United States Army, Washington, DC.

General Jordan's decorations and awards include the Distinguished Service Medal; the Silver Star; the Bronze Star Medal with "V" device and one Oak Leaf Cluster; the Bronze Star Medal with two Oak Leaf Clusters; the Defense Meritorious Service Medal; the Meritorious Service Medal with two Oak Leaf Clusters; the Army Commendation Medal with "V" device; the Army Commendation Medal with one Oak Leaf Cluster; the Army Achievement Medal with one Oak Leaf Cluster; the Combat Infantryman Badge; the Parachutist Badge; the Ranger Tab; the Joint Chiefs of Staff Identification Badge; and the Army Staff Identification Badge.

MAJOR GENERAL ALFONSO E. LENHARDT
Commanding General, United States Army Chemical and Military Police Centers, and Commandant, United States Army Chemical School, Fort McClellan, Alabama

In 1966, Lenhardt was commissioned a second lieutenant through Officers Candidate School. He earned his bachelor's degree in criminal justice from the University of Nebraska at Omaha, his master's degree in law administration from Wichita State University, and his master's degree in public administration from Central Michigan University. General Lenhardt also attended the United States Army Command and General Staff College and the National War College.

During his more than thirty years in the Army, Lenhardt has served as chief, Military Police Subjects Committee, Fourth Advanced Individual Training Brigade (Military Police), United States Army Training Center, Fort Gordon, Georgia; assistant S-2 (Intelligence) and S-3 (Operations), Fourth Advanced Individual Training Brigade (Military Police), United States Army Training Center, Fort Gordon, Georgia; action officer, Special Activity Division, Operations Directorate, United States Army Criminal Investigation Command, Washington, DC; chief, Operations Center, United States Army Criminal Investigation Command, Washington, DC; chief, Region Coordination Division, United States Army Criminal Investigation Command, Washington, DC; commander, Fort Eustis Field Office, First Regional United States Army Criminal Investigations Division Command, Fort Eustis, Virginia; operations officer, Provost Marshal Office, Fort Dix, New Jersey; executive officer, 759th Military Police Battalion, Fort Dix, New Jersey; company tactical officer, Staff and Faculty, United States Military Academy, West Point, New York; chief, Policy Branch, Office of the Provost Marshal, United States Army, Europe and Seventh Army, Germany; and commander, 385th Military Police Battalion, VII Corps, United States Army, Europe, Germany.

Returning from Germany in 1983, General Lenhardt was assigned as deputy director, Research and Special Actions, Office of the Director, Military Equal Opportunity, Office of the Secretary of Defense, Washington, DC; executive officer and assistant to director, Strategic Defense Initiative Organization, Office of the Secretary of Defense, Washington, DC; commander, Eighteenth Military Police Brigade, V Corps, United States Army, Europe, Germany; deputy provost marshal, Office of the Provost Marshal, United States Army, Europe and Seventh Army, Germany; deputy commanding general, United States Army Recruiting Command, Fort

Promotion	Date
Second Lieutenant	October 19, 1966
First Lieutenant	October 19, 1969
Captain	October 19, 1973
Major	October 19, 1980
Lieutenant Colonel	October 19, 1982
Colonel	November 1, 1984
Brigadier General	July 1, 1990
Major General	February 1, 1994

Maj. Gen. Alfonso E. Lenhardt

Sheridan, Illinois; and deputy chief of staff for personnel and installation management, Forces Command, Fort McPherson, Georgia.

General Lenhardt's numerous decorations and awards include the Distinguished Service Medal; the Defense Superior Service Medal; the Legion of Merit with one Oak Leaf Cluster; the Bronze Star Medal; the Purple Heart; the Meritorious Service Medal with two Oak Leaf Clusters; Air Medals; the Joint Service Commendation Medal; the Army Commendation Medal with two Oak Leaf Clusters; the Army Achievement Medal; the Combat Infantryman Badge; the Parachutist Badge; and the Office of the Secretary of Defense Identification Badge.

MAJOR GENERAL FRANK L. MILLER, JR.

Assistant Chief of Staff for Installation Management, Office of the Chief of Staff, United States Army, the Pentagon, Washington, DC

Born in Atchison, Kansas, General Miller is a graduate of the University of Washington with a bachelor's degree in business administration, and of Troy State University with a master's degree in management. He is also a graduate of the United States Army Command and General Staff College and the United States Naval War College.

General Miller's assignments during his more than thirty years in the military have included commander, Battery A, Second Battalion, Thirty-fourth Field Artillery, 212th Field Artillery Group, Fort Lewis, Washington; S-4 (Logistics), Seventh Battalion, Seventeenth Artillery, Second Infantry Division, United States Army, Korea; deputy G-1 (Personnel), Second Infantry Division, United States Army, Korea; motor officer, Third Battalion, Sixth Field Artillery, First Infantry Division, Fort Riley, Kansas; commander, C Battery, Third Battalion, Sixth Field Artillery, First Infantry Division, Fort Riley, Kansas; assistant S-3 (Operations) and later S-3, Third Battalion, Sixth Field Artillery, First Infantry Division, Fort Riley, Kansas; and operations and intelligence officer, Silk Purse Control Group, United States European Command, Mildenhall, England.

Returning from England in 1980, Miller was assigned as chief, Fire Support, Division Artillery, Twenty-fourth Infantry Division, Fort Stewart, Georgia; commander, First Battalion, Thirty-fifth Field Artillery, Twenty-fourth Infantry Division, Fort Stewart, Georgia; chief of staff, National Training Center, Fort Irwin, California; commander, 558th United States Army Artillery Group, United States Army, Greece; chief of staff, United States Army Field Artillery School, Fort Sill, Oklahoma; commanding general, III Corps Artillery, Fort Sill, Oklahoma; director of operations J-3 (Operations), United States Forces Command, Fort McPherson, Georgia; and deputy commanding general, III Corps and Fort Hood, Fort Hood, Texas.

General Miller's decorations and awards include the Legion of Merit with three Oak Leaf Clusters; the Distinguished Flying Cross; the Bronze Star Medal with "V" device and two Oak Leaf Clusters; the Meritorious Service Medal; Air Medals; the Joint Service Commendation Medal; the Army Commendation Medal with four Oak Leaf Clusters; the Army Achievement Medal; and the Aircraft Crew Member Badge.

Promotion	Date
Second Lieutenant	September 13, 1966
First Lieutenant	September 13, 1969
Captain	September 13, 1973
Major	July 13, 1980
Lieutenant Colonel	September 13, 1980
Colonel	November 1, 1984
Brigadier General	June 1, 1990
Major General	July 1, 1993

Maj. Gen. Frank L. Miller, Jr.

MAJOR GENERAL JAMES W. MONROE
Commanding General, United States Army Industrial
Operations Command, Rock Island, Illinois

With more than thirty-three years of commissioned service in the United States Army, General Monroe has had an interesting and rewarding career. He received his commission through Army ROTC. His hometown is Laurinburg, North Carolina. General Monroe is a graduate of West Virginia State College, where he earned a bachelor's degree in electrical engineering, and of the University of Cincinnati, where he earned a master's degree in political science. The general is also a graduate of the United States Army Command and General Staff College and the Industrial College of the Armed Forces.

General Monroe's major duty assignments have included platoon leader, Thirty-first Ordnance Company, Fort Knox, Kentucky; platoon leader, Armored Cavalry, B Troop, and later platoon leader, Troop A, Second Squadron, Ninth Cavalry, Twenty-fourth Infantry Division, United States Army, Europe, Germany; commander, 621st General Supply Company, United States Army, Europe, Germany; assistant professor of military science, First United States Army, Fort Meade, Maryland, with duty at the University of Cincinnati, Cincinnati, Ohio; strategic intelligence officer, Office of the Assistant Chief of Staff for Intelligence, United States Army, Washington DC; and commander, Sixty-first Maintenance Company, Eighth United States Army, Korea.

After returning to the United States from Korea in 1978, General Monroe was assigned to the following duties: executive officer, 709th Maintenance Company, Ninth Infantry Division, Fort Lewis, Washington; deputy commander and later commander, Division Materiel and Management Center, Division Support Command, Ninth Infantry Division, Fort Lewis, Washington; executive officer, Division Support Command, Ninth Infantry Division, Fort Lewis, Washington; commander, Seventy-first Maintenance Battalion, VII Corps, United States Army, Europe, Germany; faculty, Senior Service College, National Defense University, Fort McNair, Washington, DC; commander, Division Support Command, Twenty-fourth Infantry Division (Mechanized), Fort Stewart, Georgia; assistant chief of staff, G-4 (Logistics), Third United States Army, Fort McPherson, Georgia; G-4, United States Army Central Command, Desert Storm, Saudi Arabia; deputy commanding general for systems and logistics, United States Army Tank-Automotive Command, Warren, Michigan; and commanding general, United States Army Ordnance Center, and commandant, United States Army Ordnance School, Aberdeen Proving Ground, Maryland.

General Monroe's decorations and awards include the Legion of Merit with two Oak Leaf Clusters; the Bronze Star Medal; the Defense Meritorious Service Medal; the Meritorious Service Medal with four Oak Leaf Clusters; and the Army Commendation Medal.

Promotion	Date
Second Lieutenant	October 5, 1963
First Lieutenant	October 5, 1966
Captain	October 5, 1970
Major	October 5, 1977
Lieutenant Colonel	November 7, 1979
Colonel	February 1, 1986
Brigadier General	July 1, 1991
Major General	April 1, 1994

Maj. Gen. James W. Monroe

MAJOR GENERAL BILLY K. SOLOMON
General Officer Management Hold, the Pentagon,
Washington, DC

A native of Oakwood, Texas, General Solomon received his commission as a second lieutenant through Army ROTC. He has earned two degrees: a bachelor's degree in agriculture from Prairie View A & M University and a master's degree in procurement/contract management from the Florida Institute of Technology. General Solomon also attended the Armed Forces Staff College and the Industrial College of the Armed Forces.

During the past two decades, General Solomon served as stock control officer, 624th Supply and Service Company, 226th Supply and Service Battalion, United States Army, Vietnam; platoon leader, 506th Supply and Service Company, 266th Supply and Service Battalion, United States Army, Vietnam; S-3 (Operations), 266th Supply and Service Battalion, United States Army, Vietnam; assistant G-4 (Logistics), Second Armored Division, Fort Hood, Texas; commander, Headquarters Company, Eighty-eighth Supply and Service Battalion, United States Army, Vietnam; S-3, Logistical Support Activity, United States Army, Vietnam; supply and logistics officer, 198th Military Intelligence Group, Fort Meade, Maryland; civil affairs officer, 902d Military Intelligence Group, Fort Meade, Maryland; chief logistics officer, United States Army Communications Command Agency, Canal Zone, Fort Clayton, Panama; student, Armed Forces Staff College, Norfolk, Virginia; personnel management officer, United States Army Military Personnel Center, Alexandria, Virginia; protocol officer, Office of the Chief of Staff, Army, Washington, DC; and commander, 498th Support Battalion, Second Armored Division (Forward), United States Army, Europe and Seventh Army, Germany.

Solomon returned from duty in Germany in 1985, and was assigned as student, Industrial College of the Armed Forces, Fort McNair, Washington, DC; chief, Quartermaster/Chemical Branch, and later chief, Combat Service Support Division, Enlisted Personnel Management Directorate, United States Army Personnel Command, Alexandria, Virginia; commander, Thirteenth Corps Support Command, Fifth Infantry Division (Mechanized), Fort Polk, Louisiana; commander, Thirteenth Corps Support Command, III Corps, Fort Hood, Texas; commander, Joint Logistics Task Force, United Nations Operations, Somalia; commander, Thirteenth Corps Support Command, III Corps, Fort Hood, Texas; and assistant chief of staff, J-4/C-4/G-4 (Logistics), United States Forces Korea/United Nations Command/Combined Forces Command/Eighth United States Army, Korea.

His military decorations and awards include the Defense Superior Service Medal; the Legion of Merit with one Oak Leaf Cluster;

Promotion	Date
Second Lieutenant	August 25, 1966
First Lieutenant	August 24, 1968
Captain	October 10, 1973
Major	October 10, 1980
Lieutenant Colonel	March 1, 1982
Colonel	January 1, 1989
Brigadier General	October 1, 1992
Major General	October 1, 1995

Maj. Gen. Billy K. Solomon

the Bronze Star Medal with one Oak Leaf Cluster; the Meritorious Service Medal with three Oak Leaf Clusters; the Army Commendation Medal with one Oak Leaf Cluster; and the Army Achievement Medal.

BRIGADIER GENERAL HAROLD E. BURCH
Executive Director for Distribution, Defense Logistics Agency, Cameron Station, Alexandria, Virginia

A native of Lake Wales, Florida, General Burch received his commission as a second lieutenant through Army ROTC. He earned two degrees from Tuskegee University: bachelor's and master's degrees in soil agronomy. General Burch is also a graduate of the United States Army Command and General Staff College and the Industrial College of the Armed Forces.

During his more than thirty-two years of service, General Burch's major duty assignments have included student, Infantry Officer Basic Course, United States Army Infantry School, Fort Benning, Georgia; executive officer, Company C, Third Battalion, 199th Infantry Brigade (Separate) (Light), Fort Benning, Georgia; executive officer, Company C, and later assistant S-2 (Intelligence), Third Battalion, Seventh Infantry, 199th Infantry Brigade (Separate) (Light), United States Army, Vietnam; S-1 (Personnel) and detachment commander, Seventh Support Battalion (DIVARTY), 199th Infantry Brigade, United States Army, Vietnam; student, Quartermaster Officer Advanced School, United States Army Quartermaster School, Fort Lee, Virginia; commander, A Company, Twenty-fourth Support and Transportation Battalion, Twenty-fourth Infantry Division, Fort Riley, Kansas; and division property book officer, First Support and Transportation Battalion, First Infantry Division, Fort Riley, Kansas.

In 1971, Burch left the United States for Vietnam and was assigned as senior advisor, Nintieth Parachute Maintenance and Aerial Delivery Base Depot, United States Military Assistance Command, Vietnam; assistant G-4 (Logistics), V Corps, United States Army, Europe and Seventh Army, Germany; and general supply officer, G-4, V Corps, United States Army, Europe and Seventh Army, Germany.

Burch returned to the continental United States in 1974 and assumed his duties as instructor, United States Army Armor School, Fort Knox, Kentucky; student, United States Army Command and General Staff College, Fort Leavenworth, Kansas; division parachute officer, Company E, and later executive officer, 407th Support and Supply Battalion (Airborne), Eighty-second Airborne Division, Fort Bragg, North Carolina; chief, Maintenance and Services Division, Directorate of Industrial Operations, Honshu Sagami Depot, United States Army, Japan; commander, Seventy-fifth Support Battalion, 194th Armored Brigade, Fort Knox, Kentucky; assistant chief of staff, G-4, Second Infantry Division, Eighth United States Army, Korea; student, Industrial College of the Armed Forces, Fort McNair, Washington, DC; deputy executive director, Technical Services and

Promotion	Date
Second Lieutenant	July 10, 1964
First Lieutenant	December 11, 1967
Captain	July 10, 1971
Major	July 10, 1978
Lieutenant Colonel	September 10, 1980
Colonel	July 1, 1987
Brigadier General	October 1, 1991

Brig. Gen. Harold E. Burch

Logistics, Defense Logistics Agency, Cameron Station, Alexandria, Virginia; commander, Division Support Command, First Cavalry Division, Fort Hood, Texas; deputy commander, Twenty-first Theater Army Area Command, United States Army, Europe and Seventh Army, Germany; and commander, United States Army and Air Force Exchange, Europe.

His military decorations and awards include the Legion of Merit with two Oak Leaf Clusters; the Bronze Star Medal with one Oak Leaf Cluster; the Meritorious Service Medal with four Oak Leaf Clusters; the Army Commendation Medal with one Oak Leaf Cluster; the Army Achievement Medal; the Senior Parachutist Badge; the Parachute Rigger Badge; and the Combat Infantryman Badge.

BRIGADIER GENERAL REGINALD G. CLEMMONS
Assistant Chief of Staff for Operations, Headquarters, Land
Forces, Central Europe, APO AE

Reginald Clemmons was commissioned a second lieutenant in June of
1968 through ROTC. He received his bachelor's degree in mathematics from
North Carolina Agricultural and Technological State University, and his
master's degree in education administration from South Carolina State College. General Clemmons also attended the Field Artillery Officer Basic and
Advanced Courses, the Armed Forces Staff College, and the United States Army
War College.

During his outstanding career, General Clemmons has served in a number of staff and command positions, including forward officer and later liaison officer, Seventh Battalion, Thirteenth Field Artillery, United States Army,
Vietnam; commander, Headquarters Battery, Fifth Battalion, Eightieth Field
Artillery, Fourth Infantry Division (Mechanized), Fort Carson, Colorado; commander, Battery B, First Battalion, Twenty-seventh Field Artillery, Fourth Infantry Division (Mechanized), Fort Carson, Colorado; and student, Field Artillery Officer Advanced Course, United States Army Field Artillery School,
Fort Sill, Oklahoma.

From March 1972 until July 1975, Clemmons assumed command in Eu-
rope as assistant S-3 (Operations), Third Battalion, Twenty-first Field Artil-
lery, Seventy-second Field Artillery Group, United States Army, Europe and
Seventh Army, Germany; commander, Battery B, Third Battalion, Twenty-first
Field Artillery, United States Army, Europe and Seventh Army, Germany; as-
sistant S-3 (Operations), Third Battalion, Twenty-first Field Artillery, United
States Army, Europe and Seventh Army, Germany; and liaison officer, First
Battalion, Eightieth Field Artillery, United States Army, Europe and Seventh
Army, Germany.

Over the next two decades, Clemmons served as assistant professor of military science, United States Army ROTC Instructor Group, South Carolina State
University, Orangeburg, South Carolina; assistant fire support coordinator,
Division Artillery, and later executive officer, First Battalion, Thirty-eighth Field
Artillery, Second Infantry Division, Eighth United States Army, Korea; opera-
tions research analyst, Concepts and Doctrine Directorate, and later logistics
assessment officer, Logistics Assessment Task Group, United States Army Lo-
gistics Center, Fort Lee, Vir-
ginia; deputy assistant fire
support coordinator and op-
erations officer, XVII Airborne
Corps Artillery, XVIII Airborne
Corps, Fort Bragg, North
Carolina; executive officer,
XVII Airborne Corps Artillery,
XVIII Airborne Corps, Fort
Bragg, North Carolina; senior

Promotion	Date
Second Lieutenant	June 5, 1968
First Lieutenant	June 5, 1971
Captain	June 5, 1975
Major	March 3, 1979
Lieutenant Colonel	December 1, 1984
Colonel	December 1, 1990
Brigadier General	September 1, 1995

Brig. Gen. Reginald G. Clemmons

observer and controller, United States Army Joint Readiness Training Center, Little Rock Air Force Base, Arkansas; commander, First Battlefield Coordinated Detachment, XVIII Airborne Corps, Fort Bragg, North Carolina; commander, Division Artillery, Twenty-fifth Infantry Division (Light), Schofield Barracks, Hawaii; and director, Fire Support and Combined Operations Directorate, United States Army Field Artillery Center, Fort Sill, Oklahoma.

General Clemmons has been awarded the Legion of Merit; the Bronze Star Medal; the Meritorious Service Medal with four Oak Leaf Clusters; the Army Commendation Medal with two Oak Leaf Clusters; and the Master Parachutist Badge.

BRIGADIER GENERAL MILTON HUNTER
Commanding General, United States Army Engineering Division, North Atlantic, New York, New York

General Hunter received his commission as a second lieutenant on June 7, 1967, through Army ROTC. A native of Houston, Texas, he received his associate's degree in engineering from Compton Community College, his bachelor's degree in architectural engineering from the University of Washington, and his master's degree in civil engineering from the University of Washington. General Hunter is also a graduate of the Army Engineer School Officer Basic and Advanced Courses, the United States Army Command and General Staff College, and the Army War College.

During his twenty-nine years in the Army, he has served as construction officer and later platoon leader, Company B, 339th Engineer Battalion (Construction), Fort Lewis, Washington; executive officer and later commander, Headquarters Company, 937th Engineer Group (Combat), Nineteenth Engineer Brigade, United States Army, Vietnam; instructor and later test project officer, United States Army Engineer School, Fort Belvoir, Virginia; student, Officer Advanced Course, United States Army Engineer School, Fort Belvoir, Virginia; assignment officer, Engineer Branch, United States Army Military Personnel Center, Alexandria, Virginia; student, University of Washington, Seattle, Washington; operations officer, United States Army Command and General Staff College, Fort Leavenworth, Kansas; student, Command and General Staff Officer Course, United States Army Command and General Staff College, Fort Leavenworth, Kansas; and deputy district engineer, Engineer District, Charleston, South Carolina.

Hunter left for a tour of duty in Europe in August 1981, serving as assistant division engineer, Twelfth Engineer Battalion, Eighth Infantry Division (Mechanized), United States Army, Europe, Germany; director, Engineering and Housing, United States Army Military Community Activity, Bad Kreuznach, United States Army, Europe, Germany; special assistant to the commander, Nineteenth Engineer Brigade, United States Army, Europe, Germany; and commander, Seventy-ninth Engineer Battalion (Combat Heavy), Eighteenth Engineer Brigade, United States Army, Europe, Germany.

Back in the United States in June 1986, Hunter's assignments included program analyst, Program Analysis and Evaluation Directorate, Office of the Chief of Staff, Army, Washington, DC; assistant director for civil works (Central Region), United States Army Corps of Engineers, Washington, DC; commander, Engineer District, Seattle, Washington; chief of staff, United States Army Corps of Engineers, Office of the Chief of Engineers, United States Army, Washington, DC; and commanding general, United States Army

Promotion	Date
Second Lieutenant	June 7, 1967
First Lieutenant	June 7, 1970
Captain	June 7, 1974
Major	June 7, 1981
Lieutenant Colonel	November 1, 1982
Colonel	May 1, 1989
Brigadier General	June 1, 1993

Brig. Gen. Milton Hunter

Engineer Division, South Pacific, San Francisco, California.

General Hunter has been awarded the Legion of Merit with one Oak Leaf Cluster; the Bronze Star Medal; the Meritorious Service Medal with one Oak Leaf Cluster; the Army Commendation Medal with one Oak Leaf Cluster; the Parachutist Badge; and the Army Staff Identification Badge.

BRIGADIER GENERAL SAMUEL L. KINDRED
Commanding General, Third Support Command (Corps), United States Army, Europe and Seventh Army, Germany

General Kindred was born in Omega, Alabama. Because of his outstanding leadership qualities, he received a direct appointment to the rank of second lieutenant. He received his bachelor's and master's degrees in business administration from Hampton University. General Kindred also attended the United States Army Command and General Staff College, the Defense Systems Management College, and the Industrial College of the Armed Forces.

During his career, Kindred has served as flight training analysis officer and later instructor, United States Army Primary Helicopter School, Fort Wolters, Texas; supply platoon leader, Company E, 723d Maintenance Battalion, Twenty-third Infantry Division, United States Army, Vietnam; maintenance platoon leader, Company A, 123d Aviation Battalion, Twenty-third Infantry Division, United States Army, Vietnam; special assistant to the inspector general, Headquarters, United States Army Transportation Center, Fort Eustis, Virginia; student, Transportation Officer Advanced Course, and later Defense Procurement Management Course and Advanced Defense Procurement Management Course, United States Army Transportation School, Fort Eustis, Virginia, and Fort Lee, Virginia; commander, United States Army District Recruiting Command, Columbus, Ohio; aviation advisor, United States Army Readiness Region VI, Fort Knox, Kentucky; assistant chief, Technical Management Division, Defense Contract Administration Services Region, Defense Logistics Agency, St. Louis, Missouri; and commander, 347th Transportation Company (AVIM), Forty-fifth Support Group, Schofield Barracks, Hawaii.

General Kindred has also assumed the duties of logistics operations officer, Forty-fifth Support Group, Fort Shafter, Hawaii; commander, 124th Transportation Battalion, Forty-fifth Support Group, Schofield Barracks, Hawaii; assignment officer, Colonels Division, Officer Personnel Management Directorate, United States Total Army Personnel Agency, Alexandria, Virginia; assistant deputy chief of staff for production, United States Army Materiel Command, Alexandria, Virginia; commander, Forty-fifth Support Group, Schofield Barracks, Hawaii; chief aviation logistics officer, Office of the Deputy Chief of Staff for Logistics, United States Army, Washington, DC; executive officer to the commanding general, United States Army Materiel Command, Alexandria, Virginia; and deputy commanding general, Twenty-first Theater Army Area Command, United States Army, Europe and Seventh Army, Germany.

General Kindred's decorations and awards include the Legion of Merit with two Oak

Promotion	Date
Second Lieutenant	February 14, 1969
First Lieutenant	February 13, 1971
Captain	February 14, 1971
Major	July 7, 1979
Lieutenant Colonel	June 1, 1985
Colonel	June 1, 1990
Brigadier General	June 1, 1995

Brig. Gen. Samuel L. Kindred

Leaf Clusters; the Bronze Star Medal with two Oak Leaf Clusters; the Purple Heart; the Defense Meritorious Service Medal; the Meritorious Service Medal with two Oak Leaf Clusters; Air Medals; the Army Commendation Medal with two Oak Leaf Clusters; the Senior Army Aviator Badge; and the Army Staff Identification Badge.

BRIGADIER GENERAL ROBERT L. NABORS
Director, Single Agency Manager for Pentagon Information
Technology Services, United States Army Information Systems
Command, Washington, DC

Born in Boston, Massachusetts, Robert Nabors earned his bachelor's degree in systems engineering from the University of Arizona and his master's degree in systems management from the University of Southern California. The general is also a graduate of the Armed Forces Staff College and attended Harvard University on a United States Army War College Fellowship.

His major duty assignments have been radio systems officer, 362d Signal Company, Seventy-third Signal Battalion, United States Army Strategic Communications Command, United States Army, Vietnam; team commander, Detachment #17, 458th Signal Battalion, United States Army Strategic Communications Command, United States Army, Vietnam; commander, Company D, First Battalion, Fifty-fifth Combat Support Training Brigade, Fort Dix, New Jersey; assistant S-2/S-3 (Intelligence/Operations) and later S-2/S-3, Headquarters, Fifth Combat Support Training Brigade, Fort Dix, New Jersey; student, Signal Officer Advanced Course, United States Army Signal Center and School, Fort Monmouth, New Jersey; chief, Military Skills Branch, and later instructor, Combat Arms Branch, and chief, Allied Liaison Branch, United States Army Ordnance Center and School, Aberdeen Proving Ground, Maryland; radio officer and later chief, Transmission Systems Branch, Telecommunications Division, Deputy Chief of Staff for Operations and Plans, Fifth Signal Command, United States Army Information Systems Command, and concurrently staff action officer, Deputy Chief of Staff for Information Management, United States Army, Europe and Seventh Army, Germany; and *aide-de-camp* to the commander, VII Corps, United States Army, Europe and Seventh Army, Germany.

General Nabors returned to the United States from Germany in 1981, and was assigned as student, Armed Forces Staff College, Norfolk, Virginia; special project officer, Telecommunications Plan for the Improvement of Communications in Korea, and later S-2/S-3, Forty-first Signal Battalion, First Signal Brigade, United States Army Communications Command, Korea; operations staff officer, Joint Readiness Evaluation Division, Directorate of Plans, Programs and Policy J-5 (Management), United States Readiness Command, MacDill Air Force Base, Florida; commander, 509th Signal Battalion, Fifth Signal Command, United States Army Information Systems Command, Italy; staff officer and later division chief, Integration Division, Office of the Director for Information Systems for Command, Control, Commu-

Promotion	Date
Second Lieutenant	November 2, 1967
First Lieutenant	November 2, 1969
Captain	November 2, 1970
Major	October 6, 1978
Lieutenant Colonel	September 1, 1984
Colonel	June 1, 1990
Brigadier General	July 1, 1995

Brig. Gen. Robert L. Nabors

nications, and Computers, Office of the Secretary of the Army, Washington, DC; deputy commander, White House Communications Agency, Defense Communications Agency, Washington, DC; commander, Second Signal Brigade, Fifth Signal Command, United States Army Information Systems Command, Germany; and executive officer to the director, Information Systems for Command, Control, Communications, and Computers, Office of the Secretary of the Army, Washington, DC.

His decorations and awards include the Defense Superior Service Medal; the Legion of Merit with one Oak Leaf Cluster; the Bronze Star Medal; the Meritorious Service Medal with four Oak Leaf Clusters; the Joint Service Commendation Medal; the Army Commendation Medal with three Oak Leaf Clusters; the Presidential Service Badge; and the Army General Staff Identification Badge.

BRIGADIER GENERAL GREGORY A. ROUNTREE

Deputy Commanding General, United States Army Air Defense Artillery Center and Fort Bliss, Fort Bliss, Texas

In July 1970, Gregory Rountree was commissioned a second lieutenant through Army ROTC. A native of Jonesville, Louisiana, he earned a bachelor's degree from Southern University of A & M and a master's degree in management and human relations from Webster University. General Rountree is also a graduate of the United States Army Command and General Staff College, the Defense Systems Management College's Program Management Course, and the United States Army War College.

General Rountree's major duty assignments have included student, Air Defense Office Basis Course, United States Army Air Defense School, Fort Bliss, Texas, and later Ranger Course, United Sates Army Infantry School, Fort Benning, Georgia; assistant team commander and later team commander, Thirty-first Artillery Detachment, 559th Artillery Group, United States Army Southern European Task Force, Italy; commander, Battery B, First Battalion, Sixty-fifth Air Defense Artillery, United States Naval Air Station, Key West, Florida; student, Air Defense Artillery Officer Advanced Course, Fort Bliss, Texas; chief, Management Control Unit, C-3/J-3/G-3 (Operations), United Nations Command/United States Forces, Korea; assistant S-3 (Operations) and later project officer, Weapons System Development Branch, United States Army Air Defense Artillery School, Fort Bliss, Texas; S-4 (Logistics), 108th Air Defense Artillery Group, United States Army, Europe, Germany; executive officer, Second Battalion, Sixtieth Air Defense Artillery, Thirty-second Army Air Defense Command, United States Army, Europe, Germany; student, United States Army Command and General Staff College, Fort Leavenworth, Kansas; student, Materiel Acquisition Management Course, United States Army Logistics Management Center, Fort Lee, Virginia; staff officer, Missiles and Air Defense Systems Division, Office of the Deputy Chief of Staff for Research, Development and Acquisition, Washington, DC; student, Program Management Course, Defense Systems Management College, Fort Belvoir, Virginia; and commander, Sixth Battalion, Forty-third Air Defense Artillery, Fort Bliss, Texas, later under Sixty-ninth Air Defense Artillery Brigade, Thirty-second Army Air Defense Command, United States Army, Europe, Germany.

Rountree returned to the United States in 1989 and served as student, United States Army War College, Carlisle Barracks, Pennsylvania; commander, Sixty-ninth Air Defense Artillery Brigade, United States Army, Europe, Germany; deputy commander, United States Army Space and Strategic Defense Command, Peterson Air Force Base, Colorado; and commanding general, Second Reserve Officer Training Corps Region, Fort Knox, Kentucky.

Promotion	Date
Second Lieutenant	July 7, 1970
First Lieutenant	July 7, 1973
Captain	July 7, 1977
Major	October 1, 1981
Lieutenant Colonel	April 1, 1987
Colonel	June 1, 1991
Brigadier General	January 1, 1995

Brig. Gen. Gregory A. Rountree

His decorations and awards include the Legion of Merit with one Oak Leaf Cluster; the Meritorious Service Medal with two Oak Leaf Clusters; the Army Commendation Medal with two Oak Leaf Clusters; the Army Achievement Medal; the Ranger Tab; and the Army General Staff Identification Badge.

BRIGADIER GENERAL MICHAEL B. SHERFIELD
Commanding General, Headquarters, Joint Readiness Training Center and Fort Polk, Fort Polk, Louisiana

General Sherfield was born in Brooklyn, New York. He received his bachelor's degree in history from the University of Tampa and his master's degree in public administration from Pennsylvania State University. General Sherfield also attended the United States Army Command and General Staff College and the United States Army War College.

During his career, he has served as assistant adjutant, First Battalion, 506th Infantry, 101st Airborne Division, United States Army, Vietnam; assistant adjutant, Third Brigade, 101st Airborne Division, United States Army, Vietnam; operations officer, United States Army Atlantic Area Installation Command, Fort Sherman, Panama; commander, Company C, Third Battalion, Fifth Infantry, 193d Infantry Brigade, Fort Kobbe, Panama; S-4 (Logistics), Third Battalion, Fifth Infantry, 193d Infantry Brigade, Fort Kobbe, Panama; student, Special Forces Officer Course, United States Army Institute for Military Assistance, Fort Bragg, North Carolina; operations and training officer, United States Military Assistance Command, Thailand; assistant S-3 (Operations), First Brigade, 101st Airborne Division (Air Assault), Fort Campbell, Kentucky; S-3, Second Battalion, 327th Infantry, 101st Airborne Division (Air Assault), Fort Campbell, Kentucky; S-3, First Brigade, 101st Airborne Division (Air Assault), Fort Campbell, Kentucky; plans officer, Office of the Deputy Chief of Staff for Operations, United States Army, Europe, Germany; and deputy inspector general, Eighth Infantry Division (Mechanized), United States Army, Europe, Germany.

In June 1983, Sherfield returned from duty with the Eighth Infantry Division in Germany and assumed his assigned duty as commander, First Battalion, 502d Infantry, 101st Airborne Division (Air Assault), Fort Campbell, Kentucky; infantry assignment officer, Colonels Division, United States Army Military Personnel Center, Alexandria, Virginia; G-3 (Operations), Second Infantry Division, Eighth United States Army, Korea; staff officer and later division chief, Combat Maneuver Division, Office of the Deputy Chief of Staff for Operations and Plans, United States Army, Washington, DC; commander, Third Brigade, Second Infantry Division, Eighth United States Army, Korea; chief of staff, Second Infantry Division, Eighth United States Army, Korea; executive secretary, Department of Defense, Office of the Secretary of Defense, Washington, DC; and assistant division commander, 101st Airborne Division (Air Assault), Fort Campbell, Kentucky.

General Sherfield's decorations and awards include the Silver Star; the Legion of Merit; the Bronze Star Medal; the Purple

Promotion	Date
Second Lieutenant	December 11, 1967
First Lieutenant	December 11, 1969
Captain	August 21, 1975
Major	May 9, 1978
Lieutenant Colonel	April 1, 1984
Colonel	March 1, 1990
Brigadier General	July 1, 1993

Brig. Gen. Michael B. Sherfield

Heart; the Meritorious Service Medal with three Oak Leaf Clusters; the Air Medal; the Joint Service Commendation Medal; the Army Commendation Medal with one Oak Leaf Cluster; the Army Achievement Medal; the Combat Infantryman Badge; the Parachutist Badge; the Air Assault Badge; and the Office of the Secretary of Defense Identification Badge.

BRIGADIER GENERAL VERNON C. SPAULDING, JR.
Commanding General, Eisenhower Medical Center, Fort Gordon, Georgia

General Spaulding is a graduate of the University of California at Berkeley with a bachelor's degree in public health. He also earned a medical degree in general medicine from Howard University. Born in Los Angeles, California, the general graduated from the United States Army Command and General Staff College and the United States Army War College.

During his more than twenty-eight-year military career, his major duty assignments have been chief, Department of Medicine, United States Army Medical Activity, Fort Huachuca, Arizona; first- and second-year resident, Gastroenterology, Letterman Army Medical Center, Presidio of San Francisco, California; assistant chief and later chief, Gastroenterology Service, Madigan Army Medical Center, Tacoma, Washington; chief, Ambulatory Medicine, Second General Hospital, Seventh Medical Command, United States Army, Europe, Germany; chief, Ambulatory Care Department, and assistant deputy commander, Clinical Services, Second General Hospital, Seventh Medical Command, United States Army, Europe, Germany.

Spaulding returned from Germany in June 1986 and served as student, United States Army Command and General Staff College, Fort Leavenworth, Kansas; commander, United States Army Medical Activity, Fort Lee, Virginia; student, United States Army War College, Carlisle Barracks, Pennsylvania; commander, United States Army Medical Activity, Fort Benning, Georgia; and member, President Clinton's Health Care Services Task Force, Fort Benning, Georgia.

The general's decorations and awards include the Legion of Merit with two Oak Leaf Clusters; the Meritorious Service Medal; the Army Commendation Medal; the Expert Field Medical Badge; the Parachutist Badge; and the Air Assault Badge.

Promotion	Date
Second Lieutenant	June 12, 1968
First Lieutenant	June 12, 1968
Captain	June 5, 1972
Major	June 6, 1972
Lieutenant Colonel	June 6, 1977
Colonel	August 1, 1983
Brigadier General	November 19, 1993

Brig. Gen. Vernon C. Spaulding, Jr.

BRIGADIER GENERAL WILLIAM E. WARD
Deputy Director for Operations, National Military
Command Center, J-3 (Operations), the Joint Chiefs of Staff, the
Pentagon, Washington, DC

In 1971, General Ward was commissioned a second lieutenant through Army ROTC at Morgan State University, where he received a bachelor's degree in political science. He later earned a master's degree in political science from Pennsylvania State University. General Ward's military education includes the United States Army Command and General Staff College and the United States Army War College.

Born in Baltimore, Maryland, the general has served in a number of staff and command positions during his military career, including antitank platoon leader and later motor officer, Third Battalion, 325th Infantry, Eighty-second Airborne Division, Fort Bragg, North Carolina; liaison officer, Second Brigade, Eighty-second Airborne Division, Fort Bragg, North Carolina; rifle platoon leader, Company B, First Battalion (Mechanized), Seventeenth Infantry, Second Infantry Division, Eighth United States Army, Korea; commander, Company C, First Battalion (Mechanized), Seventeenth Infantry, Second Infantry Division, Eighth United States Army, Korea; student, Infantry Officer Advanced Course, United States Army Infantry School, Fort Benning, Georgia; instructor and later assistant professor, Social Services, Department of Social Sciences, United States Military Academy, West Point, New York; S-4 (Logistics), 210th Field Artillery Brigade, VII Corps, United States Army, Europe and Seventh Army, Germany; executive officer, United States Army Military Community Activity-Aschaffensberg, United States Army, Europe and Seventh Army, Germany; and executive officer, First Battalion (Mechanized), Seventh Infantry, Third Infantry Division, United States Army, Europe and Seventh Army, Germany.

Before assuming his current assignment, Ward also served as staff officer (Logistics), Office of the Deputy Chief of Staff for Logistics, United States Army, Washington, DC; commander, Fifth Battalion, Ninth Infantry, Second Brigade, Sixth Infantry Division (Light), Fort Wainwright, Alaska; G-4 (Logistics), Sixth Infantry Division (Light Infantry), Fort Wainwright, Alaska; commander, Second Brigade, Tenth Mountain Division (Light Infantry), Fort Drum, New York, and later Mogadishu, Somalia; and executive officer to the vice chief of staff, Office of the Joint Chiefs of Staff, United States Army, Washington, DC.

General Ward has been awarded the Legion of Merit with one Oak Leaf Cluster; the Meritorious Service Medal with five Oak Leaf Clusters; the Army Commendation Medal with three Oak Leaf Clusters; the Army Achievement Medal with one Oak Leaf Cluster; the Combat Infantryman Badge; the Expert Infantryman Badge; the Master Parachutist Badge; and the Army Staff Identification Badge.

Promotion	Date
Second Lieutenant	June 9, 1971
First Lieutenant	June 9, 1974
Captain	June 9, 1975
Major	January 1, 1983
Lieutenant Colonel	February 1, 1989
Colonel	June 1, 1992
Brigadier General	June 9, 1995

Brig. Gen. William E. Ward

BRIGADIER GENERAL RALPH G. WOOTEN
Commandant, United States Army Chemical School,
Fort McClellan, Alabama

A native of LaGrange, North Carolina, the general is a graduate of North Carolina Central University, where he earned a bachelor's degree in biology, and Central Michigan University, where he earned master's degrees in management and business administration.

During his twenty-eight years of service, General Wooten has served as chemical officer and later S-4 (Logistics), Division Artillery, Eighty-second Airborne Division, Fort Bragg, North Carolina; special projects officer, Eighty-second Airborne Division, Fort Bragg, North Carolina; commander, Fourteenth Chemical Detachment, Eighty-second Airborne Division, Fort Bragg, North Carolina; chemical officer, Eighty-second Airborne Division, Fort Bragg, North Carolina; mechanical maintenance officer, 782d Maintenance Battalion, Eighty-second Airborne Division, Fort Bragg, North Carolina; commander, Company B, 782d Maintenance Battalion, Eighty-second Airborne Division, Fort Bragg, North Carolina; chief, Combined Arms Branch, Chemical Directorate, and later assistant director, Training Department, United States Army Chemical School, Aberdeen Proving Ground, Maryland; maintenance management officer and later assistant division materiel management officer and commander, Third Armored Division Materiel Management Center, Third Armored Division, United States Army, Europe, Germany.

Wooten returned to the United States in June 1983, and was assigned as advisor and later team chief, Combat Support Branch, United States Army Reserve Readiness Group, Redstone Arsenal, Huntsville, Alabama; deputy director for research, Development and Engineering Support, United States Army Chemical, Research, Development, and Engineering Center, Aberdeen Proving Ground, Maryland; chief of staff, United States Army Chemical, Research, Development, and Engineering Center, Aberdeen Proving Ground, Maryland; commander, Second Chemical Battalion, Thirteenth Support Command (Corps), Fort Hood, Texas; logistics staff officer, G-4 (Logistics), III Corps, Fort Hood, Texas; commander, United States Army Toxic and Hazardous Materials Agency, Aberdeen Proving Ground, Maryland; commander, United States Army Environmental Center, Aberdeen Proving Ground, Maryland; and joint program manager for biological defense, Office of the Joint Program Manager for Biological Defense, Falls Church, Virginia.

General Wooten has been awarded the Bronze Star with two Oak Leaf Clusters; the Meritorious Service Medal with three Oak Leaf Clusters; Air Medals; the Army Commendation Medal with one Oak Leaf Cluster; the Army Achievement Medal; the Combat Infantryman Badge; and the Senior Parachutist Badge.

Promotion	Date
Second Lieutenant	July 29, 1968
First Lieutenant	July 29, 1971
Captain	July 29, 1975
Major	May 8, 1979
Lieutenant Colonel	April 1, 1985
Colonel	February 1, 1991
Brigadier General	December 1, 1994

Brig. Gen. Ralph G. Wooten

MAJOR GENERAL JACKSON E. ROZIER, JR.

In 1960, Jackson Rozier was commissioned a second lieutenant through Army ROTC. The general earned his bachelor's degree in educational administration from Howard University. His military training included the Signal School Basic Course and the Artillery School Advanced Course. Additionally, General Rozier is a graduate of the Armed Forces Staff College, the Industrial College of the Armed Forces, and the Defense Language Institute. General Rozier passed away in 1994.

Born in Richmond, Virginia, the general served in a variety of staff and command positions, including electronic warfare officer, Twenty-fourth Artillery Group, Coventry, Rhode Island; materiel officer and later executive officer, Seventy-first Maintenance Battalion, Europe; secretary of the general staff, Third Support Brigade, Europe; deputy director, General Supply, United States Army, Vietnam; international logistics staff officer, United States Army Materiel Command, Washington, DC; personnel management officer, United States Army Military Personnel Center, Alexandria, Virginia; commander, 801st Maintenance Battalion, 101st Airborne Division, Fort Campbell, Kentucky; executive officer, Division Support Command, 101st Airborne Division, Fort Campbell, Kentucky; student, Industrial College of the Armed Forces, Fort McNair, Washington, DC; commander, Division Support Command, Eighth Infantry Division (Mechanized), United States Army, Europe; commanding general, United States Army Ordnance Center and School, Aberdeen Proving Ground, Maryland; director of plans and operations, Office of the Deputy Chief of Staff for Logistics, Washington, DC; deputy chief of staff for logistics, United States Army, Europe and Seventh Army, Europe; and director for supply and maintenance, Office of the Deputy Chief of Staff for Logistics, United States Army, Washington, DC.

The general's decorations and awards include the Legion of Merit; the Bronze Star Medal; the Meritorious Service Medal with two Oak Leaf Clusters; the Army Commendation Medal with one Oak Leaf Cluster; the Parachutist Badge; and the Army Staff Identification Badge.

Promotion	Date
Second Lieutenant	January 11, 1960
First Lieutenant	July 11, 1961
Captain	November 20, 1963
Major	October 11, 1967
Lieutenant Colonel	June 1, 1974
Colonel	January 1, 1979
Brigadier General	November 1, 1981
Major General	July 1, 1987

LIEUTENANT GENERAL JULIUS W. BECTON, JR.
Retired

Julius Becton was commissioned a second lieutenant in August of 1945 through Officer Candidate School. He received his bachelor's degree in mathematics from Prairie View A&M College, and his master's degree in economics from the University of Maryland. General Becton also attended the United States Army Command and General Staff College, the Armed Forces Staff College, and the National War College.

During his career, General Becton was plans officer and later chief, Plans and Operations, Office of the Assistant Chief of Staff, Operations and Logistics, United States Army, Europe, personnel staff officer, Reserve Affairs and Discipline Branch, Promotion and Retention Division, Office of the Deputy Chief of Staff for Personnel, Headquarters, United States Army, Washington, DC; military analyst and later operations research analyst, Resources Systems Team, Force Planning Analysis Directorate, Office of the Assistant Vice Chief of Staff, United States Army, Washington, DC; commanding officer, Second Squadron, Seventeenth Cavalry, 101st Airborne Division, Fort Campbell, Kentucky, and United States Army, Vietnam; deputy commander, Third Brigade, 101st Airborne Division, United States Army, Vietnam; and staff officer, Deputy Chief of Staff for Personnel Special Review Board and Department of the Army Suitability Evaluation Board, Washington, DC.

He has also served as commander, Second Brigade, Second Airborne Division, Fort Hood, Texas; chief, Armor Branch, Officer Personnel Directorate, Office of Personnel Operations, United States Army, Washington, DC; deputy commander, United States Training Center, Fort Dix, New Jersey; commanding general, First Cavalry Division, Fort Hood, Texas; and commanding general, United States Army Operational Test and Evaluation Agency, Falls Church, Virginia.

In October of 1978, General Becton left the United States again to assume the duty of commanding general, VII Corps, United States Army, Europe, and brigade commander, Second Brigade, Second Armored Division. He later served as deputy commanding general for training, United States Army Training and Doctrine Command, Fort Monroe, Virginia.

General Becton has been awarded the Silver Star with one Oak Leaf Cluster; the Legion of Merit with one Oak Leaf Cluster; the Distinguished Flying Cross; the Air Medal with "V" device; the Army Commendation Medal with one Oak Leaf Cluster; the Purple Heart with one Oak Leaf Cluster; the Bronze Star with one Oak Leaf Cluster; the Combat Infantryman Badge; and the Parachutist Badge.

Promotion	Date
Second Lieutenant	November 1, 1948
First Lieutenant	May 11, 1949
Captain	June 12, 1953
Major	February 7, 1961
Lieutenant Colonel	November 18, 1964
Colonel	July 31, 1969
Brigadier General	August 1, 1972
Major General	August 1, 1974
Lieutenant General	November 1, 1978

LIEUTENANT GENERAL ANDREW P. CHAMBERS
Retired

A native of Bedford, Virginia, General Chambers received his bachelor's degree in physical education from Howard University, and his master's degree in human relations from Shippensburg State College. The general is also a graduate of several military schools, including the Infantry School Basic and Advanced Courses, the United States Army Command and General Staff College, and the United States Army War College.

During his twenty-seven years in the United States Army, the general served as commander, Company M, Third Battalion, Airborne Infantry Regiment, Eighty-second Airborne Division, Fort Bragg, North Carolina; commander, Headquarters Company, Fourth Armored Group, United States Army, Europe, Germany; assistant intelligence officer, First Brigade, Eighth Cavalry, First Cavalry Division, Eighth United States Army, Korea; operations officer, Headquarters, I Corps, First Brigade, Eighth Cavalry, Eighth United States Army, Korea; commander, Headquarters Company, First Brigade, Eighth Cavalry Division, Eighth United States Army, Korea; review analysis officer, Operations and Review Section, Company Tactics Department, Company D, United States Army Infantry School, Fort Benning, Georgia; student, United States Army Command and General Staff College, Fort Leavenworth, Kansas; assistant logistics officer, Office of the Assistant Chief of Staff, First Airborne Cavalry Division, United States Army, Vietnam; battalion executive officer, First Battalion (Airborne), Twelfth Cavalry, First Cavalry Division (Air Mobile), United States Army, Vietnam; and author/instructor, Offense Section, United States Army Command and General Staff College, Fort Leavenworth, Kansas.

Chambers also served as chief, Morale and Discipline Branch, Personnel Services Division, Office of the Deputy Chief of Staff for Personnel, United States Army, Europe; deputy commander, First Brigade, Eighth Infantry Division, United States Army, Europe; commander, First Battalion, 509th Infantry, Eighth Infantry Division, United States Army, Europe; chief, Force Programs Analysis Team, Program Analysis and Evaluation Directorate, Office of the Chief of Staff, United States Army, Washington, DC; and commander, Division Support Command, Ninth Infantry Division.

General Chambers left the United States in June 1978, and was assigned director J-1 (Personnel), Inspector General, Pacific Command, Camp H.M. Smith, Hawaii; and in October of 1980, the general returned to the United States and was assigned as assistant division commander, First Cavalry Division, Fort Hood, Texas; commanding general, United States Army Readiness and Mobilization Region VII, Fort Sam Houston, Texas; deputy commanding general, Fifth United States Army, Fort Sam Houston,

Promotion	Date
Second Lieutenant	June 4, 1954
First Lieutenant	February 13, 1956
Captain	October 17, 1960
Major	July 1, 1965
Lieutenant Colonel	July 23, 1968
Colonel	August 1, 1975
Brigadier General	September 1, 1978
Major General	January 1, 1981
Lieutenant General	February 20, 1985

Texas; commanding general, First Cavalry Division, Fort Hood, Texas; assistant deputy chief of staff for personnel, Office of the Deputy Chief of Staff for Personnel, United States Army, Washington DC; commanding general, VII Corps, United States Army, Europe; and deputy commanding general, Force Command, and commanding general, Third United States Army, Forces Command, Fort McPherson, Georgia.

General Chambers has received the Distinguished Service Medal with one Oak Leaf Cluster; the Defense Superior Service Medal; the Legion of Merit; the Soldier's Medal; the Bronze Star Medal with "V" device; the Meritorious Service Medal with one Oak Leaf Cluster; Air Medals; the Army Commendation Medal with two Oak Leaf Clusters; the Combat Infantryman Badge; and the Master Parachutist Badge.

LIEUTENANT GENERAL HENRY DOCTOR
Retired

General Doctor, a native of Oakley, South Carolina, received his bachelor's degree from South Carolina State College and his master's degree from Georgia State University. He also attended the United States War College.

Doctor has served as executive officer, First Battalion, Thirty-fifth Infantry, Fourth Division, United States Army, Vietnam; assistant operations officer, Organization and Training, Fourth Infantry Division, United States Army, Vietnam; chief, Personnel Action Section, Infantry Branch, Officer Personnel Directorate, Office of Personnel Operations, United States Army, Washington, DC; commander, First Battalion, Twenty-ninth Infantry, 197th Infantry Brigade, Fort Benning, Georgia; deputy commander, 197th Infantry Brigade, Fort Benning, Georgia; chief, Modern Volunteer Army Control Group, United States Army Infantry Center, Fort Benning, Georgia; director of psychometrics, United States Army War College, Carlisle Barracks, Pennsylvania; commander, First Brigade, Twenty-fifth Infantry Division, Schofield Barracks, Hawaii; director of enlisted personnel management, United States Army Military Personnel Center, Alexandria, Virginia; and assistant division commander, Twenty-fourth Infantry Division, Fort Stewart, Georgia; director, Personnel, Training and Force Development, United States Army Materiel Development and Readiness Command, Alexandria, Virginia.

He has also served as chief of staff, United States Army Materiel Development and Readiness Command, Alexandria, Virginia; commanding general, Second Infantry Division, Eighth United States Army, Korea; deputy, Inspector General for Investigations, Assistance, Training and Information Management, United States Army, Washington, DC; and inspector general, United States Army, Washington, DC.

General Doctor's decorations and awards include the Legion of Merit; the Bronze Star Medal; the Meritorious Service Medal; and the Army Commendation Medal with three Oak Leaf Clusters.

Promotion	Date
Second Lieutenant	July 19, 1954
First Lieutenant	February 10, 1956
Captain	September 28, 1960
Major	June 22, 1965
Lieutenant Colonel	July 17, 1968
Colonel	November 1, 1974
Brigadier General	August 1, 1977
Major General	December 1, 1980
Lieutenant General	July 1, 1986

LIEUTENANT GENERAL ARTHUR GREGG
Retired

An Officer Candidate School graduate, General Gregg is a graduate of St. Benedict's College with a bachelor's degree in business administration. He is also a graduate of the Quartermaster School Basic and Advanced Courses, the United States Army Command and General Staff College, and the United States Army War College.

During his thirty-one years of military service, General Gregg's major duty assignments included student, United States Army Command and General Staff College, Fort Leavenworth, Kansas; logistics plans officer, United States Army Materiel Command, Washington, DC; assistant secretary, General Staff, United States Army Materiel Command, Washington, DC; student, United States Army War College, Carlisle Barracks, Pennsylvania; logistics officer, Logistics Directorate, J-4 (Logistics), United States, European Command; and commander, Nahbollenbach Army Depot, United States Army, Europe.

General Gregg returned to the United States in July 1971, as deputy director and later director, Troop Support, Office of the Deputy Chief of Staff for Logistics, United States Army, Washington, DC; deputy director of supply and maintenance, Office of the Deputy Chief of Staff for Logistics, United States Army, Washington, DC; commander, European Exchange System, Munich, West Germany; deputy chief of staff, Logistics, Headquarters, United States Army, Europe and Seventh Army, Germany; deputy chief of staff for logistics directorate, J-4, the Joint Chiefs of Staff, Washington, DC; and deputy chief of staff for logistics, Headquarters, United States Army, Washington, DC.

General Gregg's decorations and awards include the Defense Distinguished Service Medal; the Distinguished Service Medal; the Legion of Merit with two Oak Leaf Clusters; the Meritorious Service Medal; the Joint Service Commendation Medal; and the Army Commendation Medal with two Oak Leaf Clusters.

Promotion	Date
Second Lieutenant	May 19, 1950
First Lieutenant	June 22, 1951
Captain	September 14, 1954
Major	December 15, 1961
Lieutenant Colonel	January 28, 1966
Colonel	January 19, 1970
Brigadier General	October 1, 1972
Major General	April 1, 1976
Lieutenant General	July 1, 1977

LIEUTENANT GENERAL EDWARD HONOR
Retired

General Honor was born in Melville, Louisiana, and received his bachelor's degree in education from Southern University A&M College. He received his commission as a second lieutenant through Army ROTC in August 1954.

His military assignments included commander, Forty-sixth Transportation Company, Seventeenth Transportation Battalion, Eighth United States Army, Korea; commander, Company A, Thirteenth Transportation Battalion, Second Infantry Division, Fort Benning, Georgia; assistant operations officer and later executive officer, Twenty-eighth Transportation Battalion, United States Army, Europe; executive officer and later chief, Sealift, 507th Transportation Group, United States Army, Vietnam; student, United States Army Command and General Staff College, Fort Leavenworth, Kansas; action officer and later chief, Personnel Movement Branch, Office of the Deputy Chief of Staff for Logistics, United States Army, Washington, DC; chief, Passenger and Unit Movement Branch, Military Traffic Management and Terminal Service, Washington, DC.

General Honor also served as commander, Thirty-sixth Transportation Battalion, United States Army Cam Ranh Bay Support Command, Vietnam; commander, Twenty-fourth Transportation Battalion, United States Army Cam Ranh Bay Support Command, Vietnam; assistant chief of staff, Security, Plans and Operations, United States Army Cam Ranh Bay Support Command, Vietnam; chief, Transportation Service Branch, Transportation Division, Office of the Deputy Chief of Staff for Logistics, United States Continental Army Command, Fort Monroe, Virginia; commander, Thirty-seventh Transportation Group, Fourth Transportation Brigade, United States Army, Europe; commander, Military Traffic Management Command, Transportation Terminal Group, Rotterdam, Netherlands, Europe; director for plans, doctrine, and systems, United States Army Materiel Development and Readiness Command, Alexandria, Virginia; deputy director for planning and deputy director for planning and resources, Logistics Directorate, J-4 (Logistics), Organization of the Joint Chiefs of Staff, Washington, DC; director of resources and management, Office of the Deputy Chief of Staff for Logistics, United States Army, Washington, DC; commanding general, Military Traffic Management Command, Eastern Area, Bayonne, New Jersey; director, Transportation, Energy and Troop Support, Office of the Deputy Chief of Staff for Logistics, United States Army, Washington, DC; commanding general, Military Traffic Management Command, Washington, DC; and director, J-4, the Joint Chiefs of Staff, Washington, DC.

His decorations and awards include the Distinguished Service Medal; the Defense Superior Service Medal; the Legion of Merit with three Oak Leaf Clusters; the Bronze Star Medal with one Oak Leaf Cluster; the Meritorious Service Medal with one Oak Leaf Cluster; the Joint Service Commendation Medal; and the Army Commendation Medal with one Oak Leaf Cluster.

Promotion	Date
Second Lieutenant	August 12, 1954
First Lieutenant	February 13, 1956
Captain	October 17, 1960
Major	January 30, 1965
Lieutenant Colonel	July 23, 1968
Colonel	February 1, 1974
Brigadier General	June 1, 1979
Major General	January 22, 1982
Lieutenant General	July 1, 1987

LIEUTENANT GENERAL JAMES F. McCALL
Retired

General McCall received his commission in March 1958 upon graduation from Officer Candidate School. The Philadelphia, Pennsylvania, native earned his bachelor's degree in economics from the University of Pennsylvania, his master's degree in military science from the United States Army Command and General Staff College, and his master of business administration degree from Syracuse University.

During his years of military service, General McCall served as commander, Company A, Twelfth Battalion, Fourth Training Regiment, United States Army Training Center, Fort Knox, Kentucky; executive officer, Mortar Battery, First Battle Group, Third Infantry, Fort McNair, Washington, DC; assistant intelligence officer, First Battle Group, Third Infantry, Fort Meyer, Virginia; intelligence officer, Second Battalion, Sixth Infantry, Berlin Brigade, United States Army, Europe; secretary of the general staff, Headquarters, Berlin Brigade, United States Army, Europe; commander, Company M, Fourth Battalion, Second Basic Training Brigade, Fort Dix, New Jersey; and advisor, United States Military Assistance Command, United States Army, Vietnam.

McCall has also served as military assistant, Office of the Secretary of the Army (Financial Management), Washington, DC; commander, First Battalion, Thirty-first Infantry Division, Korea; staff officer, Army Materiel Acquisition Review Committee-Armament, United States Army Materiel Command, Alexandria, Virginia; executive, Office of the Director of the Army Budget Office, Comptroller of the Army, Washington, DC; commander, Fourth Training Brigade, United States Army Armor School, Fort Knox, Kentucky; chief, Procurement Programs and Budget Division, Materiel Plans and Programs Directorate, Office of the Deputy Chief of Staff for Research, Development and Acquisitions, United States Army, Washington, DC; comptroller, United States Army Materiel Development and Readiness Command, Alexandria, Virginia; director, Army Budget, Office of the Comptroller, United States Army, Washington, DC; and comptroller of the Army, Office of the Secretary of the Army, Washington, DC.

McCall's military decorations and awards include the Distinguished Service Medal with one Oak Leaf Cluster; the Legion of Merit with one Oak Leaf Cluster; the Meritorious Service Medal; the Air Medal; the Army Commendation Medal with one Oak Leaf Cluster; the Combat Infantryman Badge; the Parachutist Badge; and the Army General Staff Identification Badge.

Promotion	Date
Second Lieutenant	March 4, 1958
First Lieutenant	September 4, 1959
Captain	September 4, 1962
Major	November 23, 1966
Lieutenant Colonel	November 9, 1971
Colonel	February 1, 1976
Brigadier General	March 1, 1980
Major General	September 1, 1983
Lieutenant General	July 1, 1988

LIEUTENANT GENERAL EMMETT PAIGE, JR.
Retired

General Paige received his commission as a second lieutenant on July 18, 1952, after graduating from Officer Candidate School. A native of Jacksonville, Florida, he received his bachelor's degree in business administration from the University of Maryland and his master's degree in public administration from Pennsylvania State University. General Paige also attended the United States Army Command and General Staff College and the United States Army War College.

During his twenty-nine years in the Army Paige served as executive officer and platoon officer, Company A, Fortieth Signal Battalion (Construction), Fort Devens, Massachusetts; commander, Company B, Ninth Signal Battalion, Ninth Infantry Division, Fort Carson, Colorado; officer in charge, Eighth United States Army Telephone Exchange, Fifty-seventh Signal Company, Eighth United States Army, Korea; chief, Combat Development Branch, Plans and Training Division, United States Signal Training Command, Fort Monmouth, New Jersey; acting secretary of the staff, United States Army Electronics Command, Fort Monmouth, New Jersey; systems status officer, Defense Communications Systems, Southeast Asia Region, United States Pacific Command, Clark Air Force Base, Philippines; deputy project manager, Office of the Project Manager, United States Army Communications Systems Agency, Fort Monmouth, New Jersey; and chief, Special Projects Division, Communications Systems Engineering and Management Agency, First Signal Brigade, United States Army Strategic Command, United States Army, Vietnam.

Paige also served as commander, 361st Signal Battalion, First Signal Brigade, United States Army Strategic Communications Command, United States Army, Vietnam; communications staff officer, Voice Networks Branch Operations Directorate, Defense Communications Agency, Washington, DC; deputy chief of staff, United States Army Communications Command, Fort Huachuca, Arizona; commander, Eleventh Signal Group, United States Army Communications Command, Fort Huachuca, Arizona; commanding general, United States Army Communications Systems Agency, Fort Monmouth, New Jersey; commanding general, United States Army Communications Research and Development Command, Fort Monmouth, New Jersey; commanding general, United States Army Electronic Research and Development Command, Adelphi, Maryland; and commanding general, United States Army Information Systems Command, Fort Huachuca, Arizona.

During his career, General Paige was awarded the Distinguished Service Medal with one Oak Leaf Cluster; the Legion of Merit with two Oak Leaf Clusters; the Bronze Star Medal; the Joint Service Commendation Medal; the Meritorious Service Medal; and the Army Commendation Medal.

Promotion	Date
Second Lieutenant	July 18, 1952
First Lieutenant	January 18, 1954
Captain	January 27, 1959
Major	December 31, 1963
Lieutenant Colonel	July 20, 1967
Colonel	July 16, 1973
Brigadier General	June 1, 1976
Major General	April 3, 1978
Lieutenant General	July 1, 1984

MAJOR GENERAL ROBERT B. ADAMS
Retired

Born in Buffalo, New York, General Adams earned a bachelor's degree in accounting auditing from Canisius College and bachelor's and master's degrees in automated data processing systems from George Washington University. The general is also a graduate of the United States Army Command and General Staff College, the United States Army War College, and the Advanced Management Program at the University of Houston.

His major duty assignments included finance officer, Twenty-third Infantry Division (American), United States Army, Vietnam; finance officer, 196th Infantry Brigade, United States Army, Vietnam; special projects officer, United States Army Computer Systems Command, Washington, DC; chief, Financial Management and Accounting Division, Washington, DC; comptroller, the Adjutant General Center, United States Army, Washington, DC; commandant, United States Army Institute of Administration, Fort Benjamin Harrison, Indiana; deputy commander for integration, United States Army Administration Center, Fort Benjamin Harrison, Indiana; assistant comptroller for resource policy and financial planning, Office of the Comptroller of the Army, Washington, DC; director of resources and management, Office of the Deputy Chief of Staff for Logistics, United States Army, Washington, DC; deputy commanding general, Finance and Accounting, United States Army Finance and Accounting Center, Fort Benjamin Harrison, Indiana; and deputy chief of staff, Resource Management, United States Army Materiel Command, Alexandria, Virginia.

Promotion	Date
Second Lieutenant	June 12, 1955
First Lieutenant	January 1, 1957
Captain	March 15, 1961
Major	December 13, 1965
Lieutenant Colonel	July 10, 1969
Colonel	February 1, 1975
Brigadier General	July 1, 1980
Major General	September 22, 1983

His decorations and awards include the Distinguished Service Medal; the Legion of Merit with three Oak Leaf Clusters; the Bronze Star Medal; the Meritorious Service Medal with one Oak Leaf Cluster; and the Army Commendation Medal with one Oak Leaf Cluster.

MAJOR GENERAL JULIUS W. BROOKS, JR.
Retired

General Brooks, born in Indianapolis, Indiana, received his bachelor's degree from the University of Omaha and his master's degree in human relations from the University of Oklahoma. The general is also a graduate of the United States Army Command and General Staff College and the United States Army War College.

An officer with more than twenty-five years of service, his major duty assignments included battalion commander, Second Battalion, Fortieth Artillery, 199th Infantry Brigade, Fort Benning, Georgia; student, Command and General Staff College, Fort Leavenworth, Kansas; student, the Army War College, Carlisle Barracks, Pennsylvania; commanding officer, Second Battalion, 40th Artillery, 199th Infantry Brigade, United States Army, Vietnam; special assistant to deputy commanding officer, 199th Infantry Brigade, United States Army, Vietnam; staff officer, Doctrine Branch, Doctrine and Concepts Division, Doctrine and Systems Directorate, Office of the Assistant Chief of Staff for Force Development, United States Army, Washington, DC; commanding officer, Seventy-second Field Artillery Group, United States Army, Europe; and assistant division commander, Second Infantry Division, United States Army, Pacific-Korea, Korea.

General Brooks also conducted major studies on race relations among Army troops stationed overseas in his capacity as Army director of equal opportunity programs, Office of the Deputy Chief of Staff for Personnel, United States Army, Washington, DC. He also served as commanding general, Twenty-fifth Infantry Division, Schofield Barracks, Hawaii.

General Brooks's decorations and awards include the Legion of Merit with one Oak Leaf Cluster; the Bronze Star Medal with one Oak Leaf Cluster; the Meritorious Service Medal; Air Medals (seven awards); the National Defense Service Medal; the Republic of Vietnam Campaign Medal; the Republic of Vietnam Service Medal; the Armed Forces Expeditionary Medal; the Army Occupation Medal (Japan); the Korean Service Medal; the United Nations Service Medal; the Gallantry Cross with Gold Star; the Gallantry Cross with Palm; the Republic of Vietnam Ranger Badge; the Civic Action Medal, First Class; the Army General Staff Identification Badge; and the Army Commendation Medal.

Promotion	Date
Second Lieutenant	July 1, 1949
First Lieutenant	January 19, 1951
Captain	June 30, 1954
Major	October 18, 1961
Lieutenant Colonel	December 1, 1965
Colonel	January 16, 1970
Brigadier General	July 23, 1972
Major General	August 2, 1974

MAJOR GENERAL LEO A. BROOKS
Retired

In May 1954 Leo Austin Brooks was commissioned a second lieutenant through Army ROTC. A native of Washington, DC, he earned a bachelor's degree from Virginia State College and a master's degree in financial management from George Washington University. General Brooks also attended the United States Army Command and General Staff College and the National War College.

General Brooks's major duty assignments included assistant for budget and congressional coordination, Office of the Deputy Chief of Staff for Logistics, United States Army, Washington, DC; assistant chief of staff, Supply, United States Army, Vietnam; commander, 266th Supply and Service Battalion, Twenty-ninth General Support Group, United States Army Saigon Support Command, Vietnam; deputy secretary of the general staff, United States Army Materiel Command, Alexandria, Virginia; member, Plans and Operations Branch, Logistics Directorate, J-4 (Logistics), the Joint Chiefs of Staff; Washington, DC; commander, Sacramento Army Depot, Sacramento, California; commander, Thirteenth Corps Support Command, and director of industrial operations, Fort Hood, Texas; commanding general, United States Army Troop Support Agency, Fort Lee, New Jersey; and commanding general, Defense Personnel Support Center, Philadelphia, Pennsylvania.

Promotion	Date
Second Lieutenant	May 29, 1954
First Lieutenant	March 5, 1956
Captain	October 20, 1960
Major	July 8, 1965
Lieutenant Colonel	July 25, 1968
Colonel	February 1, 1974
Brigadier General	July 1, 1978
Major General	February 1, 1982

His decorations and awards include the Legion of Merit with two Oak Leaf Clusters; the Bronze Star Medal; the Meritorious Service Medal; the Joint Service Commendation Medal; and the Army Commendation Medal with one Oak Leaf Cluster.

MAJOR GENERAL JOHN M. BROWN
Retired

General Brown was born in Vicksburg, Mississippi. He received his bachelor's degree in engineering from the United States Military Academy at West Point and his master's in business administration from Syracuse University. General Brown is also a graduate of the University of Houston's Advanced Management Program, the United States Army Command and General Staff College, and the Industrial College of the Armed Forces.

During his military career, Brown served as commander, Company C and later Combat Support Company, First Brigade, Seventeenth Infantry, Seventh Infantry Division, Eighth United States Army, Korea; comptroller, Division United States Army Airfield, Fort Belvoir, Virginia; executive officer, Fourth Battalion, Forty-seventh Infantry, Ninth Infantry Division, United States Army, Vietnam; student, United States Army Command and General Staff College, Fort Leavenworth, Kansas; chief, Cost Methodology Branch, Cost Research Division, Washington, DC; executive officer, Directorate of Cost Analysis, Office of the Comptroller of the Army, Washington, DC; assistant secretary of the general staff, Office of the Chief of Staff, United States Army, Washington, DC; commander, First Battalion, Eighty-seventh Infantry, Eighth Infantry Division, United States Army, Europe, Germany; commander, Third Brigade, Second Infantry Division, United States Army, Korea; assistant chief of staff, Comptroller, United Nations Command, United States Forces Korea, and Eighth United States Army, Korea; assistant division commander, Second Infantry Division, Korea; deputy director of materiel plans and programs, Office of the Deputy Chief of Staff for Research, Development and Acquisition, United States Army, Washington, DC; director of materiel plans and programs, Office of the Deputy Chief of Staff for Research, Development, and Acquisition, United States Army, Washington, DC; deputy chief of staff, Comptroller, United States Army Forces Command, Fort McPherson, Georgia; and deputy commanding general, III Corps and Fort Hood, Fort Hood, Texas.

General Brown has been awarded the Distinguished Service Medal; the Legion of Merit; the Bronze Star Medal; the Meritorious Service Medal; the Army Commendation Medal with two Oak Leaf Clusters; the Combat Infantryman Badge; the Parachutist Badge; and the Ranger Tab.

Promotion	Date
Second Lieutenant	June 3, 1955
First Lieutenant	December 3, 1956
Captain	February 23, 1961
Major	November 29, 1965
Lieutenant Colonel	June 11, 1969
Colonel	February 1, 1975
Brigadier General	July 1, 1979
Major General	July 1, 1984

MAJOR GENERAL EUGENE R. CROMARTIE
Retired

In 1957, Eugene Cromartie was commissioned a second lieutenant through Army ROTC at Florida A & M University, where he received a bachelor's degree in social science. Later, he earned a master's degree in education from the University of Dayton. General Cromartie's military education includes the Infantry Basic School, the Military Police School Advanced Course, the United States Army Command and General Staff College, and the National War College.

Born in Wabasso, Florida, the general served in a number of staff and command positions during his military career, including assistant provost marshal and later commander, Fifty-ninth Military Police Company, Bremerhaven, Germany; assistant provost marshal, Headquarters, United States Army Port of Entry, Bremerhaven, Germany; assistant professor of military science, University of Dayton, Dayton, Ohio; commander, Headquarters Detachment, Ninety-fifth Military Police Battalion, Vietnam; commander, Headquarters Detachment, Eighty-ninth Military Police Group, Vietnam; chief, Electives Branch, Office of the Director of Graduate Studies and Research, United States Army Command and General Staff College, Fort Leavenworth, Kansas; commander, 503d Military Police Battalion, Fort Bragg, North Carolina; provost marshal, Eighty-second Airborne Division, Fort Bragg, North Carolina; personnel management officer, Assignments Branch, Lieutenant Colonels Division, Officer Personnel Management Directorate, United States Army Military Personnel Center, Alexandria, Virginia; special assistant to the commanding general, United States Army Criminal Investigation Command,

Falls Church, Virginia; commander, First Region, United States Army Criminal Investigation Command, Fort Meade, Maryland; and deputy provost marshal, United States Seventh Army, Europe.

General Cromartie has been awarded the Distinguished Service Medal; the Bronze Star Medal with one Oak Leaf Cluster; the Meritorious Service Medal with two Oak Leaf Clusters; the Army Commendation Medal with one Oak Leaf Cluster; and the Parachutist Badge.

Promotion	Date
Second Lieutenant	June 3, 1957
First Lieutenant	January 14, 1959
Captain	January 15, 1962
Major	September 21, 1966
Lieutenant Colonel	August 9, 1971
Colonel	September 1, 1977
Brigadier General	April 1, 1982
Major General	March 1, 1985

MAJOR GENERAL JERRY R. CURRY
Retired

General Curry attended the University of Nebraska at Omaha, where he earned his bachelor's degree in general education. He also earned a master's degree in international relations from Boston University and a doctorate from Luther Rice Seminary. Curry also attended the United States Army Command and General Staff College and the United States Army War College.

General Curry served as commander, Second Battalion, Thirtieth Infantry, Third Infantry Division (Mechanized), United States Army, Europe; commander, Advisory Team Twenty-two, United States Military Assistant Command, Vietnam; operations research analyst, Programs Group, Planning and Programming Analysis Directorate, Office of the Assistant Vice Chief of Staff, United States Army, Washington, DC; commander, Third Brigade, Eighth Infantry Division (Mechanized), United States Army, Europe; deputy chief of staff and later chief of staff, V Corps, United States Army, Europe; deputy commanding general, United States Army Military District of Washington, Washington, DC; assistant division commander, Fourth Infantry Division (Mechanized), Fort Carson, Colorado; commanding general, United States Army Test and Evaluation Command, Aberdeen Proving Ground, Maryland; deputy assistant secretary of defense (Public Affairs), Washington, DC; commanding general, United States Army Military District of Washington, Washington, DC; and deputy commanding general, V Corps, United States Army, Europe.

He has been awarded the Defense Distinguished Service Medal with one Oak Leaf Cluster; the Legion of Merit with

Promotion	Date
Second Lieutenant	December 19, 1952
First Lieutenant	July 13, 1954
Captain	April 15, 1959
Major	April 1, 1964
Lieutenant Colonel	September 13, 1967
Colonel	June 12, 1973
Brigadier General	August 1, 1975
Major General	August 22, 1978

one Oak Leaf Cluster; the Bronze Star Medal; the Meritorious Service Medal with one Oak Leaf Cluster; the Air Medal; the Army Commendation Medal with two Oak Leaf Clusters; the Navy Commendation Medal; the Combat Infantryman Badge; the Parachutist Badge; and the Master Army Aviator Badge.

MAJOR GENERAL FREDRIC E. DAVISON
Retired

The first Black Army combat general, Davison was a cum laude graduate of Howard University, where he earned a bachelor's degree in 1938 and master's degree in 1940. He also attended George Washington University, where he earned a master's degree in international affairs. The general also attended the Army War College at George Washington University.

He began his military career when he received his commission as a second lieutenant through Army ROTC at Howard University. In March 1941, he was assigned to the 366th Infantry Regiment at Fort Devens, Massachusetts. From 1941 to 1944, General Davison moved up through the ranks, from platoon leader to executive officer and company commander of a heavy weapons company.

He served as chief, Personnel Services, Eighth Army, Korea; chief, Reserve Components Division, Office of the Secretary of the Army, Washington, DC; deputy commander, 199th Light Infantry Brigade, Bihn Chanh, United States Army, Vietnam. During the Tet offensive, when the brigade commander was evacuated because of injuries, Davison took his place, and led the defense of the United States base at Long Binh. For his exemplary efforts, he was promoted to brigadier general. General Creighton Abrams, the United States commander in Vietnam, pinned on his star. Abrams said, "In my judgment, I know of no officer more deserving." Fredric Ellis Davison became only the third Black in American history to wear a general's star, and the first Black American to assume combat command.

Returning to the United States in 1969, Davison served as inspector general, United States Army, Washington, DC; deputy chief of staff, Personnel, United States Army, Europe and Seventh Army, Germany; and commanding general, Military District of Washington, Washington, DC.

General Davison's decorations and awards include the Distinguished Service Medal; the Legion of Merit with one Oak Leaf Cluster; the Bronze Star Medal; the Air Medal (nineteen awards); the Army Commendation Medal with two Oak Leaf Clusters; and the Combat Infantryman Badge (two awards).

Promotion	Date
Second Lieutenant	March 17, 1939
First Lieutenant	May 29, 1942
Captain	November 3, 1943
Major	November 16, 1950
Lieutenant Colonel	April 4, 1957
Colonel	November 27, 1964
Brigadier General	October 1, 1969
Major General	April 1, 1971

MAJOR GENERAL OLIVER W. DILLARD
Retired

Born in Margaret, Alabama, Oliver Dillard was inducted into the Army during World War II. Upon graduation from Infantry Officer Candidate School at Fort Benning, Georgia, he received his commission as a second lieutenant. After completing several years of military service, he entered the University of Omaha, where he earned his bachelor's degree.

By 1965, General Dillard had earned his master's degree from George Washington University. His major duty assignments included student, Vietnam Training Center, Foreign Service Institute, Department of State, Washington, DC; senior military advisor, Advisory Team Forty-one, Military Region II, United States Military Assistance Command, Vietnam; deputy assistant chief of staff for intelligence, Office of the Assistant Chief of Staff for Intelligence, United States Army, Washington, DC; deputy assistant chief of staff, Civil Operations Revolutionary Development Support, United States Military Assistance Command, Vietnam; director of intelligence, United States Military Assistance Command, Vietnam; deputy chief of staff, Intelligence, United States Army Forces Command, Fort McPherson, Georgia; assistant division commander, Second Armored Division, Fort Hood, Texas; and deputy chief of staff for intelligence, United States Seventh Army, Europe.

General Dillard's decorations and awards include the Distinguished Service Medal; the Silver Star; the Legion of Merit with two Oak Leaf Clusters; the Bronze Star Medal with one Oak Leaf Cluster; the Air Medal; the Army Commendation Medal with one Oak Leaf Cluster; the Purple Heart; the Vietnamese Army Distinguished Service Order; and the Combat Infantryman Badge.

Promotion	Date
Second Lieutenant	December 6, 1949
First Lieutenant	March 23, 1951
Captain	October 29, 1954
Major	January 1, 1962
Lieutenant Colonel	January 2, 1969
Colonel	March 12, 1973
Brigadier General	August 11, 1974
Major General	August 1, 1975

MAJOR GENERAL ROBERT C. GASKILL
Retired

Born in Yonkers, New York, General Gaskill is a graduate of Howard University, where he earned his bachelor's degree in business administration and a commission as a second lieutenant through Army ROTC. The general is also a graduate of the United States Army Command and General Staff College, the Armed Forces Staff College, the United States Army War College, and George Washington University, where he earned a master's degree in business administration.

General Gaskill's major duty assignments have included chief, Missiles, Weapons, and Tracked Vehicles Section, Production and Industrial Facilities Branch, Procurement of Equipment and Missiles, Army Execution Branch Division, Office of the Chief of Logistics, United States Army, Washington, DC; commander, Fifth Supply and Transport Battalion, Fort Carson, Colorado; deputy chief (deputy senior advisor), Quartermaster-Commissary-Purchasing Advisory Division, Military Assistance Command, Vietnam; logistics staff officer, J-4 (Logistics), United States European Command, Supreme Headquarters Allied Powers, Europe; director, Human Relations Studies, United States Army War College, Carlisle Barracks, Pennsylvania; director, Interpersonal and Group Relations Studies, United States Army War College, Carlisle Barracks, Pennsylvania; commanding general, Letterkenny Army Depot, Chambersburg, Pennsylvania; commanding general, First Support Brigade, United States Army, Europe; deputy commanding general, Twenty-first Support Command, United States Army, Europe; deputy commandant, United States Army War College, Carlisle Barracks, Pennsylvania; and deputy director, Defense Logistics Agency, Alexandria, Virginia.

Promotion	Date
Second Lieutenant	August 25, 1952
First Lieutenant	January 18, 1954
Captain	November 12, 1958
Major	May 24, 1963
Lieutenant Colonel	February 16, 1967
Colonel	March 12, 1973
Brigadier General	September 1, 1975
Major General	May 1, 1979

General Gaskill received the Distinguished Service Medal; the Legion of Merit; the Meritorious Service Medal with one Oak Leaf Cluster; the Army Commendation Medal with one Oak Leaf Cluster; and the Army General Staff Badge.

MAJOR GENERAL EDWARD GREER
Retired

Born in the mountain state of West Virginia, General Greer received his bachelor's degree from West Virginia State College in 1948 and his master's degree in international affairs from George Washington University in 1962. He is also a graduate of the United States Army Command and General Staff College and the National War College. Having entered the Army in 1947, he achieved the rank of brigadier general in 1972.

General Greer's major permanent duty assignments included commanding officer, First Battalion, Seventeenth Artillery, United States Army, Pacific-Korea; author-instructor, Department of Command, United States Army Command and General Staff College, Fort Leavenworth, Kansas; student, the National War College, Washington, DC; member, General Operations Division, J-3 (Operations), the Joint Chiefs of Staff, Washington, DC; deputy commander, XXIV Corps Artillery, United States Army, Vietnam; commanding officer, 108th Artillery Group, United States Army, Vietnam; assistant director,

Directorate for Reserve Forces, Plans, Programs, and Budgets, Office of the Assistant Secretary of Defense (Manpower and Reserve Affairs), Washington, DC; deputy commanding general, United States Army Training Center, Fort Leonard Wood, Missouri; and deputy commanding general, United States Army Military Personnel Center, Alexandria, Virginia.

Greer was one of the first Black generals to serve as deputy commander of the United States Army Training Center, one of the Army's most prestigious jobs.

Promotion	Date
Second Lieutenant	July 12, 1948
First Lieutenant	August 18, 1950
Captain	August 3, 1951
Major	June 17, 1958
Lieutenant Colonel	January 31, 1963
Colonel	April 19, 1968
Brigadier General	October 10, 1972
Major General	September 1, 1975

General Greer's decorations and awards include the Air Medal; the Joint Service Commendation Medal; the Army Commendation Medal with one Oak Leaf Cluster; the Legion of Merit with one Oak Leaf Cluster; the Bronze Star Medal with one Oak Leaf Cluster; and the Silver Star.

MAJOR GENERAL JAMES F. HAMLET
Retired

A Native of Alliance, Ohio, General Hamlet received a bachelor's degree in business administration from Saint Benedict's College. During his military career, he also graduated from the United States Army Command and General Staff College and the United States Army War College.

His major duty assignments have included commanding general, Third Brigade, First Cavalry Division, United States Army, Vietnam; chief, Airmobility Branch, Doctrine and Systems Division, United States Army Combat Developments Command Combat Arms Group, Fort Leavenworth, Kansas; student, United States Army War College, Carlisle Barracks, Pennsylvania; commanding officer, Eleventh Aviation Group, First Cavalry Division (Airmobile), United States Army, Vietnam; assistant division Commander, 101st Airborne Division (Airmobile), United States Army, Vietnam.

In August 1972, General Hamlet returned to the United States and served as commanding general, Fourth Infantry Division, Fort Carson, Colorado; deputy to the inspector general (Inspections, Safety, and Surveys), United States Army, Washington, DC; and deputy to

Promotion	Date
Second Lieutenant	July 11, 1944
First Lieutenant	August 7, 1945
Captain	July 11, 1951
Major	November 18, 1959
Lieutenant Colonel	October 14, 1963
Colonel	September 10, 1968
Brigadier General	September 1, 1971
Major General	June 1, 1973

the inspector general (Investigations and Assistance), United States Army, Washington, DC.

General Hamlet's decorations and awards include the Distinguished Service Medal; the Legion of Merit with two Oak Leaf Clusters; the Distinguished Flying Cross; the Soldier's Medal; the Bronze Star Medal with one Oak Leaf Cluster; the Air Medal; the Army Commendation Medal with three Oak Leaf Clusters; the Combat Infantryman Badge; the Parachutist Badge; and the Senior Army Aviator Badge.

MAJOR GENERAL ARTHUR HOLMES
Retired

Born in Decatur, Alabama, General Holmes received his commission as a second lieutenant through Army ROTC. He received his bachelor's degree in chemistry from Hampton Institute and his master's degree in business administration from Kent State University. General Holmes also attended the United States Army Command and General Staff College and the United States Naval War College.

He has served as commander, 724th Maintenance Battalion, Twenty-fourth Infantry Division, Fort Benning, Georgia; chief, Materiel Program Coordination Section, Alexandria, Virginia; chief, Weapons and Combat Vehicles Section, Materiel Acquisition Directorate, Office of the Deputy Chief of Staff for Logistics, United States Army, Washington, DC; commander, Sixty-second Maintenance Battalion, United States Army Qui Nhon Support Command, Vietnam; assistant deputy chief of staff for logistics, the Joint Chiefs of Staff, Washington, DC; chief, Ordinance Branch, Officer Personnel Directorate, United States Army Military Personnel Center, Alexandria, Virginia; commander, Division Support Command, First Infantry Division (Mechanized); assistant division commander, First Infantry Division (Mechanized), Fort Riley, Kansas; executive assistant to the secretary of the Army, Washington, DC; deputy commanding general, United States Army Tank-Automotive Materiel Readiness Command, Warren, Michigan; deputy to the inspector general (Inspections), United States Army, Washington, DC; and commanding general, United States Army Tank-Automotive Command, Warren, Michigan.

Promotion	Date
Second Lieutenant	August 6, 1952
First Lieutenant	January 1, 1954
Captain	October 9, 1958
Major	December 13, 1963
Lieutenant Colonel	July 13, 1967
Colonel	July 12, 1973
Brigadier General	February 8, 1979
Major General	November 1, 1981

General Holmes' decorations and awards include the Distinguished Service Medal; the Legion of Merit; the Bronze Star Medal; the Meritorious Service Medal with one Oak Leaf Cluster; the Joint Service Commendation Medal; and the Army Commendation Medal with two Oak Leaf Clusters.

MAJOR GENERAL JULIUS PARKER, JR.
Retired

General Parker received his commission through Army ROTC upon graduation from Prairie View A&M College with a bachelor's degree in biology and chemistry. He received his master's degree in public administration for Shippensburg State College. General Parker also attended the United States Army Command and General Staff College and the United States Army War College.

A native of New Braunfels, Texas, Parker's major duty assignments included executive officer and later liaison officer and commander, Headquarters Company, First Battle Group, Twenty-second Infantry, Fourth Infantry Division, Fort Lewis, Washington; chief, Interpretation Section, 207th Military Intelligence Detachment, Sixty-sixth Instructor Training Group, Europe; executive officer, 207th Military Intelligence Detachment, Sixty-sixth Instructor Training Group, VII Corps, United States Army, Europe; operations and training staff officer; Joint Training Branch, Training Division, Directorate of Unit Training, Office of the Deputy Chief of Staff for Operations, United States Army Continental Army Command, Fort Monroe, Virginia; district senior advisor, Sadec Province, Advisory Team Sixty-five, United States Military Assistance Command, Vietnam; and student, United States Army Command and General Staff College, Fort Leavenworth, Kansas.

He also served as intelligence staff officer and later chief, Ground and Special Systems Branch, Doctrine and Systems Division, and later ground surveillance officer, Tactical Surveillance and Reconnaissance Branch, Doctrine and Surveillance Division, Office of the Assistant Chief of Staff for Intelligence, United States Army, Washington, DC; commander, 165th Military Intelligence Battalion, Sixty-sixth Military Intelligence Group, United States Army, Europe; assistant chief of staff, G-2 (Intelligence), Third Armored Division, United States Army, Europe; commander, 501st Military Intelligence Group, United States Army Intelligence and Security Command, Korea; executive to the chief of staff for intelligence, United States Army, Washington, DC; deputy chief of staff for intelligence, United States Army Forces and Command, and deputy chief of staff for intelligence, United States Seventh Army, Europe; deputy director for management and operations, Defense Intelligence Agency, Washington, DC; and commanding general, United States Army Intelligence Center, and commandant, United States Army Intelligence School, Fort Huachuca, Arizona.

General Parker's decorations and awards include the Distinguished Service Medal; the Defense Superior Service Medal; the Legion of Merit; the Bronze Star Medal with "V" device and

Promotion	Date
Second Lieutenant	November 13, 1955
First Lieutenant	May 13, 1959
Captain	May 10, 1961
Major	February 7, 1966
Lieutenant Colonel	January 14, 1970
Colonel	February 1, 1976
Brigadier General	October 1, 1980
Major General	May 1, 1984

one Oak Leaf Cluster; the Purple Heart; the Meritorious Service Medal with three Oak Leaf Clusters; the Air Medal; the Army Commendation Medal with one Oak Leaf Cluster; the Combat Infantryman Badge; and the Parachutist Badge.

MAJOR GENERAL HUGH G. ROBINSON
Retired

General Robinson was born in Washington, DC, and graduated from the United States Military Academy at West Point. He received his master's degree in civil engineering from the Massachusetts Institute of Technology. General Robinson also attended the Armed Forces Staff College and the National War College.

During his career, he has served as Army assistant to the armed forces aid to the president, Office of the President, the White House, Washington, DC; student, Armed Forces Staff College, Norfolk, Virginia; executive officer, Forty-fifth Engineer Group, United States Army, Vietnam; staff officer, Regional Capabilities Branch, War Plans Division, Washington, DC; deputy chief of staff for military operations, Plans Directorate Office, United States Army, Washington, DC; student, the National War College, Fort McNair, Washington, DC; executive officer/operations officer, Third Regiment, United States Corps of Cadets, United States Military Academy, West Point, New York; commander, Third Regiment, United States Corps of Cadets, United States Military Academy, West Point, New York; commander, United States Army Engineer School Brigade, Fort Belvoir, Virginia; district engineer, United States Army Engineering District, Los Angeles, California; deputy director of civil works, Office of the Chief of Engineers, United States Army, Washington, DC; and division engineer, United States Army Southwestern Engineer Division, Dallas, Texas.

General Robinson's decorations and awards include the Distinguished Service Medal; the Legion of Merit with one Oak Leaf Cluster; the Bronze Star Medal with one Oak Leaf Cluster; the Air Medal; the Joint Service Commendation Medal; the Army Commendation Medal with one Oak Leaf Cluster; and the Parachutist Badge.

Promotion	Date
Second Lieutenant	June 4, 1954
First Lieutenant	December 4, 1955
Captain	August 11, 1960
Major	August 5, 1964
Lieutenant Colonel	December 13, 1967
Colonel	June 14, 1973
Brigadier General	July 1, 1978
Major General	February 1, 1981

MAJOR GENERAL CHARLES C. ROGERS

In 1951 Charles Rogers was commissioned a second lieutenant through Army ROTC. He earned his bachelor's degree in mathematics from West Virginia State College and his master's degree in educational guidance from Shippensburg State College. General Rogers also attended the Advanced Artillery and Missile School, the United States Army Command and General Staff College, and the United States Army War College. General Rogers passed away in 1994.

During his military career, Rogers served as executive officer, First Battalion, Twenty-ninth Artillery, Fort Devens, Massachusetts; student, United States Army Command and General Staff College, Fort Leavenworth, Kansas; operations officer, Twenty-fourth Infantry Division Artillery, United States Army, Europe; commanding officer, First Battalion, Second Brigade, United States Army Training Center, Infantry, Fort Lewis, Washington; executive officer, First Infantry Division Artillery, United States Army, Vietnam; commander, First Battalion, Fifth Artillery, First Infantry Division, United States Army, Vietnam; operations chief, J-3 (Operations), United States Military Assistance Command, Vietnam; staff officer, Troop Operations and Readiness Division, Operations, Directorate, Office of the Deputy Chief of Staff for Military Operations, United States Army, Washington, DC; student, United States Army War College, Carlisle Barracks, Pennsylvania; assistant deputy commander, V Corps Artillery, United States Army, Europe; deputy chief of staff for ROTC, United States Army Training and Doctrine Command, Washington, DC; deputy commanding general, V Corps, United States Army, Europe; deputy chief of staff for personnel, United States Seventh Army, Europe; commanding officer, Forty-second Artillery Group, United States Army, Europe; and commanding general, VII Corps Artillery, United States Army, Europe.

This distinguished general was a recipient of the highest award a grateful nation can bestow upon its national heroes: the Congressional Medal of Honor. General Rogers's Congressional Medal of Honor citation reads, in part[1]:

> Lt. Col. Rogers' dauntless courage and heroism inspired the defenders of the fire support base to the heights of valor to defeat a determined and numerically superior enemy force. His relentless spirit of aggressiveness in action are in the highest traditions of the military service and reflects great credit upon himself, his unit, and the US Army.

Promotion	Date
Second Lieutenant	June 15, 1951
First Lieutenant	December 27, 1952
Captain	December 17, 1956
Major	November 9, 1961
Lieutenant Colonel	September 13, 1966
Colonel	March 8, 1972
Brigadier General	July 1, 1973
Major General	September 1, 1975

[1] For the complete citation, see page 219.

General Rogers's other decorations and awards include the Legion of Merit with one Oak Leaf Cluster; the Distinguished Flying Cross; the Bronze Star Medal with "V" device and one Oak Leaf Cluster; Air Medals; the Joint Service Commendation Medal; and the Army Commendation Medal with three Oak Leaf Clusters.

MAJOR GENERAL FRED C. SHEFFEY
Retired

Born in McKeesport, Pennsylvania, Fred Sheffey is a graduate of Wilberforce University, where he earned a bachelor's degree in economics and business, and of Ohio State University, where he earned a master's degree in international affairs. General Sheffey also attended the United States Army Command and General Staff College and the National War College.

General Sheffey's military assignments during his twenty-eight years in the military have included chief, Facilities Branch, Operations Research Management Office, Office of the Deputy Chief of Staff for Logistics, United States Army, Washington, DC; student, the National War College, Washington, DC; logistical plans officer and later head, Logistical Plans Section, J-4 (Logistics), United States Pacific Command, Camp H.M. Smith, Hawaii; commanding officer, Fifty-fourth General Support Group, United States Army, Vietnam; chief, Financial Resources Division, Supply and Materiel Directorate, Office of the Deputy Chief of Staff for Logistics, United States Army, Washington, DC; director of operations and maintenance resources, Office of the Deputy Director Supply and Maintenance, Office of the Deputy Chief of Staff for Logistics, United States Army, Washington, DC; director, Materiel Management, United States Army Materiel Development Readiness Command, Alexandria, Virginia; commanding general, United States Army Quartermaster Center; and commandant, United States Army Quartermaster School, Fort Lee, Virginia.

General Sheffey's decorations and awards include the Distinguished Service Medal; the Legion of Merit with two Oak Leaf Clusters; the Bronze Star; the Meritorious Service Medal; the Army Commendation Medal with one Oak Leaf Cluster; the Purple Heart; the Combat Infantryman Badge; and the General Staff Identification Badge.

Promotion	Date
Second Lieutenant	July 18, 1950
First Lieutenant	April 20, 1951
Captain	July 9, 1954
Major	November 28, 1961
Lieutenant Colonel	January 11, 1966
Colonel	November 20, 1970
Brigadier General	July 1, 1973
Major General	August 1, 1976

MAJOR GENERAL ISAAC D. SMITH
Retired

Born in Wakefield, Louisiana, Isaac Smith received his bachelor's degree in agriculture from Southern University A&M College and his master's degree in public administration from Shippensburg State College.

General Smith's assignments included commander, Headquarters Battery, Sixth Howitzer Battalion, Twenty-Ninth Artillery, Fort Lewis, Washington; commander, Headquarters Detachment, 528th United States Army Artillery Group, United States Army, Europe; operations officer, Fifth Howitzer Battalion, Sixteenth Artillery, Fourth Infantry Division, Fort Lewis, Washington; operations officer, Fifth Battalion, Eighty-third Artillery, Eighth Infantry Division, United States Army, Europe; division inspector general, Eighth Administration Company, Eighth Infantry Division, United States Army, Europe; executive officer, Tenth Battalion, Second Training Brigade, United States Army Training Center (Infantry), Fort Jackson, South Carolina; battalion commander, Tenth Battalion, Second Training Brigade, United States Army Training Center (Infantry), Fort Jackson, South Carolina; and student, United States Army Command and General Staff College, Fort Leavenworth, Kansas.

He has also served as commander, Eighth Battalion, Fourth Artillery, XXIV Corps Artillery, United States Army, Vietnam; operations advisor, Twenty-third Army of the Republic of Vietnam, Infantry Division, United States Military Assistant Command, Vietnam; commander, Second Battalion, Seventy-fifth Field Artillery, Thirty-sixth Field Artillery Group, V Corps Artillery, United States Army, Europe; staff officer, Unit Training and Readiness Division, Office of the Assistant Chief of Staff for Military Operations, United States Army, Washington, DC; deputy director of Army Equal Opportunity Programs, Human Resources Directorate, Office of the Deputy Chief of Staff for Personnel, United States Army, Washington, DC; commander, Division Artillery, First Infantry Division (Mechanized), Fort Riley, Kansas; chief, Doctrine and Systems Integration Division; Requirements Directorate, Office of the Deputy Chief of Staff for Operations and Plans, United States Army, Washington, DC; chief, Reserve Forces Division, Office of the Assistant Secretary of the Army (Manpower and Reserve Affairs), Washington, DC; commanding general, United States Army Second ROTC Region, Fort Knox, Kentucky; assistant division commander, First Armored Division, United States Army, Europe; deputy chief of staff for operations and intelligence, Allied Forces Central Europe; and deputy chief of staff for Personnel, United States Army, Europe and Seventh Army.

General Smith's decorations and awards include the Distinguished Service Medal; the Silver Star; the Defense Distinguished Service Medal; the Legion of Merit with one Oak Leaf Cluster; the Bronze Star Medal; the Meritorious Service Medal with one Oak Leaf Cluster; and the Army Commendation Medal with two Oak Leaf Clusters.

Promotion	Date
Second Lieutenant	May 11, 1954
First Lieutenant	August 13, 1956
Captain	January 13, 1961
Major	October 27, 1965
Lieutenant Colonel	February 17, 1969
Colonel	January 1, 1975
Brigadier General	July 1, 1981
Major General	September 1, 1985

MAJOR GENERAL HARVEY D. WILLIAMS
Retired

With more than thirty years of commissioned service in the United States Army, General Williams had an interesting and varied career. He received his commission through Army ROTC. A native of Whiteville, North Carolina, General Williams is a graduate of West Virginia State College with a bachelor's degree in political science and a master's degree in international relations. He is also a graduate of the Armed Forces Staff College and the United States Naval War College.

General Williams's major duty assignments included assistant G-4 (Logistics) and deputy G-4, I Field Force, United States Army, Vietnam; commander, First Battalion, Ninety-second Artillery, I Field Force, United States Army, Vietnam; chief, Security Division, Office of the Assistant Chief of Staff for Intelligence, United States Army, Washington, DC; military advisor, United States Arms Control and Disarmament Agency, Washington, DC; commander, Seventy-fifth Field Artillery Group, III Corps Artillery, Fort Sill, Oklahoma; member, Special Review Board, Office of the Deputy Chief of Staff for Personnel, United States Army, Washington, DC; commander, United States Army, Washington, DC; commander, United States Army Garrison, Fort Meyer, Virginia; deputy commanding general, United States Army Military District of Washington, Washington, DC; commanding general, United States Army Military District of Washington, Washington, DC; commanding general, VII Corps Artillery, United States Army, Europe; deputy, the Inspector General (Inspections and Compliance), United States Army, Washington, DC; and commanding general, United States Army Readiness and Mobilization Region III; and deputy commanding general, First United States Army, Fort Meade, Maryland.

General Williams's decorations and awards include the Legion of Merit; the Bronze Star Medal with one Oak Leaf Cluster; the Air Medal; and the Army Commendation Medal with three Oak Leaf Clusters.

Promotion	Date
Second Lieutenant	February 17, 1953
First Lieutenant	July 30, 1954
Captain	October 22, 1958
Major	July 30, 1965
Lieutenant Colonel	July 30, 1972
Colonel	April 15, 1976
Brigadier General	June 1, 1979
Major General	March 1, 1981

BRIGADIER GENERAL DALLAS C. BROWN, JR.
Retired

A native of New Orleans, Louisiana, General Brown received his commission as a second lieutenant through Army ROTC. He earned a bachelor's degree in history from West Virginia State College and a master's degree in government from Indiana University. General Brown also attended the United States Army Command and General Staff College and the United States Naval War College.

During his military career, General Brown served as assistant chief of staff for intelligence, United States Army, Europe; commander, 519th Military Intelligence Battalion, 525th Military Intelligence Group, United States Army, Vietnam; intelligence estimator, Soviet/East European Division, Directorate for Estimates, Defense Intelligence Agency, Washington, DC; chief, Ground

Forces/Mutual Balanced Forces Reduction Branch, Soviet/Warsaw Pact Division, Directorate for Intelligence Research, Defense Intelligence Agency, Washington, DC; commander, United States Army Field Station, United States Army Intelligence Command, Berlin, Germany; deputy chief of staff for intelligence, United States Army Forces Command, Fort McPherson, Georgia; assistant vice director for estimates and deputy vice director for foreign intelligence, Defense Intelligence Agency, Washington, DC; and deputy commandant, United States Army War College, Carlisle Barracks, Pennsylvania.

Brown's military decorations and awards include the Defense Superior Service Medal; the Meritorious Service Medal with two Oak Leaf Clusters; the Joint Service Commendation Medal; and the Army Commendation Medal.

Promotion	Date
Second Lieutenant	May 30, 1954
First Lieutenant	January 25, 1956
Captain	September 27, 1960
Major	January 22, 1965
Lieutenant Colonel	July 17, 1968
Colonel	July 1, 1975
Brigadier General	September 1, 1978

BRIGADIER GENERAL CHARLES D. BUSSEY
Retired

General Bussey entered North Carolina Agricultural and Technical State University in 1952 and graduated with a bachelor's degree in English and a commission as a second lieutenant through Army ROTC. He received a master's degree in journalism from Indiana University and a master's degree in communication science from Shippensburg State College. Born in Edgefield, South Carolina, the general also graduated from the United States Army Command and General Staff College and the United States Army War College.

During his military career, Bussey's major duty assignments included commander, Company A, First Battalion, Fifth Cavalry, First Cavalry Division, Korea; professor of military science and senior Army instructor, Indianapolis Public High Schools, Indianapolis, Indiana; manpower analyst, Force Development Division, Office of the Assistant Chief of Staff, Operations, Headquarters, United States Army, Vietnam; executive officer, First Battalion, Fifth Infantry, Twenty-fifth Infantry Division, United States Army, Vietnam; deputy operations officer, Headquarters, Twenty-fifth Infantry Division, United States Army, Vietnam; executive officer, Second Brigade, Eighty-second Airborne Division, Fort Bragg, North Carolina; special assistant to the chief of staff, Eighty-second Airborne Division, Fort Bragg, North Carolina; chief, Personnel Actions, Infantry Branch, United States Army Military Personnel Center, Alexandria, Virginia; and student, United States Army War College, Carlisle Barracks, Pennsylvania.

Bussey also served as commander, Second Battalion, 504th Infantry, Eighty-second Airborne Division, Fort Bragg, North Carolina; chief, Personnel Actions Section, Infantry Branch, Officer Personnel Directorate, United States Army Military Personnel Center, Alexandria, Virginia; chief, Operations Branch, Plans and Operations Divisions, and later executive officer, Office of the Chief, Legislative Liaison, United States Army, Washington, DC.

In October of 1976, General Bussey left the United States for assignment in Korea, where he assumed command of the Second Brigade, Second Infantry Division. He returned to the United States in December 1977, and was assigned as chief, Policy and Plans Division, Office of the Chief of Public Affairs, United States Army, Washington, DC; deputy commander/chief of staff, 172d Infantry Brigade, Fort Richardson, Alaska; deputy chief of public affairs and later chief of public affairs, Office of the Secretary of the Army, Washington, DC; and deputy chief of staff for personnel, United States Army Materiel Command, Washington, DC.

Promotion	Date
Second Lieutenant	June 28, 1955
First Lieutenant	December 28, 1956
Captain	March 14, 1961
Major	July 26, 1965
Lieutenant Colonel	August 6, 1968
Colonel	October 1, 1975
Brigadier General	October 1, 1982

General Bussey's decorations and awards include the Legion of Merit with one Oak Leaf Cluster; the Meritorious Service Medal with two Oak Leaf Clusters; the Air Medal; and the Army Commendation Medal with two Oak Leaf Clusters.

BRIGADIER GENERAL ROSCOE C. CARTWRIGHT

A native of Kansas City, Missouri, General Cartwright received his education at San Francisco State College and the University of Missouri. He joined the armed forces in 1941. After attending Officer Candidate School, he received his commission as a second lieutenant.

His numerous duty assignments included comptroller, United States Army Garrison, Fort Leavenworth, Kansas; management analyst and later chief, Research and Development Division, Office of the Director of Management, Office of the Comptroller of the Army, Washington, DC; student, Industrial College of the Armed Forces, Fort McNair, Washington, DC; commanding officer, 108th Artillery Group, United States Army, Vietnam; deputy commanding officer, United States Army Support Command, Cam Ranh Bay, Vietnam; director of management review and analysis, Office of the Comptroller of the Army, Washington, DC; chief, Budget and Five-Year Defense Program, Coordination Division, Manpower and Forces Directorate, Office of the Assistant Chief of Staff for Force Development, Washington, DC; special assistant, Office of the Assistant Chief of Staff for Force Development, United States Army, Washington, DC; and assistant division commander, United States Military Headquarters, United States Army, Europe; and Seventh Army, Third Infantry Division, United States Army, Europe; and assistant division commander, United States Army Third Infantry Division, Europe.

General Cartwright was killed in an airplane crash in Virginia in 1974. His decorations and awards included the Legion of Merit with one Oak Leaf Cluster; the Bronze Star Medal with two Oak Leaf Clusters; the Meritorious Service Medal; the Air Medal with three Oak Leaf Clusters; and the Army Commendation Medal with two Oak Leaf Clusters.

Promotion	Date
Second Lieutenant	September 25, 1950
First Lieutenant	March 23, 1951
Captain	October 29, 1954
Major	January 26, 1962
Lieutenant Colonel	January 2, 1969
Colonel	March 12, 1970
Brigadier General	August 1, 1973

BRIGADIER GENERAL DONALD J. DELANDRO
Retired

A Native of New Orleans, Louisiana, the general is a graduate of Southern University A&M College, where he earned a bachelor's degree in business administration, and the University of Chicago, where he earned a master's degree in business administration. He also attended the United States Army Command and General Staff College and the United States Army War College.

During his years of military service, General Delandro served as adjutant general, Twenty-third Infantry Division, United States Army, Vietnam; chief, Enlisted Personnel Division, Military Personnel, Directorate, Office of the Adjutant General, Headquarters, United States Army, Vietnam.

The general returned to the United States in May 1972, and was assigned as executive officer, Weapons Systems Analysis Directorate, Office of the Assistant Vice Chief of Staff, United States Army, Washington, DC; administrative executive, Office of the Deputy Chief of Staff for Military Operations, United States Army, Washington, DC; chief, Combat Support Division, and later chief, Enlisted Distribution Division, Enlisted Personnel Management Directorate, United States Army Military Personnel Center, Alexandria, Virginia; chief of staff, United States Army Military Personnel Center, Alexandria, Virginia; chief of staff, United States Army Recruiting Command, Fort Sheridan, Illinois; and deputy, Office of the Adjutant General for Administrative Systems, and executive director, Military Postal Service, the Adjutant General Center, United States Army, Washington, DC; adjutant general, United Sates Army, and commanding general, the Adjutant General Center, and commanding general, United States Army Reserve Components, Personnel and Administration Center; and commanding general, Physical Disability Agency, Washington, DC.

Promotion	Date
Second Lieutenant	August 27, 1956
First Lieutenant	February 27, 1958
Captain	August 31, 1961
Major	May 3, 1966
Lieutenant Colonel	June 26, 1970
Colonel	February 1, 1976
Brigadier General	June 1, 1981

General Delandro has been awarded the Distinguished Service Medal; the Legion of Merit with one Oak Leaf Cluster; the Bronze Star Medal; the Meritorious Service Medal; the Air Medal; the Joint Service Commendation Medal; the Army Commendation Medal with one Oak Leaf Cluster; and the Parachutist Badge.

BRIGADIER GENERAL JOHNIE FORTE, JR.
Retired

Born in New Boston, Texas, General Forte received his bachelor's degree in political science from Prairie View A&M College and his master's degree in public administration from Auburn University. The general is also a graduate of the United States Army Command and General Staff College and the Air Force War College. General Forte began his career as a second lieutenant after being commissioned through Army ROTC in July 1956.

His major duty assignments included commander, Forty-first Civil Affairs Company, Civil Operation and Rural Development Support, United States Military Assistance Command, Vietnam; assistant inspector general, First Field Force, United States Army, Vietnam; personnel management officer, Air Defense Artillery Branch, United States Army, Europe; assistant chief of staff for personnel, Fourth Infantry Division (Mechanized), Fort Carson, Colorado; officer personnel directorate, Office of Personnel Operations, United States Army, Washington, DC; commander, Fourth Battalion, Sixty-first Air Defense Artillery Division (Mechanized), Fort Carson, Colorado; liaison officer to the United States Air Force Europe, United States Army, Europe Liaison Group, Ramstein Air Force Base, Germany; commander, 108th Air Defense Artillery Group, Thirty-second Army Air Defense Command, United States Army, Europe; director of personnel, J-1/Inspector General, United States European Command, Europe; director, Personnel Plans Systems, Office of the Deputy Chief of Staff for Personnel, United States Army, Washington, DC; assistant division commander, Eighth Infantry Division (Mechanized), United States Army, Europe; deputy commanding general, Thirty-second Army Air Defense Command, United States Army, Europe; and deputy director, Civilian Personnel Study, Office of the Deputy Chief of Staff for Personnel, United States Army, Washington, DC.

His decorations and awards include the Defense Superior Service Medal; the Legion of Merit with two Oak Leaf Clusters; the Meritorious Service Medal with one Oak Leaf Cluster; the Army Commendation Medal with two Oak Leaf Clusters; the Air Force Commendation Medal; and the Aircraft Crewman Badge.

Promotion	Date
Second Lieutenant	July 29, 1956
First Lieutenant	January 29, 1958
Captain	August 23, 1961
Major	April 22, 1966
Lieutenant Colonel	September 24, 1969
Colonel	January 1, 1976
Brigadier General	May 1, 1979

BRIGADIER GENERAL GEORGE M. SHUFFER, JR.
Retired

Macon Shuffer enlisted in the Army as a private during World War II. He completed Officer's Candidate School in 1943, and was commissioned a second lieutenant. He served with the Ninety-third Infantry Division in the Pacific theater during the war. While on active duty, General Shuffer earned two degrees: an associate's degree from Monterey Peninsular College and a master's degree from the University of Maryland.

His duty assignments included training advisor, Army Section, United States Military Assistance Advisory Group, China; commanding officer, Second Battalion, Second Infantry, Fort Devens, Massachusetts; assistant for continuity of operations plans, Office of the Assistant Secretary of Defense, Washington, DC; commanding officer, 193d Infantry Brigade, United States Army Forces Southern Command, Fort Kobbe, Canal Zone, Panama; assistance intelligence officer, II Field Force, United States Army, Vietnam; student, United States Army War College, Carlisle Barracks, Pennsylvania; staff officer, Troop Operations Division, Operations Directorate, Office of the Deputy Chief of Staff for Military Operations, United States Army, Washington, DC; assistant director of individual training, Office of the Deputy Chief of Staff for Personnel, United States Army, Washington, DC; and assistant deputy chief of staff for personnel, United States Army, Europe and Seventh Army, Germany.

General Shuffer's decorations and awards include the Silver Star with two Oak Leaf Clusters; the Legion of Merit with two Oak Leaf Clusters; the Air Medal with five Oak Leaf Clusters; the Army Commendation Medal; the Bronze Star Medal with "V" device and two Oak Leaf Clusters; the Vietnamese Cross of Gallantry with Silver Star; the Purple Heart; the Combat Infantryman Badge; and the Parachutist Badge.

Promotion	Date
Second Lieutenant	February 2, 1943
First Lieutenant	October 14, 1944
Captain	June 26, 1951
Major	October 7, 1954
Lieutenant Colonel	September 25, 1963
Colonel	August 28, 1968
Brigadier General	September 1, 1972

BRIGADIER GENERAL GUTHRIE L. TURNER, JR.
Retired

A native of Chicago, Illinois, Guthrie Turner received his commission as a second lieutenant by direct appointment. A graduate of the United States Army Command and General Staff College and the United States Army War College, General Turner also has a bachelor's degree in biology from Shaw University, a medical degree from Howard University, and a master's degree in public health from Harvard University.

Some of his major duty assignments were assistant chief, Department of

Aviation Medicine, United States Army Hospital, Fort Rucker, Alabama; resident, Aerospace Medicine, United States Air Force, Brooks Air Force Base, Texas; commander, Fifteenth Medical Battalion, and surgeon, First Cavalry Division (Airmobile), United States Army Vietnam; commander and surgeon, Beach Army Hospital, and later chief, Medical Activities Division, United States Army Primary Helicopter Center and School, Fort Wolters, Texas; chief medical officer and surgeon, VII Corps, United States Army, Europe; commander, 130th General Hospital, United States Army, Europe; consultant for aviation medicine, Office of the Surgeon General, United States Army, Washington, DC; commander, United States Army Medical Command, Korea; surgeon, United Nations Command/United States Forces, Korea/Eighth United States Army, Korea; and commanding general, Madigan Army Medical Center, Tacoma, Washington.

General Turner has received the Distinguished Service Medal; the Legion of Merit; the Meritorious Service Medal; the Air Medal; the Senior Flight Surgeon Badge; the Master Parachutist Badge; and the Army Commendation Medal.

Promotion	Date
Second Lieutenant	June 23, 1951
First Lieutenant	June 23, 1953
Captain	February 10, 1956
Major	March 20, 1962
Lieutenant Colonel	April 18, 1966
Colonel	September 17, 1969
Brigadier General	May 9, 1980

BLACK UNITED STATES NAVY ADMIRALS

VICE ADMIRAL WALTER J. DAVIS, JR.
Director, Space and Electronic Warfare, Office of the Chief of
Naval Operations, Washington, DC

In June of 1951, Walter Davis was commissioned an ensign in the United States Naval Reserve and reported for active duty in July of that same year. Since being on active duty, the admiral has acquired an extensive education, including a bachelor's degree in electrical engineering from Ohio State University, a bachelor's degree in aeronautical engineering, and a master's degree in aeroelectronics from the Naval Postgraduate School. Admiral Davis is also a graduate of the Naval War College and the Industrial College of Armed Forces.

Born in Winston Salem, North Carolina, the admiral's major duty assignments have included student, Naval Air Base Training Command, Naval Air Station, Pensacola, Florida; student, Naval Auxiliary Air Station, Kingsville, Texas; student, Fighter Squadron 121, Monterey, California; fighter pilot, Fighter Squadron Fifty-three, Brunswick, Maine; fighter pilot, Fighter Squadron 143, Norfolk, Virginia; operations/maintenance officer, Fighter Squadron 143, Norfolk, Virginia; student, Naval Test Pilot School, Naval Air Training Center, Patuxent River, Maryland; project officer, Weapons Systems Test Division, Naval Air Training Center, Patuxent River, Maryland; executive officer and later commanding officer, Fighter Squadron 114, San Diego, California; assistant project manager for F-14's, Naval Air Systems Command Headquarters, Washington, DC; student, Surface Warfare Officers' School Command, Newport, Rhode Island; executive officer, USS *Kitty Hawk*, Aircraft Carrier Sixty-three, Pacific Fleet; student, Office of the Chief of Naval Personnel, Washington, DC; student and Staff Officer, Commander Naval Surface Forces, Pacific Fleet; commanding officer, USS *Sacramento*, auxiliary oiler/explosives, San Diego, California; executive assistant to the deputy chief of naval operations for air warfare, Office of the Chief of Naval Operations (Operations and Administration), Washington, DC; commanding officer, USS *Ranger*, Carrier Sixty-one, San Diego, California; assistant to the chief of naval operations, Office of the Chief of Naval Operations (Operation DOE), Washington, DC; commandant, Naval District, Washington, DC; commander, Carrier Group Six, Pacific Fleet; director, Warfare System, Architecture and Engineering, Space Warfare Systems Command, Washington, DC; and director, Space and Electronic Warfare, Office of the Chief of Naval Operations, Washington, DC.

During his outstanding career, Admiral Davis has been awarded numerous de-

Promotion	Date
Ensign	July 3, 1959
Lieutenant Junior Grade	December 3, 1960
Lieutenant	June 1, 1963
Augmented in the U.S. Navy	October 15, 1963
Lieutenant Commander	May 1, 1968
Commander	July 1, 1973
Captain	July 1, 1980
Rear Admiral Lower Half	December 1, 1988
Rear Admiral Upper Half	November 1, 1992
Vice Admiral	November 1, 1994

Vice Adm. Walter J. Davis, Jr.

corations and awards, including the Legion of Merit with two Gold Stars; the Meritorious Service Medal; the Air Medal with numeral "10"; the Navy Commendation Medal with "V" device; the Joint Meritorious Unit Award; the Meritorious Unit Commendation with one Bronze Star; the Navy "E" Ribbon; the Navy Expeditionary Medal; the National Defense Service Medal with one Bronze Star; the Armed Forces Expeditionary Medal (Korea); the Vietnam Service Medal with one Silver Star and one Bronze Star; the Republic of Vietnam Gallantry Cross Unit Citation with one Silver Star; and the Republic of Vietnam Campaign Medal.

VICE ADMIRAL J. PAUL REASON
Deputy Chief of Naval Operations, Office of the Chief of Naval
Operations, Plans, Policy and Operations

Admiral Reason is a native of Washington, DC, and a graduate of the United
States Naval Academy, class of 1965. He has a bachelor's degree in naval sci-
ence and a master's degree in computer systems management from the Na-
val Postgraduate School. His extensive military education includes the Joint
Warfighting Course, the Defense Policy Seminars at Harvard University,
CAPSTONE, and the National Defense University.

The admiral's major duty assignments have included operations officer, USS
J. Douglass Blackwood, Destroyer Escort 219, Atlantic Fleet; student, Naval
Nuclear Power School, Naval Training Center, Bainbridge, Maine; student, Na-
val Nuclear Power Training Unit, Schenectady, New York; combat systems of-
ficer, USS *Truxton*, Guided Missile Frigate Thirty-five (Nuclear Propulsion), Pa-
cific Fleet; combat systems officer, USS *Enterprise*, Attack Aircraft Carrier
Sixty-five, Pacific Fleet; student, Naval Destroyer School, Newport, Rhode Is-
land; student, Combat Systems Technical Schools Command, Mare Island,
Vallejo, California; combat systems officer, USS *Truxton*, Guided Missile Cruiser
Thirty-five (Nuclear Propulsion), Pacific Fleet; project officer, Bureau of Naval
Personnel, Surface Nuclear Junior Officer Assignment and Placement Branch,
Washington, DC; executive officer, USS *Mississippi*, Guided Missile Cruiser Forty
(Nuclear), Norfolk, Virginia; student, Surface Warfare Officers School Command,
Newport, Rhode Island; commanding officer, USS *Coontz*, Guided Missile De-
stroyer Forty, Pacific Fleet; student, Naval Reactors, Department of Energy,
Washington, DC; commanding officer, USS *Bainbridge*, Guided Missile Cruiser
Twenty-five (Nuclear), Atlantic Fleet; commander Naval Base, Seattle, Wash-
ington; commander, Cruiser-Destroyer Group One; commander, Naval Surface
Force, U.S. Atlantic Fleet; and deputy chief of naval operations, Office of the
Chief of Naval Operations, Plans, Policy, and Operations.

Admiral Reason also served as naval aide to the president of the United
States from December 1976 to June 1979.

During his illustrious naval career, Admiral Reason has been awarded nu-
merous deco-
rations and
medals, in-
cluding the
Distinguished
Service Medal;
the Legion of
Merit with two
Gold Stars; the
Navy Com-
mendation
Medal with two
Gold Stars; the

Promotion	Date
Ensign	June 9, 1965
Lieutenant Junior Grade	December 9, 1966
Lieutenant	July 1, 1968
Lieutenant Commander	July 1, 1973
Commander	September 1, 1978
Captain	October 1, 1983
Designated Rear Admiral Lower Half	June 26, 1986
Rear Admiral Lower Half	October 1, 1987
Designated Rear Admiral Upper Half	April 21, 1989
Rear Admiral Upper Half	February 1, 1991
Vice Admiral	February 1, 1991

Vice Adm. J. Paul Reason

Navy Unit Commendation; the Meritorious Unit Commendation; the National Defense Service Medal with one Bronze Star; the Armed Forces Expeditionary Medal with one Bronze Star; the Vietnam Service Medal with two Bronze Stars and one Silver Star; the Sea Service Deployment Ribbon with one Bronze Star; the Republic of Vietnam Armed Forces Honor Medal, First Class; the Republic of Vietnam Gallantry Cross Unit Citation; the Republic of Vietnam Campaign Medal; the Navy "E" Ribbon (four awards); and the El Commandante General de la Armada.

REAR ADMIRAL LOWER HALF (SELECTEE)
OSIE "V" COMBS, JR.
Program Director, Space and Naval Warfare Systems Command,
Carrier Systems Directorate, Washington, DC

Osie Combs was appointed as a lieutenant junior grade in the United States Navy in 1972 after serving a short term as an ensign in the U.S. Naval Reserve. He is a graduate of the Prairie View Agricultural and Mechanical College in Texas, where he earned a bachelor's degree in electrical engineering. He also earned a master's degree in mechanical engineering and ocean engineering from the Massachusetts Institute of Technology.

Admiral Combs's duty assignments have included assistant project manager for F-14s, Weapons Systems Test Division, Naval Air Training Command, Headquarters, Naval Air Systems Command, Patuxent River, Maryland; student, Naval Development Training Center, San Diego, California; assistant boiler officer, USS *Coral Sea*, Attack Aircraft Carrier Forty-three, Norfolk, Virginia; student, Engineering Duty Officers School, Portsmouth, Virginia; ship superintendent, Naval Shipyard, Norfolk, Virginia; assistant project officer for submarine construction, Office of the Supervisor of Shipbuilding, Newport News, Virginia; repair officer, USS *Proteus*, Submarine Tender Nineteen, Newport News, Virginia; project manager, Nuclear Submarine Twenty-one, Office of the Commander, Naval Sea Systems Command, Groton, Connecticut; program manager and representative, Office of the Supervisor of Shipbuilding, *Seawolf*, Nuclear Submarine Twenty-one, Groton, Connecticut; program manager, *Seawolf* Program, Naval Sea Systems Command, Washington, DC; and program director, Space and Naval Warfare Systems Command, Command, Control, Communications, Computers, and Information Systems Directorate, Program Directive Seventy, Washington, DC.

His military decorations and awards include the Legion of Merit; the Meritorious Service Medal with one Gold Star; the Navy Unit Commendation; the Navy Commendation Medal; the National Defense Medal with two Bronze Stars; and the Vietnam Service Medal.

Promotion	Date
Midshipman (Naval ROTC)	September 25, 1969
Ensign (U.S. Naval Reserve)	June 9, 1971
Ensign	July 3, 1971
Lieutenant Junior Grade	December 9, 1972
Augmented in the U.S. Navy	January 11, 1974
Lieutenant	July 1, 1975
Lieutenant Commander	March 1, 1980
Commander	May 1, 1986
Captain	March 1, 1992
Rear Admiral Lower Half (Frocked)	November 1, 1995

Rear Adm. Lower Half (Selectee) Osie "V" Combs, Jr.

REAR ADMIRAL LOWER HALF (SELECTEE)
MACEA E. FUSSELL
Commander, Naval Reserve Construction Forces, Gulfport, Mississippi

Admiral Fussell is a member of the Medical Corps of the United States Naval Reserve. Before assuming his current assignment, the admiral—a native of Blackshear, Georgia—served seven years of active duty. Admiral Fussell earned his bachelor's degree in chemistry from Morehouse College and his medical degree from Meharry Medical College. He served his general surgery internship at the Naval Hospital in St. Alban's, New York, and served as an orthopedic surgeon at the Naval Hospital in San Diego, California.

His major duty assignments have included general medical officer, Naval Hospital, Great Lakes, Illinois; chief of orthopedic surgery, Naval Hospital Port Hueneme, Port Hueneme, California; commanding officer, Naval Reserve, Naval Medical Clinic, Port Hueneme, California; commanding officer, Naval Reserve Naval Hospital, Camp Pendleton, California; director of health services, Naval Reserve Readiness Command Region Nineteen, San Diego, California; force medical officer and commander, Naval Reserve Construction Forces, Gulfport Mississippi; chief of orthopedic surgery, Naval Medical Clinic, Port Hueneme, California; orthopedic surgeon, Naval Hospital Bremerton, Bremerton, Washington; instructor, Naval School of Health Sciences, Executive Medicine Course, Bethesda, Maryland; assistant director, Chief of Naval Personnel, Washington, DC; Fifth and Sixth Medical Corps Reserve Selection Boards, Washington, DC; special assistant, Chief of Naval Operations, Special Projects for Operations Ninety-three (Reserves), Washington, DC; senior medical officer, Project Alpine Warrior '89 and Project Cold Winter '89, Brigade Service Support Group Four, Bethesda, Maryland; instructor, Strategic Medical Readiness Course, Naval School of Health Sciences, Bethesda, Maryland; captain and commander, Medical Corps Selection Boards, Bureau of Naval Personnel, Washington, DC; and senior medical officer, Bureau of Medicine and Surgery, Special Projects for the Bureau of Medicine Seven, Washington, DC.

His military awards and decorations include the Meritorious Service Medal; National Defense Medal with Star; and the Naval Reserve Medal with Hourglass.

Promotion	Date
Ensign	January 24, 1961
Lieutenant Junior Grade	December 15, 1961
Lieutenant	June 1, 1964
Lieutenant Commander	September 1, 1968
Commander	September 1, 1977
Captain	July 1, 1984
Rear Admiral Lower Half	September 1, 1994

Rear Adm. Lower Half (Selectee) Macea E. Fussell

REAR ADMIRAL LOWER HALF (SELECTEE)
EVERETT L. GREENE
Commander, Boat Squadron One, Special Warfare Unit, Pacific Fleet

Admiral Greene of Cincinnati, Ohio, is a graduate of the United States Naval Academy, class of 1970. The admiral earned a bachelor's degree in naval science from the academy, and a master's degree in systems technology from the Naval Postgraduate School. Rear Admiral Green is also a graduate of the prestigious United States Naval War College.

The admiral's major duty assignments have included training officer, Naval Amphibious Base, Coronado, San Diego, California; assistant platoon commander and training officer, Seal Team One, Naval Amphibious Base, Coronado, San Diego, California; plans officer, Amphibious Group One, Subic Bay, Philippines; operations officer, Underwater Demolition Team Twelve, Naval Postgraduate School, Monterey, California; special assistant to the supervisor of advising for special warfare matters, Naval Sea Systems Command, Washington, DC; executive officer, Naval Special Warfare Unit One, MacDill Air Force Base, Florida; plans officer, Joint Special Operations Support Element, MacDill Air Force Base, Florida; Navy operations officer, Joint Special Operations Command, Fort Bragg, North Carolina; commanding officer, Special Boat Unit Twelve, Fort Bragg, North Carolina; head, Sea Mobility Branch, Office of the Chief of Naval Operations, Washington, DC; director, Equal Opportunity Division, Bureau of Naval Personnel, Washington, DC; student, Ship Material Readiness Group, Newport, Rhode Island; commander, Naval Special Warfare Command, Combatant Craft United States, Coronado, California; and commander, Special Boat, First Squadron, Pacific Fleet.

Admiral Greene is a highly decorated officer. His awards and decorations include the Legion of Merit; the Defense Meritorious Service Medal; the Meritorious Service Medal with one Gold Star; the Joint Service Commendation Medal; the Navy Commendation Medal with two Gold Stars; the Navy Achievement Medal; the Combat Action Ribbon; the Presidential Unit Citation; the Joint Meritorious Unit Award; the National Defense Service Medal with one Bronze Star; the Armed Forces Expeditionary Medal; the Humanitarian Service Medal; the Sea Service Deployment Ribbon with one Bronze Star; the Navy and Marine Corps Overseas Service Ribbon with two Bronze Stars; the Republic of Vietnam Gallantry Cross Unit Citation; the Expert Rifleman Medal; and the Expert Pistol Shot Medal.

Promotion	Date
Midshipman (U.S. Naval Academy)	June 29, 1966
Ensign	June 3, 1970
Lieutenant Junior Grade	September 3, 1971
Lieutenant	July 1, 1974
Lieutenant Commander	August 1, 1979
Commander	July 1, 1985
Captain	February 1, 1992
Rear Admiral Lower Half	July 1, 1994

Rear Adm. Lower Half (Selectee) Everett L. Greene

REAR ADMIRAL LOWER HALF EDWARD MOORE, JR.
Commander, Cruiser Destroyer Group Three, San Diego, California

A native of New York City, Admiral Moore graduated from Southern Illinois University with a bachelor's degree in psychology, and from the Naval Postgraduate School with a master's degree in business administration. He has also earned the title of designated Joint Specialty Officer: Administrations.

Commissioned an ensign in the United States Naval Reserve in 1968, Moore reported for active duty that same year and was promoted to lieutenant junior grade a year later. Admiral Moore's major duty assignments have included navigator, USS *Severn,* Guns, Communications, Auxiliary Oiler Sixty-one, Pacific Fleet; student, Fleet Training Center, San Diego, California; communications and operations officer, USS *Lang,* Destroyer Escort 1060, Pacific Fleet; junior officer assignment officer, Bureau of Naval Personnel, Washington, DC; student, Surface Warfare Officers School Command, Newport, Rhode Island; student, Fleet Combat Training Center, Atlantic, Dam Neck, Virginia; student, Naval Guided Missile School, Dam Neck, Virginia; weapons/safety officer, USS *Sterett,* Guided Missile Cruiser Thirty-one, Pacific Fleet; student, Surface Warfare Officers School Command, Newport, Rhode Island; executive officer, USS *Buchanan,* Guided Missile Destroyer Fourteen, Pacific Fleet; operations officer, Office of the United States Commander-in-Chief, Pacific Fleet; student, Surface Warfare Officers School Command, Newport, Rhode Island; student, Senior Officer's Ship Material Readiness Course, Newport, Rhode Island; and commanding officer, USS *Lewis B. Puller,* Guided Missile Frigate Twenty-three, Office of the United States Commander in Chief, Pacific Fleet.

Admiral Moore is a highly decorated officer. His awards and decorations include the Legion of Merit with two Gold Stars; the Defense Meritorious Service Medal; the Meritorious Service Medal; the Navy Achievement Medal; the Meritorious Unit Commendation; the Navy "E" Ribbon; the National Defense Service Medal with one Bronze Star; the Armed Forces Expeditionary Medal; the Vietnam Service Medal with three Bronze Stars; the Southwest Asia Service Medal; the Coast Guard Special Operations Service Medal; the Sea Service Deployment Ribbon with two Bronze Stars; and the Republic of Vietnam Campaign Medal.

Promotion	Date
Ensign (U.S. Naval Reserve)	June 5, 1968
Ensign	July 7, 1968
Lieutenant Junior Grade	June 5, 1969
Lieutenant	July 1, 1971
Augmented in the U.S. Navy	February 1, 1973
Lieutenant Commander	July 1, 1974
Commander	July 1, 1980
Captain	April 1, 1987
Designated Rear Admiral Lower Half	July 7, 1993
Rear Admiral Lower Half	April 1, 1994

Rear Adm. Lower Half Edward Moore, Jr.

REAR ADMIRAL LOWER HALF (SELECTEE) LARRY L. POE
Commander, Reserve Intelligence Area Nineteen,
Washington, DC

Commissioned an ensign in August 1967, Larry Poe graduated from the University of North Carolina at Chapel Hill with a bachelor's degree in zoology. He earned a master's degree in public administration and a master's degree in national security studies at the College of Naval Warfare, the Naval War College.

Admiral Poe served on active duty February 1967 to June 1972. Prior to his current duties and assignment in the United States Naval Reserve, he served as aviation officer candidate, Aviation Officer Candidate School, Pensacola, Florida; student, Armed Forces Air Intelligence Training Center, Lowry Air Force Base, Colorado; air intelligence officer, Heavy Photographic Squadron Sixty-one, Naval Air Station, Agana, Guam; photo interpretation officer, Defense Intelligence Agency, Washington, DC; analyst, Naval Reserve, Office of the Secretary of Defense, Technology Transfer, Naval Air Facility, Washington, DC; and deputy reserve intelligence area commander, Naval Reserve Volunteer Training (Intelligence), Unit 0106, Washington, DC.

Admiral Poe's decorations and awards include the Meritorious Service Medal; the Joint Service Commendation Medal; the Navy Commendation Medal; the Armed Forces Expeditionary Medal; and the Armed Forces Reserve Medal.

Promotion	Date
Ensign	February 24, 1967
Lieutenant Junior Grade	July 1, 1968
Lieutenant	March 1, 1970
Lieutenant Commander	May 1, 1976
Commander	October 1, 1981
Captain	September 1, 1988
Rear Admiral Lower Half	March 1, 1996

Rear Adm. Lower Half (Selectee) Larry L. Poe

REAR ADMIRAL LOWER HALF ANTHONY J. WATSON
Commander, Naval Recruiting Command, Arlington, Virginia

Born in Chicago, Illinois, Admiral Watson is a graduate of the United States Naval Academy. He earned a bachelor's degree in naval science in 1970 and entered active duty as an ensign that same year. He is also a graduate of the Naval Nuclear Power School.

Admiral Watson's major duty assignments have included recruit, Naval Recruiting Training Command, Chicago, Illinois; student, Atomic Energy Commission, Schenectady, New York; naval reactors officer, Nuclear Power Training Unit, Windsor, Connecticut; damage control assistant, USS *Snook*, Nuclear Submarine 592, Pacific Fleet; electrical division officer, USS *Robert E. Lee*, Fleet Ballistic Missile Submarine (Nuclear), Atlantic Fleet; material officer, Staff of Commander, Submarine Squadron One, Atlantic Fleet; student, Naval Submarine School, Groton, Connecticut; executive officer, USS *Hammerhead*, Nuclear Submarine 663, Pacific Fleet; student, U.S. Naval Reactors, Department of Energy, Washington, DC; student, Office of the Commander of Submarine Forces, U.S. Atlantic Fleet, Atlantic Fleet; deputy commander for training, Staff of Commander, Submarine Squadron Eight, Windsor, Connecticut; commanding officer, USS *Jacksonville*, Nuclear Submarine 699, Atlantic Fleet; deputy commandant, U.S. Naval Academy, Annapolis, Maryland; commander, Submarine Squadron Seven, Pearl Harbor, Hawaii; deputy director for operations, National Military Command Center, the Joint Chiefs of Staff, Washington, DC; and commander, Navy Recruiting Command, Arlington, Virginia.

Admiral Watson's numerous military decorations and awards include the Legion of Merit; the Meritorious Service Medal with three Gold Stars; the Navy Commendation Medal with two Gold Stars; the Navy Achievement Medal; the Navy Unit Commendation with one Bronze Star; the Meritorious Unit Commendation; the Navy "E" Ribbon; the Navy Expeditionary Medal; the National Defense Medal with one Bronze Star; the Vietnam Service Medal with two Bronze Stars; the Sea Service Deployment Ribbon; the Navy Arctic Service Ribbon; the Expert Rifleman Medal; and the Expert Pistol Shot Medal.

Promotion	Date
Midshipman (U.S. Naval Academy)	June 29, 1966
Ensign	June 3, 1970
Lieutenant Junior Grade	September 3, 1971
Lieutenant	July 1, 1974
Lieutenant Commander	September 1, 1978
Released from active duty	March 22, 1982
Reported for active duty in the U.S. Naval Reserve	May 1, 1984
Augmented in the U.S. Navy	May 10, 1985
Captain	September 1, 1990
Designated Rear Admiral Lower Half	August 12, 1993
Rear Admiral Lower Half	October 1, 1994

Rear Adm. Lower Half Anthony J. Watson

REAR ADMIRAL LOWER HALF DAVID L. BREWER, III

Commander, Naval Forces, United States Commander-in-Chief, Pacific, Republic of Guam, Commonwealth of the Northern Marianas Island, Federated States of Micronesia, Republic of Palau

Born in Farmville, Virginia, Admiral Brewer is a graduate of Prairie View Agricultural and Mechanical College, with a bachelor's degree in pre-medicine. He also attended Naval Schools Command and the United States Naval War College.

Admiral Brewer's major duty assignments have included student, Naval Schools Command, Norfolk, Virginia; student, Fleet Anti-Air Warfare Training Center, Dam Neck, Virginia; electronics warfare officer, USS *Little Rock*, Guided Missile Light Cruiser, Norfolk, Virginia; student, Recruiting Officer Management Orientation, Norfolk, Virginia; minority affairs officer, Naval Recruiting District, Nashville, Tennessee; student, Fleet Combat Training Center Atlantic, Dam Neck, Virginia; combat information center officer, USS *California*, Guided Missile Cruiser Thirty-six (Nuclear), Norfolk, Virginia; student, Surface Warfare Officers School Command, Newport, Rhode Island; student, Naval Guided Missiles School, Dam Neck, Virginia; weapons nuclear safety officer, USS *William H. Standley*, Guided Missile Cruiser Thirty-two, Atlantic Fleet; student, Naval Amphibious School, Little Creek, Virginia; executive officer, USS *Fresno*, Landing Ship Transport 1182, Norfolk, Virginia; manager, Enlisted Community Surface Combat Systems Ratings, Operations, Office of the Chief of Naval Operations, Washington, DC; student, Senior Officer Ship Material Readiness Course, Norfolk, Virginia; student, Surface Warfare Officers School Command, Newport, Rhode Island; commanding officer, USS *Bristol County*, Landing Ship Transport 1198, Norfolk, Virginia; special assistant, Office of the Chief of Naval Operations, Washington, DC; commanding officer, USS *Mount Whitney*, Amphibious Command Ship Twenty, Atlantic Fleet; and special assistant, Bureau of Naval Personnel, Washington, DC.

The admiral left the United States for his current Far East assignment as commander, Naval Forces, United States Commander-in-Chief, Pacific, Republic of Guam, Commonwealth of the Northern Marianas Island, Federated States of Micronesia, Republic of Palau in August 1994.

His military decorations and awards include the Legion of Merit; the Meritorious Service Medal with one Gold Star; the Navy Achievement Medal; the Navy "E" Ribbon; the Navy Expeditionary Medal; the National Defense Medal with one Bronze Star; and the Sea Service Deployment Ribbon with one Gold Star.

Promotion	Date
Ensign (U.S. Naval Reserve)	September 18, 1968
Ensign (U.S. Naval Reserve)	June 3, 1970
Lieutenant Junior Grade	September 3, 1971
Lieutenant	July 1, 1974
Augmented in the U.S. Navy	August 16, 1974
Lieutenant Commander	August 1, 1979
Commander	July 1, 1985
Captain	September 1, 1990
Designated Rear Admiral Lower Half	June 1, 1994

REAR ADMIRAL LAWRENCE C. CHAMBERS
Retired

Born in Bedford, Virginia, Admiral Chambers is a graduate of the United States Naval Academy, class of 1952. He is also a graduate of the Naval Air Base Training Command and Stanford University's Naval ROTC Unit.

Admiral Chambers's major duty assignments have included pilot, Attack Squadron 125, Norfolk, Virginia; officer in charge, Attack Squadron Twenty-two, Detachment Romeo, San Diego, California; assistant curriculas officer, Aeronautical Engineering Program, Naval Postgraduate School, Monterey, California; combat information officer, USS *Ranger*, Attack Aircraft Carrier Sixty-one, San Diego, California; prospective commanding officer, Attack Squadron Sixty-seven, Everett, Washington; commander, Attack Squadron Sixty-seven, Everett, Washington, commander, Attack Squadron Fifteen, Alameda, California; assistant air officer and later air officer, USS *Oriskany*, Attack Aircraft Carrier Thirty-four, San Diego, California; deputy project manager, Attack Aircraft Seven E, Project Office, Naval Air Systems Command, Washington, DC; commander, USS *White Plains*, Sarebo, Japan; commander, USS *Midway*, Aircraft Carrier Forty-one, Sarebo, Japan; assistant chief, Naval Personnel for Enlisted Personnel Development and Distribution, Bureau of Naval Personnel, Washington, DC; assistant commander, Chief of Naval Personnel, Personnel Distribution, Washington, DC; student, Naval Nuclear Power Training Unit, Instruction in Senior Officers Ship Material Readiness Course, Idaho Falls, Idaho; commander, Carrier Group Three, Alameda, California; and vice commander, Naval Air Systems Command Headquarters, with additional duty as deputy commander, Antisubmarine Warfare, Washington, DC.

Chambers's military decorations and awards include the Bronze Star Medal; the Meritorious Service Medal; the Navy Unit Commendation; the China Service Medal; the National Defense Service Medal with one Bronze Star; the Armed Forces Expeditionary Medal; the Vietnam Service Medal with three Bronze Stars; and the Republic of Vietnam Campaign Medal with "V" device.

Promotion	Date
Midshipman	June 30, 1948
Ensign	June 6, 1952
Lieutenant Junior Grade	December 6, 1953
Lieutenant	July 1, 1956
Lieutenant Commander	September 1, 1961
Commander	July 1, 1966
Captain	July 1, 1972
Rear Admiral	August 1, 1977

REAR ADMIRAL BENJAMIN T. HACKER
Retired

Admiral Hacker, who was born in Washington, DC, was appointed as a lieutenant junior grade in the United States Navy in 1962, after serving a short term as an ensign in the U.S. Naval Reserve. He is a graduate of the Naval Postgraduate School and has earned a master's degree in business administration from George Washington University.

Admiral Hacker's major duty assignments have included pilot, Patrol Squadron Ten, Corpus Christi, Texas; pilot, Patrol Squadron Twenty-one, Brunswick, Maine; operations officer, United States Naval Facility, Argentina, Newfoundland; executive officer, United States Naval Facility, Barbados, West Indies; student, Fleet Airborne Electronics Training Unit, Pacific Fleet; administration officer/patrol plane tactical coordinator, Patrol Squadron Forty-seven, Moffett Field, California; commanding officer, Naval ROTC Unit, and professor of naval science, Florida A & M University, Tallahassee, Florida; flight instructor, Patrol Squadron Thirty, Moffett Field, California; executive officer, Patrol Squadron Twenty-four, and patrol plane tactical coordinator/mission commander, Jacksonville, Florida; director, Equal Opportunity Division, and special assistant to the chief of naval personnel, Bureau of Naval Personnel, Washington, DC; student, National Defense University, Fort McNair, Washington, DC; commanding officer, Naval Air Station, Brunswick, Maine; commander, Military Enlistment Processing Command, Fort Sheridan, Illinois; commander, Fleet Air Mediterranean; and commander, Maritime Surveillance and Reconnaissance Force, United States, Sixth Fleet, Naples, Italy.

Admiral Hacker was designated rear admiral in September of 1980. His decorations and awards include the Defense Superior Service Medal; the Legion of Merit with one Gold Star; the Meritorious Service Medal; the Navy Unit Commendation; the National Defense Service Medal; and the Armed Forces Expeditionary Medal.

Promotion	Date
Ensign	September 19, 1958
Lieutenant Junior Grade	March 19, 1960
Lieutenant	October 1, 1962
Lieutenant Commander	September 1, 1967
Commander	November 1, 1971
Captain	September 1, 1977
Rear Admiral	September 1, 1980

REAR ADMIRAL WENDELL N. JOHNSON
Retired

Born in Boston, Massachusetts, Wendell Johnson graduated from the New England College of Pharmacy, Northeastern University, and American University, where he earned a master's degree in international communications. Commissioned an ensign in May of 1957, Johnson's major duty assignments have included officer, USS *Lookout*, Radar Picket Ship Two, San Diego, California; gunnery officer, Fire Control, USS *Coral Sea*, Aircraft Carrier Forty-three, Norfolk, Virginia; weapons officer, USS *Ingraham*, Destroyer 938, Everett, Washington; commanding officer, USS *Dahlgren*, Guided Missile Destroyer Forty-three, Everett, Washington; commanding officer, USS *Jason*, Auxiliary Repair Ship Eight, San Diego, California; commander, Destroyer Thirty-five, Pacific Fleet; officer in charge, United States Navy Branch Oceanographic Office, Boston, Massachusetts; special projects officer, Recruiting Division, Bureau of Naval Personnel, Washington, DC; plans officer, Military Assistance Office, Military Assistance Command, Vietnam; head, Surface Officer Retention Group, and special assistant to the chief of naval personnel, Bureau of Naval Personnel, Washington, DC; assistant branch head, Europe and NATO Plans and Policy Branch, Office of the Chief of Naval Operations, Washington, DC; and director, Undersea and Strategic Warfare and Nuclear Energy Development Division, Office of the Chief of Naval Operations, Washington, DC.

Admiral Johnson is also a graduate of the United States Postgraduate School Engineering Curriculum and the Armed Forces Staff College. He also attended the National War College, where he was cited for outstanding scholarship by the college commandant and the chief of naval operations.

Admiral Johnson's military decorations and awards include the Legion of Merit; the Meritorious Service Medal with one Gold Star; the Navy Commendation Medal with one Gold Star; the Navy Achievement Medal; the Navy Combat Action Ribbon; the Republic of Vietnam Honor Medal First Class; and the Order of Sikatuna, Philippine Government.

Promotion	Date
Ensign	May 2, 1957
Lieutenant Junior Grade	November 3, 1958
Lieutenant	May 1, 1961
Lieutenant Commander	October 25, 1962
Commander	February 1, 1972
Captain	September 1, 1977
Rear Admiral Lower Half	June 1, 1983

REAR ADMIRAL GERALD E. THOMAS
Retired

Gerald Thomas was born in Natick, Massachusetts. In June of 1951, he was commissioned an ensign in the United States Navy. He graduated from the Naval War College in 1966 and, that same year, he was awarded his master's degree in international affairs by George Washington University.

The admiral's major duty assignments prior to his retirement included executive officer, USS *Lowe*, Destroyer Escort Radar 325, Pacific Fleet; commanding officer, USS *Impervious*, Mine Sweeper, Open Ocean, Pacific Fleet; assistant head, College Training Programs Section, Officer Programs Branch, Bureau of Naval Personnel, Washington, DC; commanding officer, USS

Bausell, Destroyer 845, Pacific Fleet; professor of naval science, executive officer, and later commanding officer, Naval ROTC Unit, Prairie View A & M College, Prairie View, Texas; commander, Destroyer Squadron Nine, Long Beach, California; commander, Cruiser Destroyer Group Five, San Diego, California; and assistant commander, Office of the Assistant Secretary of Defense, International Security Affairs, Washington, DC.

Aside from being a brilliant naval officer, Admiral Thomas is also an intellectual who speaks Russian fluently, is well-versed in German, and holds a doctorate in diplomatic history from Yale University.

Admiral Thomas has been awarded the Meritorious Service Medal; the Navy Commendation Medal with "V" device; the Navy Occupation Service Medal with Europe Clasp; the National Defense Service Medal with one Bronze Star; the Vietnam Service Medal with two Bronze Stars; and the Republic of Vietnam Campaign Medal with "V" device.

Promotion	Date
Midshipman (U.S. Naval Academy)	September 17, 1947
Ensign	June 1, 1951
Lieutenant Junior Grade	January 1, 1953
Lieutenant	November 1, 1955
Lieutenant Commander	November 1, 1960
Commander	September 1, 1965
Captain	July 1, 1971
Rear Admiral	June 1, 1975

REAR ADMIRAL LOUIS A. WILLIAMS
Retired

Louis Williams, who holds a bachelor's degree in business administration and attended the Naval Postgraduate School, enlisted in the United States Naval Reserve in 1949. After several tours of duty and honorable discharges, he was appointed an ensign in the United States Naval Reserve in March of 1954 and was augmented into the United States Navy in December 1957.

A native of Ypsilanti, Michigan, Admiral Williams's varied duty assignments have included fighter pilot, Air Antisubmarine Squadron Forty-nine, Naval Auxiliary Air Station, Saufley Field, Pensacola, Florida; fighter pilot, Naval Air Training Center, Glynco, Georgia; assistant combat information center officer, USS *Hancock*, Attack Air Craft Carrier Nineteen, Alameda, California; aviation maintenance officer, Air Antisubmarine Squadron Twenty-three, San Diego, California; operations officer, Carrier Airborne Early Warning Squadron 114, Pacific Fleet; executive officer, Carrier Airborne Early Warning Squadron 114, Pacific Fleet; commanding officer, Carrier Early Warning Squadron 110, Pacific Fleet; commanding officer, Naval Air Station, Agana, Guam; deputy director, Aviation Programs Division, Office of the Chief of Naval Operations,

Washington, DC; commander, Training Command, Atlantic, Norfolk, Virginia; commander, Antisubmarine Warfare Wing, United States Pacific Fleet, San Diego, California; and deputy commander in chief, Iberian Atlantic Area, Norfolk, Virginia.

Admiral Williams was designated rear admiral in August 1978.

His military decorations and awards include the Air Medal with Numeral 2; the Joint Service Commendation Medal; the Navy Commendation Medal with one Gold Star; the Navy Unit Commendation; the National Defense Service Medal with one Bronze Star; the Armed Forces Expeditionary Medal; the Vietnam Service Medal with three Bronze Stars; the Republic of Vietnam Meritorious Unit Citation Gallantry Cross Color; and the Republic of Vietnam Campaign Medal with "V" device.

Promotion	Date
Ensign	March 1, 1954
Lieutenant Junior Grade	September 1, 1955
Lieutenant	February 1, 1958
Lieutenant Commander	August 1, 1963
Commander	February 1, 1968
Captain	July 1, 1973
Rear Admiral	August 1, 1978

BLACK UNITED STATES
AIR FORCE GENERAL OFFICERS

LIEUTENANT GENERAL ALBERT J. EDMONDS
Director, Defense Information Systems Agency, and Manager,
National Communications System, Arlington, Virginia

In his present assignment, General Edmonds is responsible for providing command, control, communications, computer, and intelligence support to the nation's warfighters. The general began his career in the Air Force in August 1964, after graduating from Officer Training School at Lackland Air Force Base, Texas.

General Edmonds is a graduate of several institutions of higher education, including Morris Brown College, where he earned a bachelor's degree in chemistry, and Hampton Institute, where he earned a master's degree in counseling psychology. He also attended the United States Air Force Air War College, from which he is a distinguished graduate, and the National and International Security Program at the John F. Kennedy School of Government at Harvard University.

During his more than thirty years of distinguished service, General Edmonds has held a number of highly critical positions, including deputy chief of staff for communications-computer systems, Tactical Air Command, and commander, Air Force Communication Commands' Tactical Communications Division, Langley Air Force Base, Virginia; assistant chief of staff, Command, Control, Communications, and Computer Systems Directorate, Headquarters, United States Air Force, Washington, DC; and director, Command, Control, Communications, and Computer Systems Directorate, the Joint Chiefs of Staff, Washington, DC.

The general's other assignments have included student, Basic Communications-Electronics Course, Kessler Air Force Base, Mississippi; data systems officer, Tactical Communications Area, Langley Air Force Base, Virginia; inspection team chief and contributing editor, Project Corona Harvest, Pacific Communications Area Inspector General Office, Hickam Air Force Base, Hawaii; director, Emergency Mission Support, Pacific Communications Area, Hickam Air Force Base, Hawaii; chief of operations, 2083d Communications Squadron (Provisional), Takhli Royal Thai Air Base, Thailand; communications systems staff officer, Command, Control, Communications, and Computer Systems Directorate, Headquarters, United States Air Force, Washington, DC; chief, Commercial Communications Policy Office, Defense Communications Agency, Arlington, Virginia; director, Communications-Electronics, Third Air Division, Andersen Air Force Base, Guam; Commander, Twenty-seventh Communications Squadron, Andersen Air Force Base, Guam; student, Air War College, Maxwell Air Force Base, Alabama; chief, Joint Mat-

Promotion	Date
Second Lieutenant	November 10, 1964
First Lieutenant	May 10, 1966
Captain	May 2, 1968
Major	December 1, 1973
Lieutenant Colonel	April 1, 1976
Colonel	February 1, 1980
Brigadier General	July 1, 1988
Major General	February 1, 1991
Lieutenant General	March 26, 1993

Lt. Gen. Albert J. Edmonds

ters Group, Directorate of Command, Control, and Telecommunications, Deputy Chief of Staff, Plans, and Operations, Headquarters, United States Air Force, Washington, DC; vice commander, Tactical Communications Division, Langley Air Force Base, Virginia; and assistant deputy chief of staff, Communications and Electronics, Headquarters, Tactical Air Command, Langley Air Force Base, Virginia.

General Edmonds's decorations and awards include the Defense Distinguished Service Medal; the Defense Superior Service Medal; the Legion of Merit; and the Meritorious Service with three Oak Leaf Clusters.

LIEUTENANT GENERAL LESTER L. LYLES
Commander, Odgen Air Logistics Center, Hill Air Force Base, Utah

General Lyles was commissioned a second lieutenant in February of 1968, through Air Force ROTC. He received his bachelor's degree in mechanical engineering from Howard University and his master's degree in mechanical and nuclear engineering form the Air Force Institute of Technology in conjunction with New Mexico State University. General Lyles also attended the Defense Systems Management College, the Armed Forces Staff College, the National War College, and the National and International Security Management Course at Harvard University.

Currently, the command responsibilities of General Lyles include the worldwide logistical support of the F-16 Fighting Falcon and F-4 Phantom, as well as the entire array of Minuteman and Peacekeeper intercontinental ballistic missiles.

During his outstanding career, General Lyles has served as propulsion and structures engineer, Standard Space Launch Vehicles Program Office, Los Angeles Air Force Station, California; propulsion engineer, Headquarters, Aeronautical Systems Division, Wright-Patterson Air Force Base, Ohio; program element monitor, Short-Range Attack Missile, Headquarters, United States Air Force, Washington, DC; executive officer to the deputy chief of staff for research and development, Headquarters, United States Air Force, Washington, DC; aide-de-camp and special assistant to the commander, Headquarters, Air Force Systems Command, Andrews Air Force Base, Maryland; student, Defense Systems Management College, Fort Belvior, Virginia; chief, Avionics Divisions, F-16 Systems Programs Office, Headquarters, Aeronautical Systems Division, Wright-Patterson Air Force Base, Ohio; deputy director, Special and Advanced Projects, F-16 Systems Program Office, Headquarters, Aeronautical Systems Division, Wright-Patterson Air Force Base, Ohio; director, Tactical Aircraft Systems, Headquarters, Air Force Systems Command, Andrews Air Force Base, Maryland; director, Medium Launch Vehicles Program Office, Headquarters, Space Systems Division, Los Angeles Air Force Station, California; assistant deputy commander for launch systems, Headquarters, Space Systems Division, Los Angeles Air Force Station, California; assistant deputy chief of staff for requirements and later deputy chief of staff for requirements, Headquarters, Air Force Systems Command, Andrews Air Force Base, Maryland; and vice commander, Ogden Air Logistics Center, Hill Air Force Base, Utah.

General Lyles has been awarded the Legion of Merit with one Oak Leaf Cluster; the

Promotion	Date
Second Lieutenant	February 2, 1968
First Lieutenant	August 2, 1969
Captain	February 2, 1971
Major	November 1, 1979
Lieutenant Colonel	December 1, 1982
Colonel	December 1, 1985
Brigadier General	May 1, 1991
Major General	August 6, 1993
Lieutenant General	December 1, 1995

Lt. Gen. Lester L. Lyles

Meritorious Service Medal with three Oak Leaf Clusters; the Air Force Commendation Medal; the Senior Missileman Badge; the Space Badge; and was named the Astronautics Engineer of the Year by the National Space Club in 1990.

LIEUTENANT GENERAL LLOYD W. "FIG" NEWTON
Assistant Vice Chief of Staff, Headquarters, United States Air Force, Washington, DC

A distinguished graduate of Air Force ROTC, Lloyd Newton was commissioned a second lieutenant in March 1966. General Newton is a graduate of Tennessee State University, where he earned a bachelor's degree in aviation education, and of George Washington University, where he earned a master's degree in public administration. In addition, the general is a graduate of the Armed Forces Staff College, the Industrial College of the Armed Forces, and the National Security Senior Executives Course at Harvard University. In his present position, General Newton is responsible for the organization and administration of the Air Staff and is the Air Force Accreditation Official for the Corps of Air Attaches.

General Newton is also a command pilot of great skill. He flew 269 combat missions during the Vietnam War. In 1974, the general was one of the elite members of the legendary United States Air Force Aerial Demonstration Squadron, the Thunderbirds. He has also commanded three wings and an air division. A highly versatile aviator, General Newton has logged more than four thousand flying hours in the C-12, F-4, F-15, F-16, F-117, T-37, and T-38.

During his thirty years of military service, General Newton has served in a number of command and staff positions, including pilot and systems operator, Da Nang Air Base, Vietnam; student, F-4D Upgrade Qualification Training, George Air Force Base, California; F-4D pilot, 523d Tactical Fighter Squadron, Clark Air Base, Philippines; F-4D flight instruction pilot, Luke Air Force Base, Arizona; narrator and slot pilot, United States Air Force Thunderbirds, Nellis Air Force Base, Nevada; right wingman and narrator, United States Air Force Thunderbirds, Nellis Air Force Base, Nevada; congressional liaison officer, United States House of Representatives, Washington, DC; student, F-16 Qualification Training, MacDill Air Force Base, Florida; assistant deputy commander for operations, Eighth Tactical Fighter Wing, Junsan Air Base, South Korea; assistant deputy commander for operations, 388th Tactical Fighter Wing, Hill Air Force Base, Utah; assistant deputy director for operations and training, Headquarters, United States Air Force, Washington, DC; assistant director of special projects, Directorate of Plans, Headquarters, United States Air Force, Washington, DC; commander, Seventy-first Air Base Group, Vance Air Force Base, Oklahoma; commander, Seventy-first Flying Training Wing, Vance Air Force Base, Oklahoma; commander, Twelfth Flying Training Wing, Randolph Air Force Base, Texas; commander, 833d Air Division, Holloman Air Force Base, New

Promotion	Date
Second Lieutenant	March 23, 1966
First Lieutenant	December 12, 1967
Captain	June 12, 1969
Major	January 1, 1978
Lieutenant Colonel	October 1, 1980
Colonel	December 1, 1983
Brigadier General	August 3, 1991
Major General	August 10, 1993
Lieutenant General	May 25, 1995

Lt. Gen. Lloyd W. "Fig" Newton

Mexico; commander, Forty-ninth Fighter Wing, Holloman Air Force Base, New Mexico; and director of operations, J-3 (Operations), United States Special Operations Command, MacDill Air Force Base, Florida.

General Newton's decorations and award include the Defense Superior Service Medal; the Legion of Merit with one Oak Leaf Cluster; the Distinguished Flying Cross with one Oak Leaf Cluster; the Meritorious Service Medal with one Oak Leaf Cluster; the Air Medal with sixteen Oak Leaf Clusters; the Air Force Commendation Medal; the Air Force Outstanding Unit Award; the Philippines Presidential Unit Citation; the Vietnam Service Medal; and the Republic of Vietnam Campaign Medal.

MAJOR GENERAL MARCELITE J. HARRIS
Director of Maintenance, Deputy Chief of Staff, Logistics, Headquarters, United States Air Force, Washington, DC

In 1965, Marcelite Harris was commissioned a second lieutenant through the Air Force Officer Training School at Lackland Air Force Base in Texas. She earned her bachelor's degree in business management from the University of Maryland. General Harris also graduated from the Squadron Officers School (by correspondence), the Air University, the Air War College (by seminar), the Air University Senior Officer in National Security Course at Harvard University, the CAPSTONE General and Flag Officer Course, and the National and International Security Management Course at Harvard University.

In her present position, General Harris supervises a workforce of more than 125,000 technicians and managers with a budget of more than $260 billion for maintenance of a "Global Reach-Global Power" aerospace weapons system inventory.

This pioneering dynamo has blazed a fiery trail for other women to follow. She was the first female aircraft maintenance officer, one of the first two female air officers commanding at the United States Air Force Academy, and the first female deputy commander for maintenance.

During her thirty-one years in the Air Force, the General has served as administrative officer, Seventy-first Tactical Missile Squadron, Bitburg Air Base, West Germany; maintenance analysis officer, Thirty-sixth Tactical Fighter Wing, Bitburg Air Base, West Germany; student, Aircraft Maintenance Officer Course, Chanute Air Force Base, Illinois; maintenance supervisor, Forty-ninth Tactical Fighter Squadron, Korat Royal Thai Air Force Base, Thailand; job control officer and later field maintenance supervisor, 916th Air Refueling Squadron, Travis Air Force Base, California; personnel staff officer and white house social aide, Headquarters, United States Air Force, Washington, DC; air officer commanding, Cadet Squadron Thirty-nine, United States Air Force Academy, Colorado Springs, Colorado; maintenance control officer, 384th Air Refueling Wing, McConnell Air Force Base, Kansas; commander, 384th Avionics Maintenance Squadron, McConnell Air Force Base, Kansas; commander, 384th Field Maintenance Squadron, McConnell Air Force Base, Kansas; director of maintenance, Pacific Air Forces Logistic Support Center, Kadena Air Base, Japan; deputy commander for maintenance, Keesler Air Force Base, Mississippi; commander, 3300th Technical Training Wing, Keesler Air Force Base, Mississippi; vice commander, Oklahoma City Air Logistics Center, Tinker Air Force Base, Oklahoma; director of technical training, Headquarters, Air Education and Training Command, Randolph Air Force Base, Texas; and direc-

Promotion	Date
Second Lieutenant	December 21, 1965
First Lieutenant	December 21, 1967
Captain	December 21, 1969
Major	April 1, 1975
Lieutenant Colonel	October 1, 1981
Colonel	September 1, 1986
Brigadier General	May 1, 1991
Major General	May 25, 1995

SECRETARY OF THE AIR FORCE

Maj. Gen. Marcelite J. Harris

tor of maintenance, Headquarters, United States Air Force, Washington, DC.

General Harris's decorations and awards include the Legion of Merit with one Oak Leaf Cluster; the Bronze Star Medal; the Meritorious Service Medal with three Oak Leaf Clusters; the Air Force Commendation Medal with one Oak Leaf Cluster; the Presidential Unit Citation; the Air Force Outstanding Unit Award with "V" device and eight Oak Leaf Clusters; the National Defense Service Medal with one Oak Leaf Cluster; the Vietnam Service Medal with three Oak Leaf Clusters; the Republic of Vietnam Gallantry Cross with Palm; and the Republic of Vietnam Campaign Medal.

MAJOR GENERAL JOHN F. PHILLIPS
Commander, Sacramento Air Logistics Center, McClellan Air Force Base, California

On December 20, 1963, John Phillips was commissioned a second lieutenant through the Air Force Officer Training School at Lackland Air Force Base in Texas. General Phillips has an extensive academic background. He received a bachelor's degree with honors in biology and chemistry from Jarvis Christian College and is an honors graduate of the Institute of Aerospace Safety Engineering, the University of Southern California, and the Air Command and Staff College. He earned a master's degree in logistics management from the Air Force Institute of Technology and attended the Industrial College of the Armed Forces, the Defense Systems Management College, the National War College, and the Senior Managers in Government Course at Harvard University.

In his present command position, General Phillips is responsible for the worldwide logistics support to numerous aircraft, including the F-117 Stealth Fighter, the F-22, the F-111 Series, the A-10, the F-15, and the KC135. He supervises more than two hundred communications systems and eight space systems, and repairs, overhauls, and modifies entire categories of complex avionics components, hydraulic and pneudraulic systems, and flight control systems. His command has an annual budget of more than $3.2 billion.

General Phillips is rated a senior pilot/navigator and has logged more than three thousand flight hours, including more than three hundred combat hours over Vietnam. His impressive duty assignments have included instructor/navigator, KC135, Travis Air Force Base, California; student, Pilot Training, Williams Air Force Base, Arizona; T-37 instructor pilot, First German Squadron, Sheppard Air Force Base, Texas; inspector and flight examiner, Office of the Inspector General, Headquarters, Air Training Command, Randolph Air Force Base, Texas; student, Air Force Institute of Technology, Wright-Patterson Air Force Base, Ohio; program manager, F100 and J85 Engines, San Antonio Air Logistics Center, Kelly Air Force Base, Texas; logistics systems analyst, Doshan Tappeh Air Base, Iran; deputy program manager for logistics, KC10 Joint Program Office; TR-1 system program director, Wright-Patterson Air Force Base, Ohio; director, Airlift and Trainer Systems, Headquarters, Air Force Logistics Command, Wright-Patterson Air Force Base, Ohio; student, National War College, Fort McNair, Washington, DC; deputy division chief and later chief, Weapons System Program Division, Programs, Headquarters, United States Air Force, Washington, DC; military assistant to the secretary, Office of the Assistant Secretary of the Air Force for Research, Development,

Promotion	Date
Second Lieutenant	December 20, 1963
First Lieutenant	December 20, 1966
Captain	December 20, 1970
Major	August 1, 1977
Lieutenant Colonel	November 6, 1981
Colonel	October 1, 1982
Brigadier General	October 1, 1988
Major General	August 1, 1991

Maj. Gen. John F. Phillips

and Logistics, Washington, DC; vice commander, Logistics Management Systems Center, Wright-Patterson Air Force Base, Ohio; deputy chief of staff, Communications-Computer Systems, Headquarters, Air Force Logistics Command, Wright-Patterson Air Force Base, Ohio; and assistant to the commander and later commander, Joint Logistics Systems Center, Wright-Patterson Air Force Base, Ohio.

His decorations and awards include the Distinguished Service Medal; the Legion of Merit; the Meritorious Service Medal with two Oak Leaf Clusters; the Air Medal; the Air Force Commendation Medal with one Oak Leaf Cluster; the Air Force Outstanding Unit Award; the Combat Readiness Medal; and the Republic of Vietnam Gallantry Cross with Palm.

BRIGADIER GENERAL CLAUDE M. BOLTON, JR.
Commandant, Defense Systems Management College, Fort Belvoir, Virginia

General Bolton entered the Air Force as a student pilot and a second lieutenant, and received his wings in 1970. He earned a bachelor's degree in electrical engineering from the University of Nebraska and a master's degree in national security and strategic studies from the Naval War College. The general is also a graduate of the Air Command and Staff College, the Naval War College, and the Program Management Course at the Defense Systems Management College.

General Bolton has held a full range of positions as one of the Air Force's finest command pilots with more than twenty-seven hundred flying hours in twenty-seven different aircraft. He has served in a variety of positions, including squadron and wing safety officer; instructor pilot, wing standardization and evaluation flight examiner, scheduler, test pilot, and acquisition professional. A combat veteran of the Vietnam War, Bolton has flown 232 combat missions, forty of which were over North Vietnam.

In his present position, General Bolton is responsible for the adoption of practices of sound systems management principles through education, research, consulting, and information dissemination.

Before assuming his present duties, General Bolton served as pilot, F-105D, McConnell Air Force Base, Kansas; pilot, F-4, Davis-Monthan Air Force Base, Arizona; pilot, F-4D/E, 497th Tactical Fighter Squadron (Nite Owls), Ubon Royal Thai Air Force Base, Thailand; pilot, F-111D, instruction pilot and safety officer, Cannon Air Force Base, New Mexico; pilot, F-111E, Fifty-fifth Tactical Fighter Squadron, Royal Air Force Upper Heyford, England; student, Air Force Test Pilot School, Edwards Air Force Base, California; F-4, F-111, and F-16 test pilot, 325th Test Wing, and F-111 flight test manager, Armament Division, Eglin Air Force Base, Florida; program manager, Advanced Tactical Fighter Technologies Program, F-22 Systems Program Office, Aeronautical Systems Division, Wright-Patterson Air Force Base, Ohio; F-16 program element monitor, and deputy division chief, Aircraft Division, and later, division chief, Low Observable Vehicle Division, Office of Special Programs, the Pentagon, Washington, DC; deputy program director, B-2 System Program Office, Aeronautical Systems Division, Wright-Patterson Air Force Base, Ohio; program director, Advanced Cruise Missile System Program Office, Aeronautical Systems Division, Wright-Patterson Air Force Base, Ohio; and inspector general, Headquarters, Air Force Materiel Command, Wright-Patterson Air Force Base, Ohio.

The General has been awarded the Legion of Merit;

Promotion	Date
Second Lieutenant	May 31, 1969
First Lieutenant	November 30, 1970
Captain	May 30, 1972
Major	May 1, 1980
Lieutenant Colonel	March 1, 1984
Colonel	July 1, 1988
Brigadier General	August 1, 1993

Brig. Gen. Claude M. Bolton, Jr.

the Distinguished Flying Cross with one Oak Leaf Cluster; the Meritorious Service Medal with two Oak Leaf Clusters; the Air Medal with seventeen Oak Leaf Clusters; the Vietnam Service Medal with three Service Stars; the Republic of Vietnam Gallantry Cross; and the Republic of Vietnam Campaign Medal.

BRIGADIER GENERAL JOHN D. HOPPER, JR.
Commandant of Cadets and Commander, Thirty-fourth Training Wing, United States Air Force Academy, Colorado

John D. Hopper, Jr., graduated from the Air Force Academy as a second lieutenant in 1969, with a bachelor's degree in general studies. He is also a distinguished graduate of the Squadron Officer School, the Air Force Institute of Technology, where he earned a master's degree in logistics management, the Air Force Command and Staff College, and the Industrial College of the Armed Forces. In his present position, General Hopper commands and administers the four thousand-member Cadet Wing. His responsibilities include cadet military training and airmanship education, supervision of cadet life activities, and facilities and logistic support.

General Hopper is rated a command pilot and has flown combat missions in Vietnam, and as commander of the 1660th Tactical Airlift Wing (Provisional) during Operation Desert Storm. The general has logged more than thirty-five hundred flying hours.

During his outstanding career, General Hopper has served as C130 pilot, Ching Chuan Kang Air Base, Taiwan and Vietnam; T-37 instructor pilot, academic instructor, and class commander, Seventy-first Flying Training Wing, Vance Air Force Base, Oklahoma; student, Air Force Institute of Technology School for Systems and Logistics, Wright-Patterson Air Force Base, Ohio; deputy director, Cadet Logistics, and aide to the superintendent, Air Office Commanding, Cadet Squadron Twelve, United States Air Force Academy, Colorado Springs, Colorado; chief, pilot and assistant operations officer, Eighteenth Military Airlift Squadron, McGuire Air Force Base, New Jersey; chief, Wing Command Post, 438th Military Airlift Wing, McGuire Air Force Base, New Jersey; commander, 438th Field Maintenance Squadron, McGuire Air Force Base, New Jersey; chief, Exercises Division, Headquarters, United States Force Command, Fort McPherson, Georgia; deputy commander for operations, Sixty-third Military Airlift Wing, Norton Air Force Base, California; commander, Eighty-ninth Operations Group, Andrews Air Force Base, Maryland; commander, Sixty-third Airlift Wing, Norton Air Force Base, California; and commander, 375th Airlift Wing, Scott Air Force Base, Illinois.

General Hopper's decorations and awards include the Defense Superior Service Medal; the Legion of Merit; the Distinguished Flying Cross; the Meritorious Service Medal with two Oak Leaf Clusters; the Air Medal with two Oak Leaf Clusters; the Air Force Commendation Medal with one Oak Leaf Cluster; the Southwest Asia Service Medal with two Bronze Stars; and the Kuwait Liberation Medal.

Promotion	Date
Second Lieutenant	June 4, 1969
First Lieutenant	December 4, 1970
Captain	June 4, 1972
Major	October 10, 1979
Lieutenant Colonel	March 1, 1984
Colonel	July 1, 1988
Brigadier General	July 15, 1994

Brig. Gen. John D. Hopper, Jr.

GENERAL BERNARD P. RANDOLPH
Retired

Born in New Orleans, Louisiana, General Randolph is an honors graduate with three degrees: a bachelor's degree in chemistry from Xavier University; and bachelor's and master's degrees in electrical egineering from the University of North Dakota at Grand Forks, through the Air Force Institute of Technology program. The general is also a distinguished graduate of the Air Command and Staff College and the Air War College.

The general's major duty assignments after completing aviation cadet training at Ellington Air Force Base, Texas, and Mather Air Force Base, California, were instructor and evaluator of KC-97 and B-47 flight crews, Strategic Air Command, Lincoln Air Force Base, Nebraska; chief, On-Orbit Operations, Space Systems Division, Los Angeles Air Force Station, California; assistant deputy program director, Launch and Orbital Operations, Los Angeles Air Force Station, California; and assistant deputy program director, Launch and Orbital Operations, Space Systems Division, Los Angeles Air Force Station, California.

General Randolph also attended the Air Command and Staff College at Auburn University. Upon completion of his studies there, he was assigned to the Republic of Vietnam as an airlift operations officer in Chu Lai and as airlift coordinator at Tan Son Nhut Air Base. He also served as coordinator of operations for all airlift control elements throughout the Republic of Vietnam.

Returning to the United States, his next duty assignments were as chief, Command Plans/Test Evaluation, Headquarters, Air Force Systems Command, Andrews Air Force Base, Maryland; executive officer, Deputy Chief of Staff for Operations, Andrews Air Force Base, Maryland; director, Space Systems Planning for the Space and Missile Systems Organization, Los Angeles Air Force Station, California; deputy program director and later program director, Air Force Satellite Communications System, Los Angeles Air Force Station, California; vice commander, Warner Robins Air Logistics Center, Robins Air Force Base, Georgia; director, Space Defense Systems, Space Division Headquarters, Los Angeles Air Force Station, California. As the director of Space Defense Systems, Randolph managed a program to design and develop the United States' antisatellite system with its supporting surveillance, command control, and survivability aspects.

General Randolph was the second Black four-star general in the United States Air Force. When he retired from active military service in April 1990, he was director, Space Systems, Command, Control, and Com-

Promotion	Date
Second Lieutenant	November 9, 1955
First Lieutenant	May 9, 1957
Captain	February 5, 1960
Major	January 20, 1967
Lieutenant Colonel	April 1, 1971
Colonel	July 1, 1975
Brigadier General	September 8, 1980
Major General	November 1, 1982
Lieutenant General	June 28, 1984
General	August 1, 1987

munications, Office of the Deputy Chief of Staff, Research Development and Acquisition, Headquarters United States Air Force, Washington, DC. In this capacity, he controlled more than $30 billion dollars and a staff of more than fifty-three hundred people.

General Randolph's decorations and awards include the Distinguished Serivce Medal; the Legion of Merit with one Oak Leaf Cluster; the Bronze Star Medal; the Meritorious Service Medal; the Air Force Commendation Medal; the Presidential Unit Citation Emblem; the Air Force Organizational Excellence Award; the Air Force Good Conduct Medal; the National Defense Service Medal; the Vietnam Service Medal with four Service Stars; the Air Force Longevity Service Award Ribbon with seven Oak Leaf Clusters; the Small Arms Expert Marksmanship Ribbon; the Air Force Training Ribbon; the Republic of Vietnam Gallantry Cross with Palm; and the Republic of Vietnam Campaign Medal.

LIEUTENANT GENERAL WILLIAM E. BROWN
Retired

A native of the empire state of New York, General Brown was born in the Bronx. He is a command pilot with more than fifty-one hundred hours of flying time in everything from the F-84 Thunderjet to the F-102 Delta Dagger. General Brown is a graduate of several institutions of higher education, including Pennsylvania State University, the Harvard Business School Advanced Management Program, the Armed Forces Staff College, and the Armed Forces Industrial College.

The general's major duty assignments have included combat fighter pilot, F-86 Saberjets, Fourth Fighter Interceptor Wing, South Korea; combat fighter pilot, Ubon Royal Thai Air Force, Thailand; special assistant for domestic action, Office of the Assistant Secretary of Defense, Department of Defense Manpower and Reserve Affairs Office, the Pentagon, Washington, DC; deputy commander, Operations, Sixty-fourth Flying Training Wing, Reese Air Force Base, Texas; commander, First Composite Wing, Military Airlift Command, Andrews Air Force Base, Maryland; chief of security police, Headquarters, United States Air Force, Washington, DC; commander, Air Defense Weapons Center, Tyndall Air Force Base, Florida; commander, Seventeenth Air Force, Sembach Air Base, Germany; commander, Allied Air Forces Southern Europe; and deputy commander in chief, United States Air Forces in Europe, Naples, Italy.

General Brown's numerous decorations and awards include the Distinguished Service Medal; the Legion of Merit with two Oak Leaf Clusters; the Distinguished Flying Cross with one Oak Leaf Cluster; the Air Medal with four Oak Leaf Clusters; the Air Force Commendation Medal with one Oak Leaf Cluster; the Purple Heart; the Presidential Unit Citation Emblem; the Air Force Outstanding Unit Award Ribbon with "V" device and Oak Leaf Cluster; the Combat Readiness Medal; the Good Conduct Medal; the National Defense Service Medal with one Service Star; the Korean Service Medal with three Service Stars; the Vietnam Service Medal with two Service Stars; the Air Force Longevity Service Award Ribbon with six Oak Leaf Clusters; the Republic of Korea Presidential Unit Citation; the Republic of Vietnam Gallantry Cross with Palm; the United Nations Service Medal; and the Republic of Vietnam Campaign Medal.

Promotion	Date
Second Lieutenant	December 15, 1951
First Lieutenant	July 14, 1952
Captain	February 10, 1956
Major	July 15, 1964
Lieutenant Colonel	February 20, 1967
Colonel	May 1, 1971
Brigadier General	August 1, 1975
Major General	April 1, 1979
Lieutenant General	September 15, 1982

LIEUTENANT GENERAL WINSTON D. POWERS
Retired

A graduate of McKendree College in Illinois, General Powers also attended George Washington University and the Industrial College of the Armed Forces. He is a master navigator with more than four thousand flying hours.

The general began his military career in November 1950, when he enlisted in the United States Air Force. He served in numerous staff and command positions. After basic training, his first duty assignment was with the Air Defense Command at Hancock Field, New York. Subsequently, he volunteered for navigator training at Ellington Air Force Base in Texas, and wound up the initial stages of his training at Randolph Air Force Base, also in Texas.

His major duty assignments have included communications engineer, Defense Communications Agency, Royal Air Force Station Croughton, England, United Kingdom; director, Tactical Communications Operations Tactical Communications Area, Langley Air Force Base, Virginia; combat fighter pilot, EC-47s, 460th Renaissance Wing, Tan Son Nhut Air Base, Vietnam; member, the Joint Chiefs of Staff, Plans and Policy Division, J-6 (Communications), Washington, DC; special assistant for joint matters, Directorate of Command, Control, and Communications, Office of the Deputy Chief of Staff, Programs and Resources, Washington, DC.

General Powers returned to South Korea in February 1974, and assumed the positions of commander, 2146th Communications Group, Osan Air Base, South Korea; director, Communications/Electronics, 314th Air Division, Osan Air Base, Korea; chief, Plans and Programs Division, Directorate of Command, Control, and Communications Panel, Headquarters, United States Air Force, Washington, DC; member, Program Review Committee of the Air Staff Board, Washington, DC; deputy director and later director, Telecommunications and Command and Control Resources, Office of the Assistant Chief of Staff, Communications and Computer Resources, Control and Communications, Headquarters, United States Air Force, Washington, DC; deputy chief of staff, Communications, Electronics, and Computer Resources for the North American Air Defense Command and United States Aerospace Defense Command, Peterson Air Force Base, Colorado; chief, Systems Integration Office, Aerospace Defense Center, Peterson Air Force Base, Colorado.

His decorations and awards include the Distinguished Service Medal; the Meritorious Service Medal with two Oak Leaf Clusters; the Legion of Merit; the Air Medal with one Oak Leaf Cluster; the Air Force Commendation Medal; the Presidential Unit Citation Emblem; the Air Force Outstanding Unit Award Ribbon with "V" device; the Air Force Organizational Excellence Award Ribbon; and the National Defense Service Medal with one Service Star.

Prmotion	Date
Second Lieutenant	August 3, 1953
First Lieutenant	February 4, 1955
Captain	March 30, 1959
Major	January 20, 1966
Lieutenant Colonel	February 1, 1970
Colonel	October 1, 1973
Brigadier General	August 1, 1978
Major General	July 1, 1981
Lieutenant General	October 1, 1983

MAJOR GENERAL RUFUS L. BILLUPS
Retired

General Billups earned a bachelor's degree from Tuskegee Institute, a master's degree from the University of Colorado, and an honorary doctorate from Guadalupe College of Texas. A distinguished graduate of Air Force ROTC, Billups received his early training at the Air Tactical School at Tyndall Air Force Base in Florida.

From January 1953 to December 1955, the general was assigned as a transportation officer in several units at New Castle Airport in Wilmington, Delaware, and later entered the University of Colorado under the Air Force Institute of Technology program and graduated with a master's degree in business in 1957.

General Billups's major duty assignments have included Air Force liaison officer, Pusan and Inchon, Korea; transportation, 7100th Transportation Squadron, Lindsey Air Station, Wiesbaden, Germany; director of transportation, 803d Transportation Squadron, Davis-Monthan Air Force Base, Arizona; student, Hughes Aircraft Company, Culver City, California; staff officer, Air Force Inspector General's Office, Norton Air Force Base, California; director, Aerial Port Operations, Second Aerial Port Group, Tan Son Nhut Air Base, Vietnam; combat fighter pilot, Aerial Port Operations, Second Aerial Port Group, Tan Son Nhut Air Base, Vietnam; staff transportation officer, Headquarters, United States European Command, Vaihingen, Germany; and director of transportation, Headquarters, United States Air Forces in Europe, Lindsey Air Station, Wiesbaden, Germany.

General Billups returned to the United States in May 1973, and served as commander, Twelfth Air Base Group, Randolph Air Base, Texas; deputy director of transportation, Office of the Deputy Chief of Staff, Systems and Logistics, Headquarters, United States Air Force, Washington, DC; commander, Defense General Supply Center, Defense Supply Agency, Richmond, Virginia; and director, Logistics Plans, Programs, and Transportation, Office of the Deputy Chief of Staff, Logistics and Engineering, Headquarters, United States Air Force, Washington, DC.

General Billups's military decorations and awards include the Defense Superior Service Medal; the Legion of Merit; the Bronze Star Medal; the Meritorious Service Medal; the Air Medal; the Air Force Commendation Medal; and the Air Force Outstanding Unit Award Ribbon.

Promotion	Date
Second Lieutenant	August 31, 1949
First Lieutenant	August 19, 1952
Captain	August 20, 1956
Major	August 19, 1963
Lieutenant Colonel	August 19, 1970
Colonel	August 1, 1972
Brigadier General	January 18, 1977
Major General	February 8, 1979

MAJOR GENERAL THOMAS E. CLIFFORD
Retired

A cum laude graduate of Howard University, General Clifford received his commission as a distinguished military graduate of Air Force ROTC. He also earned a master's of business administration and is an honors graduate of the Industrial College of the Armed Forces. Born in Washington, DC, General Clifford entered active military service in 1949, as a supply officer in the 2225th Overseas Replacement Depot at Camp Kilmer, New Jersey. After completing Air Tactical School at Tyndall Air Force Base, he entered pilot training at Connally Air Force Base and earned his wings in 1951.

General Clifford's major duty assignments have included pilot and later flight commander, F-94 and F-89, Fifth Fighter-Interceptor Squadron, Ladd Air Force Base, Fairbanks, Alaska; flight commander, 437th Fighter-Interceptor Squadron, Oxnard Air Force Base, California; chief, Twenty-seventh Air Division Jet Instrument School, Oxnard Air Force Base, California; flight commander and later weapons training officer and assistant operations officer, 329th Fighter-Interceptor Squadron, George Air Force Base, California; assistant chief, Directorate of Management Analysis, Headquarters, United States Air Force Europe, Lindsey Air Station, Wiesbaden, Germany; and chief, Progress Analysis Division, Headquarters, United States Air Force Europe, Lindsey Air Station, Wiesbaden, Germany.

In 1966, General Clifford was assigned to the Pentagon as assistant deputy of chief of staff for programs and resources, Directorate of Aerospace Programs, Washington, DC; military assistant, Office of the Assistant Secretary of Defense for Administration, Directorate of Organizational and Management Planning, Washington, DC; deputy commander for operations, 366th Tactical Fighter Wing, Da Nang Air Base, Vietnam; wing vice commander, 366th Tactical Fighter Wing, Da Nang Air Base, Vietnam; commander, Fifty-second Tactical Fighter Wing, Spangdahlem Air Base, Germany; vice commander, Seventeenth United States Air Force, Sembach Air Base, Germany; director of inspection, United States Air Force, Norton Air Base, California; commander, Twenty-sixth North American Air Defense Command Region, Headquarters, Air Division, Luke Air Force Base, Arizona; and deputy assistant secretary of defense for public affairs, the Pentagon, Washington, DC.

General Clifford's decorations and awards include the Legion of Merit with two Oak Leaf Clusters; the Distinguished Flying Cross; the Air Medal with four Oak Leaf Clusters; the Air Force Commendation Medal with one Oak Leaf Cluster; the Air Force Outstanding Unit Award Ribbon; and the Republic of Vietnam Gallantry Cross with Palm.

Promotion	Date
Second Lieutenant	May 27, 1949
First Lieutenant	March 9, 1953
Captain	March 11, 1957
Major	March 9, 1964
Lieutenant Colonel	March 9, 1971
Colonel	October 1, 1969
Brigadier General	October 1, 1973
Major General	January 22, 1977

MAJOR GENERAL ARCHER L. DURHAM
Retired

General Durham received his bachelor's degree in political science from Utah State University in 1960, and his master's degree in international affairs from George Washington University in 1975. He is also a graduate of the Squadron Officer School at Maxwell Air Force Base, the Advanced Management Program at Columbia University, the National War College, and the Executive Program in National and International Security at Harvard University. A native of Pasadena, California, General Durham is a command pilot with more than six thousand flying hours. He received his wings in 1954, at Laredo Air Force Base, Texas.

During his military career, General Durham has served in a variety of command and staff positions. His major duty assignments have included commander and squadron plans and mobility officer, Twenty-eighth Logistics Support Squadron, Hill Air Force Base, Utah; flight test maintenance officer, 2720th Maintenance Group, Air Force Logistics Command, Clark Air Base, Philippines; air light command post controller, 1622d Support Squadron, Paris, France; chief, Advanced Programming and Policy Division, Office of the Deputy Chief of Staff for Plans, Scott Air Force Base, Illinois; assistant deputy director, Plans and Policy, the Joint Chiefs of Staff, Washington, DC; and director, Plans and Programs, 314th Air Division, Osan Air Base, South Korea.

In October 1966, General Durham returned to the United States after an extensive tour of duty overseas, and was assigned as chief, Advanced Programming and Policy Division, Office of the Deputy Chief of Staff for Plans, Headquarters, Military Airlift Command, Scott Air Force Base, Illinois. Subsequent duty assignments included deputy base commander and later base commander, McGuire Air Force Base, New Jersey; commander, 1606th Air Base Wing, Kirtland Air Force Base, New Mexico; commander, 436th Military Airlift Wing, Dover Air Force Base, Delaware; commander, Seventy-sixth Airlift Division, Military Airlift Wing, Andrews Air Force Base, Maryland; vice commander, Military Traffic Management Command, Washington, DC; and director of deployment, United States Air Force Transportation Command, MacDill Air Force Base, Florida.

The general's decorations and awards include the Defense Superior Service Medal; the Legion of Merit with two Oak Leaf Clusters; the Meritorious Service Medal with one Oak Leaf Cluster; the Air Force Commendation Medal with one Oak Leaf Cluster; the Air Force Outstanding Unit Award with three Oak Leaf Clusters; the National Defense Service Medal with one Service Star; the Armed Forces Expeditionary Medal; the Air Force Longevity Service Award Ribbon with six Oak Leaf Clusters; the Armed Forces Reserve Medal; and the Small Arms Expert Marksmanship Ribbon.

Promotion	Date
Second Lieutenant	April 28, 1954
First Lieutenant	October 28, 1955
Captain	December 17, 1959
Major	September 26, 1966
Lieutenant Colonel	August 1, 1970
Colonel	March 1, 1974
Brigadier General	July 1, 1980
Major General	June 1, 1984

MAJOR GENERAL TITUS C. HALL
Retired

A master navigator with more than four thousand flying hours, General Hall received his bachelor's degree in electrical engineering from Tuskegee Institute in Alabama in 1952. He was a distinguished graduate of Air Force ROTC and eventually earned a master's degree in systems engineering management from the University of Southern California at Los Angeles in 1971. He is also a graduate of the Basic Navigational Flying School and Advanced Bombing and Navigation School.

A native of Texas, Hall began his active duty career with the United States Air Force in March 1952. Upon completion of Communications Officer Training at Scott Air Force Base, Illinois, in June 1953, his first duty assignment was overseas with the United States Air Force Security Service in Japan as communications intelligence operations officer at Johnson and Shiroi air bases.

His subsequent assignments included flying duty, Strategic Air Command Units, Davis-Monthan Air Force Base, Arizona; commander, Satellite Tracking Station, Kodiak, Alaska; executive officer, Space and Missile Systems Organization (now Air Force Space Division), Los Angeles, California. In 1972, General Hall assumed command as chief, Avionics Engineering, B-1 Strategic Manned Bombers, Headquarters, Aeronautical Systems Division, Wright-Patterson Air Force Base, Ohio; deputy for systems, Reconnaissance and Electronic Warfare Systems, Headquarters, Aeronautical Systems Division, Wright-Patterson Air Force Base, Ohio; systems program director, Avionics Program Office, Wright-Patterson Air Force Base, Ohio; assistant deputy, Reconnaissance/Strike/Electronic Warfare System Program Office, Wright-Patterson Air Force Base, Ohio; vice commander, 2750th Air Base Wing, Wright-Patterson Air Force Base, Ohio; commander, Kelly Air Force Base, Texas; deputy, Systems/Reconnaissance/Electronics Warfare Systems, Headquarters, Aeronautical Systems Division, Wright-Patterson Air Force Base, Ohio; and commander, Lowry Technical Training Center, Lowry Air Force Base, Colorado.

General Hall's decorations and awards include the Distinguished Service Medal; the Legion of Merit; the Distinguished Flying Cross; the Bronze Star Medal; the Meritorious Service Medal with one Oak Leaf Cluster; and the Air Medal with two Oak Leaf Clusters.

Promotion	Date
Second Lieutenant	August 7, 1949
First Lieutenant	January 22, 1954
Captain	January 22, 1958
Major	October 5, 1962
Lieutenant Colonel	March 8, 1973
Colonel	October 1, 1975
Brigadier General	December 4, 1980
Major General	July 1, 1981

MAJOR GENERAL LUCIUS THEUS
Retired

General Theus came up through the ranks the hard way. Born in Madison County, Tennessee, Lucius Theus enlisted in the United States Army Air Corps in 1942, as a private. In 1946, he was commissioned a second lieutenant. The general has a bachelor's degree from the University of Maryland, a master's degree in business administration from George Washington University, and is a graduate of the Harvard Advanced Management Program, Harvard University Graduate School of Business Administration.

During his military career, General Theus also attended the Statistical Control Officers School at Lowry Air Force Base, Colorado, in 1948, and the Armed Forces Staff College in Norfolk, Virginia, in 1960. He was an honor graduate of the Industrial College of the Armed Forces correspondence course in 1964, and in 1966 he graduated with distinction from the Air War College at Maxwell Air Force Base, Alabama.

In his capacity as director of accounting and finance, the general was responsible for the worldwide operation of the United States Air Force accounting and finance network.

His major duty assignments have included statistical services staff officer, Headquarters, Central Air Materiel Forces, Europe, Chateauroux Air Base, France; technical statistical advisor to the comptroller, Headquarters, Air Materiel Forces, Europe, Chateauroux Air Base, France; chief, Management Services Office, Eastern Air Logistics Office, Athens, Greece; chief, Management Analysis, Headquarters, Spokane Air Defense Sector, Larson Air Force Base, Washington; base comptroller, Kingsley Field, Oregon; base comptroller, Cam Ranh Bay Air Base, Vietnam; acting deputy base commander, Cam Ranh Bay Air Base, Vietnam; data automation staff officer, Directorate of Data Automation, Office of the Comptroller of the Air Force, Denver, Colorado; chief, Technology and Standards Branch, Washington, DC; chief, Plans, Policy, and Technology Division, Washington, DC; chief, Program Management Division, Washington, DC; chairman, Inter-Service Task Force, Education in Race Relations, Office of the Secretary of Defense, the Pentagon, Washington, DC; director, Management Analysis, Office of the Comptroller of the Air Force, Denver, Colorado; special assistant for social actions, Directorate of Personnel Plans, Deputy Chief of Staff, Personnel, Headquarters, United States Air Force, Washington, DC; director of accounting and finance, Office of the Comptroller of the Air Force, Denver, Colorado; and commander, Air Force Accounting and Finance Center, Denver, Colorado.

Promotion	Date
Second Lieutenant	January 26, 1946
First Lieutenant	August 25, 1947
Captain	September 1, 1951
Major	April 24, 1956
Lieutenant Colonel	March 27, 1962
Colonel	January 23, 1967
Brigadier General	July 2, 1972
Major General	May 1, 1975

General Theus's military decorations and awards included the Legion of Merit; the Distinguished Service Medal; the Bronze Star Medal; the Air Force Commendation Medal with one Oak Leaf Cluster; the Air Force Outstanding Unit Award Ribbon; and the Republic of Vietnam Commendation Medal.

MAJOR GENERAL JOHN H. VOORHEES
Retired

General Voorhees was born in New Brunswick, New Jersey, and received his bachelor's degree in chemistry from Rutgers University in 1958, and his master's degree in management from the University of Southern California in 1967. The general is also a graduate of the National War College and was designated a senior executive fellow of Harvard University in 1981.

After receiving his commission as a distinguished military graduate of Air Force ROTC, Voorhees's major duty assignments included student, United States Air Force School of Naviation, Connally Air Force Base, Texas, and Mather Air Force Base, California; navigator systems operator, Fourteenth Tactical Fighter Squadron, Udorn Royal Thai Air Force Base, Thailand. While stationed in Thailand, Voorhees flew 176 combat missions, including one hundred over Vietnam. Upon his return to the United States in May 1969, General Voorhees was assigned as chief, Systems Effectiveness Branch, Space and Missile Systems Organization Headquarters, Los Angeles Air Force Station, Los Angeles, California; chief, Test Support Division, Los Angeles Air Force Station, Los Angeles, California; Research and Development Planner, the Joint Chiefs of Staff, Washington, DC; chief, Strategic Plans Division, Air Force Logistics Command Headquarters, Wright-Patterson Air Force Base, Ohio; director, Plans, Air Force Logistics Command Headquarters, Wright-Patterson Air Force Base, Ohio; chief, Strategic Plans Division, and later director, Plans, Air Force Logistics Command Headquarters, Wright-Patterson Air Force Base, Ohio; chief, Missiles Systems Management Division, Oklahoma City Air Logistics Center, Tinker Air Force Base, Oklahoma; director, Materiel Management, Sacramento Air Logistics Center, McClellen Air Force Base, California; and commander, Defense Contract Administration Services Region, Los Angeles, California.

General Voorhees is a master navigator with more than thirty-eight hundred flying hours. His military decorations and awards include the Defense Distinguished Service Medal; the Defense Superior Service Medal with one Oak Leaf Cluster; the Legion of Merit with two Oak Leaf Clusters; the Distinguished Flying Cross; the Meritorious Service Medal; the Air Medal with twelve Oak Leaf Clusters; and the Air Force Commendation Medal with one Oak Leaf Cluster.

Promotion	Date
Second Lieutenant	June 1, 1958
First Lieutenant	May 9, 1959
Captain	February 1, 1962
Major	January 21, 1968
Lieutenant Colonel	April 1, 1973
Colonel	September 1, 1978
Brigadier General	November 1, 1982
Major General	June 1, 1986

BRIGADIER GENERAL JAMES T. BODDIE
Retired

A graduate of Howard University, General Boddie was an award-winning cadet who received his commission through Air Force ROTC. Born in Baltimore, Maryland, he is also a graduate of the Industrial College of the Armed Forces; the Air War College, and Auburn University, where he earned a master's degree in public administration.

General Boddie earned his wings in 1956, at Laredo Air Force Base, Texas. His major duty assignments have included pilot, F-84F Thunderstreak, 560th Strategic Fighter Squadron, Bergstrom Air Base, Texas; instructor, United States Air Force in Europe Weapons Center, Wheelus Air Base, Tripoli, Libya; commandant of cadets, Air Force ROTC, Tuskegee Institute, Alabama; flight instructor, 4453d Combat Crew Training Wing, David-Monthan Air Force Base, Arizona; combat pilot, 559th Tactical Fighter Squadron, Cam Ranh Bay Air Base, Vietnam; commander, F-4 Replacement Training Unit Weapons School, 4457th Tactical Training Squadron, Arizona; provisional squadron commander, Fortieth Tactical Fighter Squadron, Davis-Monthan Air Force Base, Arizona; chief, Flying Status Branch, Directorate of Personnel Program Action, Randolph Air Force Base, Texas; chief, Maintenance Standardization and Evaluation Division, Directorate of Maintenance Engineering, Headquarters, Tactical Air Command, Langley Air Force Base, Virginia; deputy commander, Operations, 347th Tactical Fighter Wing, Moody Air Force Base, Georgia; vice commander, 347th Tactical Fighter Wing, Moody Air Force Base, Georgia; vice commander, Fifty-first Composite Wing, Osan Air Base, South Korea; commander, Fifty-first Composite Wing, Osan Air Base, South Korea; and deputy director of operations, J-3 (Operations), National Military Command Center, the Joint Chiefs of Staff, Washington, DC.

A command pilot with more than four thousand hours in jet fighter craft, General Boddie's flew seventy-five missions during the Vietnam War. His military decorations and awards include the Air Medal with thirteen Oak Leaf Clusters; the Air Force Commendation Medal; the Meritorious Service Medal with two Oak Leaf Clusters; the Legion of Merit; the Distinguished Flying Cross; the Air Force Outstanding Unit Award Ribbon with three Oak Leaf Clusters and "V" device; the Combat Readiness Medal; the National Defense Service Medal with one Service Star; the Combat Readiness Medal; the Armed Forces Expeditionary Medal; the Vietnam Service Medal with three Silver Stars; the Small Arms Expert Marksmanship Ribbon; the Republic of Vietnam Gallantry Cross with Palm; and the Vietnam Campaign Medal. General Boddie also wears the Organization of the Joint Chiefs of Staff Badge.

Promotion	Date
Second Lieutenant	June 4, 1954
First Lieutenant	June 3, 1957
Captain	April 3, 1962
Major	January 22, 1969
Lieutenant Colonel	January 1, 1976
Colonel	October 1, 1978
Brigadier General	August 1, 1980

BRIGADIER GENERAL ELMER T. BROOKS
Retired

General Brooks is a graduate of Miami of Ohio University with a bachelor's degree in zoology. He was commissioned a second lieutenant through Air Force ROTC. In 1973, General Brooks received a master's degree from George Washington University; he also completed the Executive Program of the Colgate Darden Graduate School of Business Administration at the University of Virginia through the Air Force's Advanced Management Program in 1978, and attended the Industrial College of the Armed Forces. General Brooks also has the distinction of being one of the first Black officers to serve as flight control technician at the Houston Space Center during the *Gemini* and *Apollo* space missions for the National Aeronautical and Space Administration (NASA) Manned Spacecraft Center.

General Brooks held a number of executive positions, including unit adjutant and later base director, Continental Air Command, Air Reserve Flying Center, Pittsburgh, Pennsylvania; commander, Radar Station, Thirteenth Air Force, Philippines; division chief, Personnel, Headquarters, Thirteenth Air Force, Philippines; commander, Combat Crew, Atlas F, Intercontinental Ballistic Missile System, Lincoln Air Force Base, Nebraska; executive officer, Office of the Secretary of the Air Force, Space Systems Office, Washington, DC; military assistant to special assistant and later military assistant, Secretary and Deputy Secretaries of Defense, the Pentagon, Washington, DC; vice commander, 381st Strategic Missile Wing, McConnell Air Force Base, Kansas; assistant deputy director, International Negotiations, the Joint Chiefs of Staff, Washington, DC; deputy commissioner, Standing Consultative Commission, Washington, DC; and deputy director for international negotiations, Plans and Policy Directorate, the Joint Chiefs of Staff, Washington, DC.

General Brooks's decorations and awards include the Meritorious Service Medal with one Oak Leaf Cluster; the Legion of Merit; the Air Force Commendation Medal; the Defense Superior Service Medal with two Oak Leaf Clusters; the Joint Service Commendation Medal with one Oak Leaf Cluster; the Air Force Outstanding Unit Award Ribbon with two Oak Leaf Clusters; the Combat Readiness Medal; the Master Missile Badge; and the Space Badge.

Promotion	Date
Second Lieutenant	October 5, 1954
First Lieutenant	October 4, 1957
Captain	October 4, 1961
Major	April 11, 1969
Lieutenant Colonel	February 1, 1976
Colonel	October 1, 1978
Brigadier General	September 1, 1981

BRIGADIER GENERAL ALONZO L. FERGUSON
Retired

A graduate of Howard University, where he earned a degree in psychology, and of the Armed Forces Staff College, General Ferguson began his active duty service in 1952, after receiving his commission as a second lieutenant through Air Force ROTC.

The general's major duty assignments after completing jet fighter training include forward air controller, T-6 Mosquito, Korea; and instructor, 4520th Combat Crew Training Wing, Nellis Air Force Base, Nevada.

Leaving the United States in June 1961, General Ferguson served as F-105 weapons instructor, Wheelus Air Base, Libya; liaison officer, Thirty-sixth Tactical Fighter Wing, Bitburg Air Base, Germany.

Returning to the United States in 1966, the general was again assigned to Nellis Air Force Base. This time as an F-105 instructor pilot and operations officer for the 4523d Combat Training Squadron. In August of 1966, after attending the Armed Forces Staff College, he was assigned to Takhli Royal Thai Air Force Base, Thailand, where he flew 103 combat missions in F-105s with the famed 355th Tactical Fighter Wing over North Vietnam.

General Ferguson returned from Thailand in 1968, and served as chief, Weapons Systems Branch, Headquarters, Tactical Air Command, Langely Air Force Base, Virginia; directorate of operations, Air Force Board Structure, Tactical Weapons Systems Branch, Headquarters, United States Air Force, Washington, DC; vice commander and later commander, Fifty-first Air Base Wing, Osan Air Base, South Korea; commander, Fifty-first Combat Support Group, Fifty-first Composite Wing, Osan Air Base, South Korea; vice commander and later commander, 355th Tactical Fighter Wing, Davis-Montham Air Force Base, Arizona; deputy director, J-3 (Operations), National Military Command Center, the Joint Chiefs of Staff, Washington, DC; deputy director, Readiness Development, Directorate of Operations and Readiness, Deputy Chief of Staff for Operations and Plans, Headquarters, United States Air Force, Washington, DC; commander, Twenty-first North American Air Defense Command Region at Hancock Field, New York; commander, Twenty-first Aerospace Defense Command Region, New York; and commander, Twenty-first Air Division, Air Defense Component, Tactical Air Command, New York.

A command pilot, General Ferguson's decorations and awards include the Silver Star with one Oak Leaf Cluster; the Legion of Merit; the Defense Meritorious Service Medal; the Meritorious Service Medal with one Oak Leaf Cluster; the Air Medal with thirteen Oak Leaf Clusters; and the Air Force Commendation Medal with one Oak Leaf Cluster.

Promotion	Date
Second Lieutenant	May 23, 1952
First Lieutenant	June 20, 1955
Captain	July 13, 1959
Major	July 12, 1966
Lieutenant Colonel	July 12, 1973
Colonel	October 1, 1975
Brigadier General	August 1, 1977

BRIGADIER GENERAL DAVID M. HALL
Retired

Born in Gary, Indiana, General Hall is a graduate of Howard University with a bachelor's degree in business administration and a master's degree in educational sociology from the Agricultural and Technical State University of North Carolina at Greensboro. He is also a graduate of Air Command and Staff College, the Air War College, the Industrial College of the Armed Forces, and the Advanced Management Program at Massachusetts Institute of Technology.

The general enlisted in the Air Force in August 1951, and was commissioned a second lieutenant in June 1953 through the Air Force's Officers' Candidate School. During the early stages of his career, the general served in several different capacities, which included accounting and finance, supply, data processing, and Air Force ROTC instruction. Finding data processing to his liking, he cross-trained into this field while stationed at Oxnard Air Force Base in California, and was later assigned to the Clark Air Base in the Philippines as a data processing officer.

Returning to the United States in June 1962, the general became an assistant professor, Aerospace Science, Air Force ROTC, Agricultural and Technical State University of North Carolina, Greensboro, North Carolina; comptroller, Eighth Tactical Fighter Wing, Ubon Royal Thai Air Force Base, Thailand; chief, Computer Operations Division, Directorate of Data Automation, Air Force Accounting and Finance Center, Denver, Colorado; director, Data Processing, Ubon Royal Air Force Base, Thailand; chief, Computer Operations Division, Military Airlift Command Headquarters, Scott Air Force Base, Illinois; assistant, Office of the Deputy of Staff for Personnel, Scott Air Force Base, Illinois; deputy base commander and later base commander, Scott Air Force Base, Illinois; assistant deputy chief of staff, Comptroller, Headquarters, Air Force Logistic Command, Wright-Patterson Air Force Base, Ohio; and deputy chief of staff, Comptroller, Air Force Logistics Command, Wright-Patterson Air Force Base, Ohio.

His military decorations and awards include the Legion of Merit; the Meritorious Service Medal with one Oak Leaf Cluster; and the Air Force Commendation Medal with one Oak Leaf Cluster.

Promotion	Date
Second Lieutenant	January 19, 1953
First Lieutenant	January 18, 1956
Captain	April 22, 1959
Major	January 3, 1967
Lieutenant Colonel	March 1, 1971
Colonel	October 1, 1976
Brigadier General	December 4, 1980

BRIGADIER GENERAL AVON C. JAMES
Retired

A master electronics specialist, General James was born in Hampton, Virginia, and received his bachelor's degree from Morgan State University. After graduation, he enlisted in the Air Force and served as a weather observer with the Air Weather Service prior to entering Officer Candidate School. He received his commission as a second lieutenant in 1953.

General James's major duty assignments included personnel officer, Eighty-first Fighter Wing, Royal Air Force Station, Bentwater, England; personnel officer, 1001st Air Base Wing, Andrews Air Force Base, Maryland; personnel officer, Field Maintenance Squadron, Operations Group, Maintenance and Supply Group, Andrews Air Force Base, Maryland; chief, Consolidated Base Personnel Office, Andrews Air Force Base, Maryland; chief, Personnel and Administration, 304th Munitions Maintenance Squadron, Royal Air Force Station, Alconbury, England; student, Command and Control System Computer Programmer Course, Kessler Air Force Base, Mississippi; chief, Personnel and Administration Division, 7232d Munitions Maintenance Group, Ramstein Air Base, Germany; chief, Analysis and Programming Branch, Air Force Command Post's Systems Division, Headquarters, United States Air Force, Washington, DC; chief of staff, Electronics System Division, Air Force Systems Command, Hanscom Air Force Base, Massachusetts; and first deputy commander, Data Automation, Headquarters, Air Force Communications Command, Scott Air Force Base, Illinois. In this last position, General James was responsible for the overall management of eight data automation organizations that provided services to the Office of the Secretary of Defense, United States Air Force Headquarters, major commands, bases, and designated government agencies. He also served as director, Computer Resources, Office of the Comptroller of the Air Force, Headquarters, United States Air Force, Washington, DC.

The general's military decorations and awards include the Legion of Merit with one Oak Leaf Cluster; the Meritorious Service Medal; the Air Force Commendation Medal with one Oak Leaf Cluster; and the Air Force Organizational Excellence Award.

Promotion	Date
Second Lieutenant	June 19, 1953
First Lieutenant	June 18, 1956
Captain	March 10, 1959
Major	June 19, 1967
Lieutenant Colonel	June 19, 1974
Colonel	October 1, 1976
Brigadier General	December 4, 1980

BRIGADIER GENERAL CHARLES B. JIGGETTS
Retired

General Jiggetts was born in Henderson, North Carolina. He received a bachelor's degree in political science from Howard University. The general is also a graduate of the Squadron Officer School, the Air Command and Staff College, the Air War College, and the Industrial College of the Armed Forces.

His major duty assignments have included group adjutant and supply officer, Basic Military Training Center, Sampson Air Force Base, New York; squadron operations officer, Twenty-seventh Communication Squadron, Andersen Air Force Base, Guam; student, Communications-Electronic Staff Officer Course, Kessler Air Force Base, Mississippi; chief, Maintenance, and wing communications-electronic officer, Ninety-second Strategic Aerospace Wing, Fairchild Air Base, Washington; communications-electronic requirements officer, Headquarters, Seventh Air Force, Tan Son Nhut Air Base, Vietnam; joint communications staff officer, United States Strike Command, MacDill Air Force Base, Florida; technical assistant to director, Telecommunications Policy, Office of the Assistant Secretary of Defense (Installations and Logistics), Washington, DC; director of communications and data processing (later reorganized as Directorate of Command, Control and Communications System), J-6 (Communications), Pacific Command, Camp H.M. Smith, Hawaii; deputy commander, Combat Communications and Reserve Force Matters, Air Force Communications Command, Scott Air Force Base, Illinois; military assistant to the director, Office of Telecommunications Policy, Executive Office of the President of the United States, Washington, DC; vice commander, Northern Communications Area, Air Force Communications Service, Griffin Air Force Base, New York; and vice commander, Air Force Communications Command, Headquarters, Scott Air Force Base, Illinois.

General Jiggetts's decorations and awards include the Distinguished Service Medal; the Defense Superior Service Medal; the Legion of Merit with one Oak Leaf Cluster; the Bronze Star Medal; the Meritorious Service Medal; the Defense Superior Service Medal; the Joint Service Commendation Medal; and the Air Force Commendation Medal. He also wears the Air Traffic Controller's Badge.

Promotion	Date
Second Lieutenant	May 27, 1949
First Lieutenant	September 3, 1953
Captain	August 19, 1957
Major	August 19, 1964
Lieutenant Colonel	August 19, 1971
Colonel	October 1, 1973
Brigadier General	February 24, 1978

BRIGADIER GENERAL NORRIS W. OVERTON
Retired

A graduate of Indiana University, General Overton was a distinguished military graduate of Air Force ROTC. Born in Clarkville, Tennessee, his higher education includes a master's degree in business administration from the Air Force Institute of Technology. He also attended the Air Command and Staff College, the Industrial College of the Armed Forces, the Air War College, and the Advanced Management Program at Harvard University's School of Business Administration.

The general's major duty assignments included finance officer, Eighteenth Fighter Bomber Wing, Chinhai, Korea; deputy finance officer, Forbes Air Force Base, Kansas; finance officer, Greiner Air Force Base, New Hampshire; finance officer, Bordeaux Air Base, France; deputy accounting and finance officer, Lindsey Air Base, Germany; chief, Comptroller Services Division, Air Force Plant Representative Office, Curtiss-Wright Corporation, Woodside, New Jersey; chief, Comptroller, Milwaukee Contract Management District, Milwaukee, Wisconsin; finance officer, Karamursel Common Defense Installation, Turkey; associate professor, Aerospace Studies, University of Iowa, Iowa City, Iowa; base comptroller, Tan Son Nhut Air Base, Vietnam; executive officer, Deputy Assistant Comptroller, Accounting and Finance, Headquarters, United States Air Force, Washington, DC; assistant deputy comptroller, Accounting/Finance, Headquarters, United States Air Force, Washington, DC; deputy chief of staff, Comptroller, United States Air Force Academy, Colorado Springs, Colorado; deputy chief of staff, Comptroller, Headquarters, Pacific Air Forces, Hickam Air Force Base, Hawaii; and vice commander, Army Air Force Exchange Services, Dallas, Texas.

The general's military decorations and awards include the Legion of Merit with one Oak Leaf Cluster; the Bronze Star Medal with one Oak Leaf Cluster; the Air Force Commendation Medal; the Air Force Outstanding Unit Award Ribbon; the Republic of Korea Presidential Unit Citation; and the Republic of Vietnam Gallantry Cross with Palm.

Promotion	Date
Second Lieutenant	January 1, 1951
First Lieutenant	September 24, 1952
Captain	March 15, 1955
Major	June 25, 1958
Lieutenant Colonel	June 25, 1965
Colonel	October 20, 1972
Brigadier General	May 1, 1979

BRIGADIER GENERAL HORACE L. RUSSELL
Retired

General Russell, a native New Yorker, is a graduate of Bradley University, where he earned a bachelor's degree, the Air Force Institute of Technology, where he earned a master's degree, and Purdue University, where he earned a doctorate. He also attended the Air Command and Staff College, the Air War College, and the Industrial College of the Air Force.

During his years of military service, General Russell's major duty assignments included weather officer, Detachment Twelve, Third Weather Squadron, Seymour Johnson Air Force Base, North Carolina; missile combat crew member and later deputy missile combat crew commander and missile combat crew commander, Tenth Strategic Missile Squadron, Malmstrom Air Force Base, Montana; mechanical engineer, Air Force Aero Propulsion Lab, Wright-Patterson Air Force Base, Ohio; staff development engineer and later chief, Laboratory, Aerospace Dynamics Branch, Air Force Flight Dynamics Lab, Wright-Patterson Air Force Base, Ohio; research manager and later manager, Mechanical Physical Engineering Science Division, Physical Engineering, Andrews Air Force Base, Maryland; chief, Physical and Engineering Science Division, Andrews Air Force Base, Maryland; deputy director, Plans and Operations, Office of Scientific Research, Bolling Air Force Base, Washington, DC; staff development engineer, Tactical Systems Division, assistant chief of staff, Studies and Analysis, Headquarters, United States Air Force, Washington, DC; chief, Programs Division, Director of Programs Integration, Washington, DC; deputy chief of staff, Research, Development and Acquisition, Headquarters, United States Air Force, Washington, DC; and policy analysis, the White House, Washington, DC.

General Russell's decorations and awards include the Defense Superior Service Medal with one Oak Leaf Cluster; the Meritorious Service Medal with three Oak Leaf Clusters; the Air Force Commendation Medal; the Air Force Commendation Unit Award with one Bronze Oak Leaf Cluster; the Combat Readiness Medal; the National Defense Service Medal; and the Air Force Longevity Service Award Ribbon with one Silver Oak Leaf Cluster.

Promotion	Date
Second Lieutenant	January 8, 1958
First Lieutenant	December 28, 1959
Captain	December 28, 1962
Major	February 1, 1969
Lieutenant Colonel	October 1, 1974
Colonel	May 1, 1979
Brigadier General	January 1, 1984

BLACK UNITED STATES
MARINE CORPS GENERAL OFFICERS

BRIGADIER GENERAL CHARLES F. BOLDEN, JR.

Assistant Wing Commander, Third Marine Aircraft Wing, Naval
Air Station, Miramar, California

Born in Columbia, South Carolina, General Bolden is a graduate of the
United States Naval Academy, where he earned a bachelor's degree. He also
earned a master's degree in systems management from the University of
Southern California. General Bolden is also the recipient of honorary doctor-
ates from Johnson C. Smith University, the University of South Carolina,
Winthrop College, and an Alumni Award of Merit from the University of Southern California.

The general flew more than one hundred missions over North and South
Vietnam, Cambodia, and Laos while assigned to all-weather fixed wing marine attack plane 533 in Thailand.

An extraordinary naval pilot and astronaut, General Bolden has flown four
missions as a member of NASA's space shuttle program. He was selected by
NASA for the space program in 1981, and in 1986, the general flew his first
mission on board the space shuttle *Columbia*. During this mission, the
SATCOM KU Satellite was deployed and a variety of experiments in astro-
physics and materials processing were conducted.

In 1990, Astronaut-General Bolden conducted a number of experiments
involving a series of cameras, including both the IMAX in-cabin and cargo
bay cameras, aboard the space shuttle *Discovery*. During this mission, the
Discovery flew at a record-setting altitude of more than four hundred miles
and deployed the Hubble Telescope.

In 1992, on his third mission, General Bolden commanded the space
shuttle *Atlantis*. During this nine-day mission, Commander Bolden and his
crew successfully conducted numerous ATLAS-1 (Atmospheric Laboratory
for Application and Science) experiments. As a result of this mission, a multi-
tude of detailed measurement of the earth's atmospheric, physical, and chemical elements were obtained for the first time. This information made a major
contribution to the greater understanding of planet earth's climate and atmosphere.

Then in 1994, General Bolden commanded the space shuttle *Discovery*
on the historic eight-day mission that was the first joint U.S./Russian space
shuttle mission. This highly delicate mission was the first time two nations
had cooperated in such a joint scientific venture. The experiments conducted
involved the Space Habitation Module-2 and the Wake Shield Facility 0-1.

Promotion	Date
Second Lieutenant	October 1, 1969
First Lieutenant	November 1, 1969
Captain	March 1, 1973
Major	March 1, 1979
Lieutenant Colonel	June 1, 1985
Colonel	June 1, 1990
Brigadier General	September 1, 1995

Bolden flew 130 orbits of mother
earth before landing at the
Kennedy Space Center. Upon
completion of his historic mission, the general had logged
more than 680 hours in outer
space and more than six thousand hours of conventional aircraft flight time.

Brig. Gen. Charles F. Bolden, Jr.

General Bolden's other major duties and assignments include: Marine Corps officer selection and recruiting officer, Los Angeles, California; three years of various assignments, Marine Corps Air Station, El Toro, California; student, United States Naval Test Pilot School, Patuxent River, Maryland; Naval Air Test Center's Systems Engineering and Strike Aircraft Test Directorate; test pilot, A-6E, EA-6B, and A-7C/EA; and deputy commandant, United States Naval Academy, Annapolis, Maryland.

General Bolden's awards and decorations include the Legion of Merit; the Distinguished Flying Cross; the Defense Meritorious Service Medal; the Air Medal; the Strike/Flight Medal (eighth award); the NASA Outstanding Leadership Medal; and three NASA Exceptional Service Medals.

BRIGADIER GENERAL CLIFFORD L. STANLEY
Assistant Deputy Chief of Staff for Manpower and Reserve Affairs (Manpower Plans & Policy), Headquarters Marine Corps, Washington, DC

General Stanley was promoted to his present rank on August 1, 1994, after only twenty-five years as a member of the United States Marine Corps. He was commissioned in October 1969, after graduating from South Carolina State University. The general received his master's degree from John Hopkins University in 1977. He is also a graduate of the Amphibious Warfare School, the Naval War College, the United States Marine Corps Command and General Staff College, and the National War College.

The general's command and staff assignments have included student, the Marine Corps Basic School, Quantico, Virginia; supply officer/fiscal officer, overseas and continental United States Command; commanding officer, Company M, Third Battalion, Eighth Marines; commanding officer, Headquarters Company, Fourth Marines; executive officer, First Battalion, Sixth Marines; commanding officer, First Marine Regiment; instructor, Leadership and Technology, United States Naval Academy, Annapolis, Maryland; executive officer, Marine Corps Institute, and parade commander, Marine Barracks, Washington, DC; special assistant and Marine Corps aide for the assistant secretary of the Navy, Headquarters, United States Navy, Washington, DC; desk officer, Office of the Assistant Secretary of Defense, East Asia and Pacific Region, the Pentagon, Washington, DC.

General Stanley also served as depot inspector and commander, First Recruit Training Battalion, Parris Island; member, White House Fellowship Program, Special Assistant to the Director of the FBI; and fleet Marine officer, Second Fleet, USS *Mt. Whitney*, LCC-20, Norfolk, Virginia.

His decorations and awards include the Legion of Merit; the Defense Meritorious Service Medal; the Meritorious Service Medal with Gold Star; the Navy Commendation Medal; and the Navy Achievement Medal.

Promotion	Date
Second Lieutenant	September 1, 1969
First Lieutenant	December 1, 1970
Captain	April 1, 1974
Major	April 1, 1980
Lieutenant Colonel	July 1, 1986
Colonel	July 1, 1991
Brigadier General	August 1, 1994

Brig. Gen. Clifford L. Stanley

CHRONOLOGY OF MAJOR EVENTS IN BLACK MILITARY HISTORY 1492–1996

1492   Black ship's pilot, Pedro Alonso Niño, accompanies Columbus on his voyage to America.

1538   Estevanico, a Black conquistador, leads an expedition into the Southwest and discovers Arizona and New Mexico.

1652   Blacks are trained in Virginia as militiamen and fight in the French and Indian War.

1770   On March 5, Crispus Attucks, a Black seaman from Framingham, Massachusetts, is the first American to die in the struggle for liberty from England when British troops fire on the citizens of Boston in what has become known as the Boston Massacre.

1774   In Massachusetts, Black minutemen enlist in companies being organized by the Committee of Safety.

1775   Black minutemen see action at the first battles of the Revolution at Lexington and Concord. Among the Black minutemen were Peter Salem, Lemuel Haynes, Pompey, Cato Stedman, Cuff Whittemore, Pomp Blackman, Cato Wood, and Prince Esterbrooks.

William Flora enlists in the American forces. Flora is eventually cited for bravery at the Great Bridge, which he defended against the British attack in the winter of 1776. He fights throughout the Revolutionary War and joins the American forces again during the War of 1812.

Samuel Charlton enlists in the American forces at the age of sixteen and sees service at the battles of Brandywine, Germantown, and Monmouth. He is also with General Washington at Valley Forge.

Barzillai Lew enlists in the Revolutionary Army and serves for the duration of the hostilities. Lew is at Bunker Hill and the Boston Massacre and leads many commando assignments against the British in New England.

Saul Matthews, soldier and spy, joins the American forces. He leads one of the most successful behind-the-lines raids of the Revolutionary War. Commandos led by Saul Matthews took so many British prisoners at Portsmouth that Gen. Charles Cornwallis had to abandon the position.

Black patriots take part in the capture of the Fort Ticonderoga with the Green Mountain Boys.

Peter Salem and Salem Poor are heroes of the Battle of Bunker Hill.

The Continental Congress prohibits Blacks from joining the American Revolutionary Army.

Lord John Murray Dunmore offers freedom and equal pay to all male Blacks who will join the British Army.

Because of the massive response by Blacks to Lord Dunmore's proclamation, Gen. George Washington reverses the decision of the Continental Congress and issues orders authorizing the enlistment of free Blacks into the Revolutionary Army.

1776   The United States Cavalry is formed. John Banks, a free Black American from Virginia, is a member of this elite fighting force. Banks later rides for several years with Theodorick Blands's regiment.

Black militiamen are among the victorious American troops at the Battle of Trenton.

General George Washington makes his famous Delaware River crossing. Two Black patriots are with him: Prince Whipple and Oliver Cromwell.

Tack Sisson, commando, leads a daring surprise raid on the headquarters of British Maj. Gen. Samuel Prescott and captures him.

Oliver Cromwell, a member of the Second New Jersey Regiment, fights at Trenton and Princeton from 1776-1777, at Brandywine in 1777, at Monmouth in 1778, and at Yorktown in 1781.

1777   Scipio Africanus and Cato Carlile enlist in the Navy and serve with Capt. John Paul Jones.

Black troops are among the American forces that suffer through the terrible winter with General Washington at Valley Forge.

"The Negro can take the field instead of his master," reads a Hessian officer's diary. The diary continues, "…and therefore no regiment is to be seen in which there are not Negroes in abundance, and among them are able-bodied and strong fellows."

Edward Hector enlists in the Third Pennsylvania Artillery and is later cited for conspicuous bravery at the Battle of Brandywine.

1778   Seven hundred Black troops are among the patriots who defeat the British at the Battle of Monmouth Courthouse.

The Rhode Island Black Regiment is organized.

At the Battle of Rhode Island on August 29, a battalion of four hundred Black men holds off three separate charges from fifteen hundred Hessians under the command of Count Emil Kurt Von Donop.

1781   James Robinson, Black soldier, is awarded a gold medal for valor at the Battle of Yorktown.

James Armistead risks his life behind enemy lines on numerous occasions to supply the American forces with intelligence data on British Gen. Charles Cornwallis's troop strength and disposition. Armistead's information was a major contributing factor in General Washington's victory at Yorktown.

Jordan Freeman gives his life in a courageous stand with other American patriots who were finally overcome by numerically superior British forces at the Battle of Groton Heights. Lambo Latham, another Black patriot, died at Jordan Freeman's side on the same day.

1782   "L" Company of the Bucks of America is the first Black military organization formed in America. The unit was made up of Black Revolutionary War veterans from the Boston area. John Hancock, the governor of Massachusetts and a signer of the Declaration of Independence, presented the Bucks with their colors.

1783   The heroic Black Regiment commanded by Col. Christopher Green is deactivated at the end of the Revolutionary War. More than ten thousand Black Americans saw service during the war.

1812   During the War of 1812, many Blacks see action aboard American ships. In fact, one-sixth of the naval force during this war is Black.

1814   Two battalions of Black soldiers serve with Gen. Andrew Jackson and contribute to the defeat of the British at the Battle of New Orleans. The Black troops won high praise from Jackson.

1861   Nicholas Biddle is shot and wounded on April 18, while his Pennsylvania company is on its way to defend the nation's capital, becoming the first casualty of the Civil War.

1862   Harriet Tubman becomes America's first female soldier, Black or White. She also becomes the first American woman to lead troops in an armed assault against an enemy force when she leads Union troops against the Confederates. Harriet Tubman serves the Union as a scout, spy, and volunteer nurse, but she spends most of her time in the fields with the troops. She is such a great leader of men that she is referred to as "General Tubman" because of the admiration and respect the Union soldiers felt for her.

Susan King Taylor, an African-American woman, becomes the most well-known volunteer nurse of the Civil War era. Taylor served with the Thirty-third United States Colored Troops, her husband's combat unit.

On May 13, Robert Smalls, a Black ship's pilot, sails the Confederate steamer *Planter* out of the Charleston Harbor and turns it over to the Union forces. He later becomes a congressman from South Carolina.

Black volunteers attempt to fight for the Union, but are officially rejected. By the fall of 1863, however, Black Americans have fought in both land and sea battles.

On August 12, free Black men in the First Regiment Louisiana National Guard are armed, becoming the first armed Black men in the Union Army.

Colonel Thomas Higginson organizes the First South Carolina Volunteers, the second Black regiment mustered into service during the Civil War, in November.

1863   Only after constant agitation by African-American Frederick Douglass does President Lincoln ask congress to authorize the enlistment of more than 180,000 Blacks to fight for the Union. The date is May 22. This enlistment of African-Americans shifts the balance of power to the Union and is one of the major reasons for the Union victory in the Civil War. President Abraham Lincoln calls these men a crucial fighting force. He adds, "Keep them and you can save the Union. Throw them away and the Union goes with it."

On May 22, the War Department of the United States of America officially establishes the Bureau of Colored Troops.

Capt. Andre Cailloux, Company E, leads an attack on Port Hudson by the Black First Louisiana Native Guards. This is one of the few instances in the Civil War when Black troops are led by a Black officer.

The Black Ninth and Eleventh Louisiana, the First Mississippi, and about sixty troops of the Twenty-Third Iowa (White), hold off six Confederate regiments at Milliken's Bend.

The Fifty-fourth Massachusetts Regiment, an all-Black regiment, wins fame and glory at Fort Wagner, South Carolina. It was here that Flag Sgt. William H. Carney, though critically wounded, brought the flag back in honor. Falling exhausted from a loss of blood, he exclaimed, "Boys, the old flag never touched the ground!" Carney becomes the first Black American to win the Congressional Medal of Honor.

Congress approves the enlistment of free Blacks for Civil War service. Some 186,000 Black men are eventually inducted.

Maj. Gen. David Hunter, commander of the Department of the South, issues written permission for free access to all government property for the famed Civil War scout, nurse, and spy for the Union, Harriet Tubman. The permit read "Pass the bearer, Harriet Tubman, wherever she wishes to go, and give her free passage, at all times, on all government transports."

Dr. A. T. Augusta becomes the first Black commissioned medical officer when he is appointed surgeon of the Seventeenth Regiment,

U.S. Colored Volunteers. He later attains the rank of lieutenant colonel, the highest rank achieved by a Black American during the Civil War.

The United States Colored Troops are formed with the official authorization of the War Department.

Robert Blake wins the Navy Medal of Honor for displaying extraordinary courage and intelligence in discharging his duties aboard the USS *Marblehead*.

1864   John Lawson, James Miffin, and William Brown are awarded the Navy Medal of Honor for heroic action aboard a Union gunboat during the Battle of Mobile Bay.

Despite the efforts of the War Department, Black troops are denied their wages by commanders in the field.

After the loss of their officers at New Market Heights, Virginia, six non-commissioned officers lead their men so gallantly that they are awarded Medals of Honor. The non-commissioned officers were: Milton M. Holland, James H. Bronson, Powhattan Beatty, Robert Pinn, Edward Ratcliff, and Samuel Gilchrist.

Fourteen Black soldiers are awarded the Congressional Medal of Honor for their heroism in the Battle of Chapin's Farm.

1865   Martin R. Delaney, a graduate of Harvard Medical School, is personally recommended by President Lincoln as the first field grade Black line officer in American history. On February 26, he is commissioned a major in the 104th Regiment, United States Colored Troops, by Secretary of War Edwin M. Stanton.

Desperate for troops, Jefferson Davis, the president of the Confederacy, authorizes the enlistment of Black men into the Southern militia.

Gen. Robert E. Lee surrenders at Appomattox, ending the Civil War. Approximately 180,000 Blacks had served in the Union Army.

Black soldiers and civilians demand the right to vote.

1866   Due to the desire to expand westward and occupy Native American Indians' land, the United States Congress passes legislation forming the All African-American Calvary and Infantry units on July 28. They were: the Ninth and Tenth Cavalry Regiments, and the Thirty-eighth, Thirty-ninth, Fortieth, and Forty-first Infantry Regiments.

The Thirty-eighth and Forty-first African-American Regiments are consolidated into one unit, the Twenty-fourth Infantry Regiment, and the Thirty-ninth and Fortieth African-American Regiments are merged to form the Twenty-fifth Infantry Regiment.

1872   John H. Conyers becomes the first Black admitted to the United States Naval Academy.

President Johnson concedes the right to vote to Black Americans who are either educated or veterans.

Black Civil War veteran P. B. S. Pinchback becomes the first Black governor in the history of the United States when he serves forty-three days as the acting governor of Louisiana.

1877   Henry O. Flipper, after four years of taunts and abuse, finally graduates from West Point on June 15, as the first African-American ever to graduate from one of the service academies.

1887   The second Black graduate of West Point, John H. Alexander, is assigned as a second lieutenant to Fort Robinson, Nebraska.

1889   Cadet Charles Young becomes the third Black West Point graduate. Upon receiving his commission, he is assigned to the Tenth United States Cavalry.

1898   At the battle of El Caney, the Black Twenty-fifth Infantry sweeps up the hill of El Caney to rescue Col. Theodore Roosevelt and his Rough Riders from certain annihilation. In saving them, the Black regiment saves a future New York governor and United States president.

Black regiments compile a brilliant combat record during the Spanish-American War. During the charge up San Juan Hill, with Col. Theodore Roosevelt's Rough Riders, Black troops perform heroically. Five of them are awarded the Congressional Medal of Honor.

Daniel Atkins and Robert Penn win the Navy Medal of Honor for gallantry in action abroad the USS *Cushing* and the USS *Iowa* respectively.

1902   The only written record of services rendered by African-American women in the Civil War is documented in the memoirs of Susan King Taylor, a famous Black nurse from that period.

1906   In Brownsville, Texas, a racial incident involving the Black infantrymen of the Twenty-fifth Infantry erupts. President Roosevelt dishonorably discharges three entire companies when the men of the Twenty-fifth refuse to identify those who participated. This decision is not reversed by the Army until 1972.

1916   Maj. Charles Young leads a squadron in a military expedition against Pancho Villa in Mexico.

1917   On October 24, the War Department authorizes the formation of the first African-American division, the Ninety-second Division. Up until this time, there was an unwritten law dating back to the Civil War that no Black unit larger than a regiment was to be formed. The reasoning behind this rule was that the members of a Black unit larger than a regiment might rebel against their racist tormentors.

The 369th Infantry arrives in Europe, becoming the first Black unit to arrive there. In 191 days of fighting, the 369th never loses a man, a trench, or a foot of ground, and is nicknamed the "Hell Fighters" by the Germans.

More than seven hundred thousand Black Americans register for the draft during World War I.

Black leadership establishes an all-Black officers' training base in Des Moines, Iowa.

1918   The German general staff knows of the intolerance suffered by African-Americans and tries to convince the soldiers of the all-Black Ninety-second Division to desert. The Germans circulate propaganda leaflets asking: "Can you eat where White people eat? Do you enjoy the same rights as the White people in America? Why fight Germans for the benefit of the fat, White, Wall Street robbers?"

The French croix de guerre is awarded to two Black Infantry battalions.

Two Black American officers win the French Legion of Honor.

The French government awards Needham Roberts and Henry Johnson of the New York Fifteenth Division the croix de guerre for their bravery in action.

The legendary men of the all African-American Tenth Cavalry Regiment, which played a major role in America's conquest of the West, make the last mounted cavalry charge against Native Americans by the armed forces of the United States.

1919   The famed all-Black 369th marches up Fifth Avenue to Harlem through a cheering crowd of thousands. The 369th was on the front line for a longer span of time than any other American outfit during World War I.

1936   Benjamin O. Davis, Jr., graduates from West Point as the fourth Black cadet ever accorded that honor. He is the first Black cadet to graduate since Charles Young did so in 1889.

1940   Benjamin O. Davis, Sr., becomes the first Black general in United States history.

1941   The first—and perhaps the best-known—of the Black Air Force combat units, the Ninety-ninth Fighter Squadron, is formed at Army Air Field, Tuskegee, Alabama.

Messman Dorie Miller, who served on the USS *Arizona*, shoots down four Japanese planes during the surprise Japanese invasion of Pearl

Harbor and is awarded the Navy Cross.

The 366th Infantry is activated and becomes the first all-Black regular Army unit staffed with Black officers.

The 275th Construction Company, the first Black Signal Unit, is activated.

The first Black Tank Battalion, the 758th, is formed.

1942   The United States Army forms the African-American Ninety-third Division, which was the only Black division to see combat in the Pacific theater.

African-American women suffer the same racial injustice as Black men, and it is not until July 20, that they are accepted into the Women's Auxiliary Army Corps (WAAC).

America's first African-American Division, the Ninety-second Division, which was formed during World War I, is activated again on October 15.

Following the inception of the all African-American Ninety-ninth Fighter Squadron and its brilliant record, the larger 332d Fighter Group is formed on October 13. The 332d is made up of the 99th, 100th, 301st, and 302d Fighter Squadrons, and the 616th, 617th, and 619th Bombardment Squadrons.

Ensign Joseph C. Jenkins becomes the first Black officer commissioned by the United States Coast Guard.

Executive Order 9279 is issued, requiring all services to accept recruits processed through the Selective Service System regardless of ethnic origin.

Bernard W. Robinson is commissioned an ensign in the United States Navy, becoming the first Black man to win a commission in that branch of the military service.

In the Solomon Islands, Leonard Roy Harmon receives the Navy Cross for extraordinary action aboard the USS *San Francisco.*

1943   William Pinckney is awarded the Navy Cross for heroic action while serving aboard the USS *Enterprise* during the Battle of Santa Cruz Islands.

The USS *Leonard Roy Harmon* is commissioned. It is the first United States fighting ship named for a Black man. Leonard Roy Harmon won the Navy Cross for heroism in the Solomon Islands during World War II.

Lieutenant Charles Hall of the Ninety-ninth Fighter Squadron becomes the first member of that legendary squadron to shoot down a

German plane during World War II. Gen. Dwight D. Eisenhower personally congratulates Lieutenant Hall.

The men of the First Marine Depot Company, which is activated on March 8, become the first African-American Marines sent overseas during World War II on April 16. This occurs only after civil rights advocate A. Philip Randolph threatens the president with a march on Washington if Black troops are not given a chance to take a more active role in the war overseas. As a result, President Roosevelt issues Executive Order 8802, prohibiting discrimination on the basis of race in defense industries.

The Ninety-ninth Pursuit Squadron, the first Black flying unit, flies its first combat mission in the Mediterranean theater.

The third Black Air Force unit, the 477th Bomber Group, is formed.

Messman Dorie Miller, a Pearl Harbor hero, is lost at sea.

1944   On January 1, the first sixteen Black officer candidates enter Great Lakes Training Base for segregated training. All sixteen pass the course with an exceptional overall class G.P.A. of 3.89—a record that has yet to be broken. At the last moment, the Bureau of Naval Personnel decides that only twelve will be commissioned with a thirteenth, the only candidate without a college degree, becoming a warrant officer. The "Golden Thirteen" receive their commissions as the first Black officers in the history of the United States Navy.[1]

Black American troops are among the invasion force that lands on Omaha Beach in France on D-Day.

The legendary Red Ball Express is formed on August 21. This trucking company transports supplies that are desperately needed by the First and Third Armies, particularly Gen. George Patton's mechanized Third Army. The Black men of the Red Ball Express serve not only as truck drivers, but often get out of their vehicles and fight alongside the regular combat troops.

On October 19, the Office for War Information announces that the Navy has lifted the color ban against African-American women and that these women are welcome to join the WAVES (Women Accepted for Volunteer Emergency Service).

The African-American 555th Parachute Infantry Company is formed with First Sgt. Walter Morris as the first Black paratrooper in American military history. The 555th becomes known as "the Triple Nickel" and is later redesignated as the Third Battalion, 505th Airborne Infantry Regiment, Eighty-second Airborne Division.

---

[1] On April 6, 1982, the eight surviving members of the "Golden Thirteen" were honored by the Navy with a three-day cruise off the coast of Virginia aboard the Navy's newest Guided Missile Destroyer, the USS *Kidd*.

The USS *Mason* and Patrol Craft 1264 become the first antisubmarine vessels commissioned and manned by all-Black crews.

Secretary of the Navy James V. Forrestal orders all naval vessels to be integrated.

The exclusion of Black Americans from the Coast Guard and Marine Corps is officially terminated by the War Department.

The Ninety-ninth Fighter Squadron achieves an outstanding record over the Anzio-Nettuno beachhead.

1945   Even though President Franklin D. Roosevelt has already signed Public Law 554, allowing African-Americans to serve in the armed forces, the Navy drags its feet until March 8, when Phyllis Mae Daily becomes the first African-American woman to serve in the Navy Nurse Corps.

The United States Navy lifts all racial restrictions on vessel assignments on April 13. Before this date, Blacks were not assigned to combat vessels such as destroyers, cruisers, and submarines, in any capacity other than as messmen.

Charles F. Anderson is promoted to sergeant major, the U.S. Army's highest non-commissioned rank.

Three other all-Black squadrons join the Ninety-ninth Fighter Squadron to form the 332d Fighter Group assigned to the Twelfth and Fifteenth Air Forces.

Col. Benjamin O. Davis, Jr. is appointed commander of Godman Field, becoming the first Black to command a U.S. Army air base.

The first Black Marine Corps officer, Fredrick C. Branch, is commissioned a second lieutenant in the Marine Corps Reserve.

Despite a plethora of racially motivated incidents that plague Blacks in the military and the wider society, Black troops are conspicuous in the Allies' victorious assaults in the European theater.

1946   Secretary of the Navy James V. Forrestal issues orders prohibiting restriction of Blacks from certain types of assignments throughout the U.S. Navy on February 27. Secretary Forrestal announces, "Effective immediately, all restrictions governing the types of assignments for which Negro Navy personnel are eligible are hereby lifted. Henceforth, they shall be eligible for all types of assignments in all ratings in all activities and all ships of the naval services."

Thirty-one Black officers are integrated into the regular U.S. Army.

1947   Ensign John W. Lee becomes the first Black officer to transfer to the regular U.S. Navy.

1948   President Harry S. Truman issues Executive Order 9981, desegregating the armed forces of the United States of America.

John Earl Rudder becomes the first Black commissioned regular Marine Corps officer.

President Truman issues a civil rights message to Congress in which he states that all branches of the armed forces will provide equal opportunity for all their members, regardless of ethnic or racial background.

A. Philip Randolph forms the Committee Against Jim Crow in the Military.

The first African-American nurse is integrated into the regular U.S. Army Nurse Corps. Up until this time, Black nurses had been restricted to treating Black soldiers.

The Navy's first Black aviator, Ensign Jesse Brown, is commissioned and assigned to the Thirty-second Fighter Squad.

1949   Secretary of the Army Gordon Gray issues orders stating that the policy of establishing Black quotas will be abolished. Until this time, Blacks were mainly placed in the infantry, where the mortality rate is much higher than in service units such as the Signal Corps or Quartermaster Corps, and the number of Blacks per unit was limited out of fear of mutiny.

Wesley A. Brown becomes the first Black midshipman to graduate from the United States Naval Academy at Annapolis.

Secretary of the Navy Francis Matthews declares that the Navy's policy is that there shall be equality of treatment for all personnel in the Navy and Marine Corps regardless of ethnic origin.

With the passage of the Armed Services Integration Act of 1948, African-American women became eligible to serve in the Marine Corps. Annie L. Graham becomes the first Black woman to enlist in the United States Marine Corps.

1950   The Ninth and Tenth Cavalry units, which date back to the frontier wars in the West, are modernized and converted to mechanized warfare as the 509th and 510th African-American Tank Battalions.

The first U.S. victory in Korea is won by the all-Black Twenty-fourth Infantry Regiment on July 22. The *New York Daily News* headline announced "Negroes Gain 1st Korea Victory!"

Ensign Jesse L. Brown wins the Navy's Distinguished Flying Cross for heroic action in Korea, becoming the first Black to win this award. He was honored posthumously for this award.

In Korea, Pfc. William Thompson becomes the first Black American since the Spanish-American War to be awarded the Congressional Medal of Honor, the nation's highest honor.

1951   Sgt. Cornelius H. Charlton, Twenty-fourth Infantry Regiment, Twenty-fifth Division, is awarded the Congressional Medal of Honor for his courageous action near Chipo-Ri, Korea, on June 2. Sergeant Charlton and Pvt. William Thompson were the only African-Americans to be awarded the Congressional Medal of Honor during the Korean conflict. Both were members of the highly decorated Twenty-fourth African-American Infantry Regiment.

The Defense Advisory Committee On Women In The Service (DACOWITS), holds its first meeting in September. The committee is founded by Secretary of Defense Gen. George C. Marshall. The purpose of DACOWITS is to plan and organize a more efficient use of women and minorities in the armed forces. African-American women play a major role in the organization from its inception. One of its first members is Dorothy I. Height, who later becomes chairperson of the National Council of Negro Women.

1952   Frank E. Petersen, Jr., the Marine Corps' first Black pilot, receives his wings.

1953   Secretary of Defense Charles Wilson announces that all school facilities on U.S. military installations throughout the world are to be desegregated.

1954   Benjamin O. Davis, Jr., becomes the first Black general in the history of the United States Air Force on October 27.

1962   Lt. Comdr. Samuel L. Gravely assumes command of the USS *Falgout*, becoming the first Black naval warship commander.

1966   On February 1, Thomas D. Parham, Jr., becomes the first African-American chaplain to attain the rank of captain in the United States Navy.

1968   Pfc. James A. Anderson, Jr., is posthumously awarded the Congressional Medal of Honor for conspicuous bravery at Cam Lo, Vietnam, on February 28, 1967. Pfc Anderson was a member of Second Platoon, Company F, Second Battalion, Third Marine Division. He was the first African-American Marine so honored in the history of this nation.

1969   In Saigon, the U.S. Army releases a report that there has been an increase in racial tensions. The root cause: lack of Black officers and unfair punishment of Black soldiers.

1970   An investigative committee appointed by the Pentagon reports that Black servicemen are being subjected to racial indignities at the hands of former U.S. enemies, the Germans.

The Chief of Naval Operations, Admiral E.R. Zumwalt, issues Z-66, a directive detailing the action to be taken by all naval personnel to ensure equal opportunity.

Secretary of Defense Laird announces a program to end discrimination in the armed forces.

Eighty colonels are promoted to brigadier general, but only three are Black. The total number of Black generals in 1970 is four.

Navy Capt. Samuel L. Gravely is named the first Black admiral.

1972   During the months of October and November, interracial violence erupts on the USS *Kitty Hawk*, USS *Hassayampa*, USS *Forrestal*, USS *Ranger*, and USS *Constellation*. Chief of Naval Operations Adm. E. R. Zumwalt reprimands more than ninety Navy admirals and Marine Corps generals for their failure to implement effective racial policies in their respective commands.

1973   Gen. Daniel "Chappie" James, Jr., becomes the highest ranking Black in the U.S. Armed Forces when he is promoted to lieutenant general in the U.S. Air Force.

He is designated commander in chief of the North American Air Defense Command (NORAD) and receives his fourth star—becoming the first Black four-star general in U.S. military history—on the same day.

A destroyer escort is named in honor of Ensign Jesse L. Brown, the first African-American Navy aviator. Ensign Brown was an inspiration for many other African-American Navy aviators and other African-American military personnel, including a little known seaman by the name of Frank E. Petersen, Jr., who would, many years later, become the first Black Marine Corps general.

1974   Camp Johnson in North Carolina, becomes the first Marine Corps facility to be named for a Black soldier. Camp Johnson is dedicated to the memory of Sgt. Maj. Gilbert H. "Hashmark" Johnson, United States Marine Corps (Ret.).

Capt. Gerald Thomas becomes the second Black admiral in U.S. Navy history.

Two Black brigadier generals, Julius W. Becton and Harry W. Brooks, Jr., are promoted to the rank of major general in the United States Army.

1975   The U.S. Navy, which had one of the poorest records in the area of equal opportunity for African-Americans, finally admits Lt. Donna P. Davis as the first Black physician in the history of the Naval Medical Corps.

1976   Mason C. Reddix, Jr., achieves the distinction of being the highest ranking midshipman at Annapolis, the first Black in the history of the United States Naval Academy to hold this position.

Col. Emmett Paige, Jr., makes history when he is promoted to brigadier general in the U.S. Army Signal Corps, becoming the first African-American ever to reach general in that branch of service.

1977   Clifford Alexander, Jr., becomes the first Black Secretary of the Army. In this capacity, he supervises 1.3 million regular Army personnel and 370,000 civilians.

1978   Maj. Fredrick D. Gregory and Guion S. Bluford, Jr., along with Dr. Ronald McNair, begin astronaut training.

U.S. Air Force four-star general, Daniel "Chappie" James, Jr., dies.

1979   Secretary of the Army Clifford Alexander promotes five Black colonels to the rank of brigadier general. They are: Arthur Holmes, John Michel Brown, Colin Powell, John Forte, and Edward Honor.

Frank E. Petersen, Jr., becomes the first Black General in the Marine Corps history.

The Navy announces that all ship and shore commanders are ordered to fight racism with the full power of their office.

Second Lt. Marcella A. Hayes earns her aviator wings and becomes the first Black woman pilot in United States Armed Forces history.

1980   Hazel W. Johnson becomes the first Black female brigadier general and chief of the U.S. Army Nurse Corps.

1982   General Roscoe Robinson, Jr., becomes the first African-American four-star general in the United States Army, and the second Black to achieve that rank in the U.S. Armed Forces.

1983   Col. Guion S. Bluford, Jr., a jet fighter pilot with a doctorate in mechanical engineering, becomes America's first Black astronaut in space when the space shuttle, *Challenger,* is launched on August 20.

1985   Brig. Gen. Sheridan Cadoria becomes the second African-American woman to be promoted to that rank and the first woman—Black or White—who was not a nurse to be promoted to general. As director of manpower and personnel of the Joint Chiefs of Staff, Brig. Gen. Sheridan Cadoria is the highest ranking African-American woman in the U.S. Army.

1986   Ronald E. McNair, a physicist and graduate of the Massachusetts Institute of Technology, is killed, along with the rest of the space shuttle crew aboard the ill-fated *Challenger* in January.

Lt. Gen. Colin Powell takes command of the 72,000-member Fifth U.S. Corps in Frankfurt, West Germany, in July 1986. A few months later, President Ronald Reagan summons Colonel Powell to the White House to serve as deputy to National Security Advisor Frank Carlucci.

1987   Mae C. Jemison becomes the first Black female astronaut when she is selected as a candidate in June. Dr. Jemison holds two degrees: a bachelor of science in chemical engineering and a doctorate in medicine.

Brig. Gen. Fred A. Gorden is appointed commandant of cadets at the U.S. Military Academy, at West Point, becoming the first African-American commandant in the school's 185-year history.

Bernard P. Randolph, a four-star general, becomes the highest ranking African-American officer in the military. The general is the second Black four-star general in the Air Force and only the third in the nation's history.

Gen. Colin Powell succeeds Frank Carlucci as National Security Advisor, becoming the first African-American to hold that position. In this highly sensitive position, General Powell is the president's eyes and ears for coordinating all activities of the State Department, the Central Intelligence Agency, the Department of Defense, and other major government agencies.

1988   Brig. Gen. Clara Adams-Ender becomes the second African-American to be appointed chief of the U.S. Army Nurse Corps.

Lieutenant General Frank E. Petersen, Jr., Commanding General of Marine Corps Development and Education at Quantico, Virginia, retires. General Petersen leaves the service as the senior ranking aviator in the U.S. Marine Corps and the U.S. Navy.

1989   Lt. Gen. Colin L. Powell is promoted to four-star general in April. He returns to field duty at his headquarters at Fort McPherson, Georgia, where he is in command of more than 250,000 active duty soldiers and more than 300,000 Reservists and National Guardsmen.

Gen. Colin Powell makes military history when he is sworn in by Defense Secretary Dick Cheney as the twelfth chairman of the Joint Chiefs of Staff and the first African-American ever to hold that position.

Maj. Gen. Wallace C. Arnold is appointed as the Army's ROTC Cadet Commander at Fort Monroe, Virginia. In this capacity, the General is responsible for the recruiting and training of seventy percent of the Army's future officers. According to General Arnold, the purpose of the ROTC program is to "create better young Americans by teaching them self-respect, respect for each other, self-discipline, and teamwork."

1990   Brig. Gen. Marcelite J. Harris becomes the first Black woman to earn the rank of brigadier general in U.S. Air Force history, and the first female vice commander of Oklahoma City Logistics Center at Tinker Air Force Base.

Col. Frederick Gregory becomes the first African-American to command a space shuttle mission. When the space shuttle *Discovery* swoops down over the Mojave Desert and makes a perfect landing at Edwards Air Force Base, Colonel Gregory is at the controls. The Colonel not only commands the shuttle *Discovery*, he also directs the deployment of the shuttle's highly classified payload.

Saddam Hussein's Iraqi Army invades Kuwait on August 2. Chairman of the Joint Chiefs of Staff Gen. Colin Powell plays an integral role in the ultimate success of Operation DESERT STORM.

1991   Forty percent of the thirty-five thousand women who fight in this war are African-American; three of these women give their lives to the cause.

Cynthia Mosely receives the Bronze Star for Meritorious Service for her outstanding effort in Operation DESERT STORM.

1993   Anthony Weston is promoted to Rear Admiral, becoming one of the youngest admirals in the U.S. Navy and the first African-American Submarine Commander to attain the rank of admiral. He serves as Deputy Director for Operations at the National Military Command Center at the Pentagon.

1995   Retired chairman of the Joint Chiefs of Staff, Colin L. Powell, publishes his memoirs, *My American Journey*. His book jumps to number one on the *New York Times'* best seller list.

On November 22, Colin Powell ends weeks of speculation about his presidential aspirations when he announces that he will not be a candidate for the office.

BLACK CONGRESSIONAL MEDAL OF HONOR RECIPIENTS

It is interesting to note that there were no African-American recipients of the Congressional Medal of Honor during World War I, World War II, or the Gulf War. The Department of Defense (DOD) has initiated a review of the records of decorated African-American servicemen and women who served in these wars to determine whether or not this is due to racial discrimination. At the time of the publication of this volume, the DOD had not yet reached any conclusions.

The reasons indicated for each of the following awards are—in every instance—those given in the official records.

THE CIVIL WAR 1861-1865:

Landsman Aaron Anderson, USS *Wyandank*, Mattox Creek, Virginia, March 17, 1865. Wounded and lying on his back. Anderson rendered gallant assistance by loading his cannon and firing with great precision, killing and wounding many of the enemy.

Pvt. William H. Barnes, Company C, Thirty-eighth U.S. Colored Troops, Chapin's Farm, Virginia, September 29, 1864. Barnes was among the first to penetrate the enemy fortification despite the fact that he was severely wounded.

1st Sgt. Powhattan Beatty, Company G, Fifth U.S. Colored Troops, Chapin's Farm, Virginia, September 29, 1864. Sergeant Beatty gallantly assumed command of Company G after all the officers were killed or wounded.

Robert Blake, contraband (a slave who had escaped the Union forces, not an enlisted man) USS Marblehead, Stone River, South Carolina, December 25, 1862. Cited for displaying extraordinary courage and intelligence in the discharge of his duty under extremely hazardous circumstances.

1st Sgt. James E. Bronson, Company D, Fifth U.S. Colored Troops, Chapin's Farm, Virginia, September 29, 1864. Bronson gallantly assumed the command of Company D after all the officers were killed or wounded.

Landsman William H. Brown, USS Brooklyn, Mobile Bay, Alabama, August 5, 1864. During successful attacks against Fort Morgan, rebel gunboats, and the ram Tennessee, Brown was stationed in the immediate vicinity of the shell whips, which were twice cleared of men by bursting shells. Brown remained steadfast at his post and performed his duties in the powder division throughout the furious action, which resulted in the surrender of the prized rebel ram *Tennessee*, and in the damaging and destruction of batteries at Fort Morgan.

Landsman Wilson Brown, USS *Hartford*, Mobile Bay, Alabama, August 5, 1864. During successful attacks against Fort Morgan, rebel gunboats, and the ram *Tennessee*, Brown was knocked unconscious into the hold of the ship when enemy shell bursts fatally wounded a man on the ladder above him. Upon regaining consciousness, Brown promptly returned to the shell whip on the berth deck and zealously continued to perform his duties although four of the six men at this station had been either killed or wounded by the enemy's terrific fire.

Sgt. William H. Carney, Company C, Fifty-fourth Massachusetts Colored Infantry, Ft. Wagner, South Carolina, June 18, 1863. During the Battle of Fort Wagner, Carney seized the colors from a dying companion, threw away his rifle, and led the assault even though he had been wounded three times. Sergeant Carney was the first Black American to win the Congressional Medal of Honor.

Seaman Clement Dees, USS *Pontoosuc*, Cape Fear River, North Carolina, December 24, 1864. Dees was cited for extraordinary personal valor during a confrontation with enemy forces.

Sgt. Decatur Dorsey, Company B, Thirty-ninth U.S. Colored Troops, Petersburg, Virginia, June 15, 1864. Dorsey was cited for conspicuous gallantry while acting as regimental color sergeant.

Sgt. Maj. Christian A. Fleetwood, Fourth U.S. Colored Troops, Chapin's Farm, Virginia, September 29, 1864. After two color bearers were mortally wounded, Fleetwood seized the colors and carried them nobly throughout the battle.

Pvt. James Gardiner, Company I, Chapin's Farm, Virginia, September 29, 1864. Gardiner gallantly charged along, ahead of his brigade, shot a rebel officer who was on the parapet, and then ran him through with his bayonet.

Sgt. James H. Harris, Company B, Thirty-eighth U.S. Colored Troops, Chapin's Farm, Virginia, September 29, 1864. Sergeant Harris was cited for conspicuous gallantry during battle.

Sgt. Maj. Thomas Hawkins, Sixth U.S. Colored Troops, Deep Bottom, Virginia, July 21, 1864. While in the face of a murderous line of fire, the sergeant gallantly rescued the regimental colors from the grasp of the enemy

Sgt. Alfred B. Hilton, Company H, Fourth U.S. Colored Troops, Chapin's Farm, Virginia, September 29, 1864. Seizing the flag from a fellow sergeant who fell mortally wounded, Hilton carried the colors until the was shot down. As he fell, he held up the flag and shouted, "Boys, save the colors!"

Sgt. Maj. Milton M. Holland, Company C, Fifth U.S. Colored Troops, Chapin's Farm, Virginia, September 29, 1864. Sergeant Holland gallantly assumed command of Company C after all the officers were killed or wounded.

Cpl. Miles James, Company B, Thirty-sixth U.S. Colored Troops, Chapin's Farm, Virginia, September 29, 1864. Although his arm was shattered and required amputation, James continued to fight, urging his men on, loading and firing his piece with one arm. At the time, Corporal James was only thirty yards away from the enemy's front line.

1st Sgt. Alexander Kelly, Company F, Sixth U.S. Colored Troops, Chapin's Farm, Virginia, September 29, 1864. Sergeant Kelly displayed extraordinary courage by rallying his men at a time of confusion and in a place of great danger. He seized the colors that had fallen under the enemy's murderous line of fire and led his men in battle.

Landsman John H. Lawson, USS *Hartford*, Mobile Bay, Alabama, August 5, 1864. Though severely wounded in the leg by an exploding shell, Landsman Lawson refused to go below and remained at his station throughout the battle.

Seaman Joachim Pease, USS *Kearsarge*, Cherbourg, France, June 19, 1864. Pease was cited for extraordinary coolness and valor while under fire.

1st Sgt. Robert Pinn, Company I, Fifth U.S. Colored Troops, Chapin's Farm, Virginia, September 29, 1864. Pinn gallantly assumed command of Company I and led it in battle after all the officers were killed or wounded.

1st Sgt. Edward Radcliff, Company C, Thirty-eighth U.S. Colored Troops, Chapin's Farm, Virginia, September 29, 1864. Sergeant Radcliff took command of Company C and led it in battle after all the officers were killed or wounded.

Pvt. Charles Veal, Company D, Fourth U.S. Colored Troops, Chapin's Farm, Virginia, September 29, 1864. After two color bearers were killed close to the enemy's line of fire, Veal seized the colors and held them high throughout the battle.

THE INDIAN WARS 1870-1890:

Sgt. Benjamin Brown, Company C, Twenty-fourth U.S. Infantry, Cedar Springs and Fort Thomas, Arizona, May 11, 1889. Although shot in the abdomen in a fight between a paymaster's escort and robbers, Brown did not leave the field until wounded through both arms.

Sgt. Thomas Boyne, Troop C, Ninth U.S. Cavalry, Mimbus Mountains, New Mexico, May 29, 1879, and the Cuchillo Negro Mountains, New Mexico, September 27, 1879. Cited for extraordinary courage under fire.

Sgt. John Denny, Troop B, Ninth U.S. Cavalry, Las Animas Canyon, New Mexico, September 18, 1879. Though subjected to heavy enemy fire, Sergeant Denny rescued a wounded comrade.

Pvt. Pompey Factor, Indian Scout, Pecos River, Texas, April 25, 1875. With three other men, Factor participated in a charge against twenty-five hostiles while on a scouting patrol.

Cpl. Clinton Greaves, Troop C, Ninth U.S. Cavalry, Florida Mountains, New Mexico, January 24, 1877. Greaves was cited for conspicuous gallantry in hand-to-hand fighting against the hostiles.

Sgt. Henry Johnson, Troop D, Ninth U.S. Cavalry, Milk River, Colorado, October 2, 1879. Under heavy close-range fire, the sergeant fought his way to a creek and back to bring water to the wounded.

Sgt. George Jordan, Troop K, Ninth U.S. Cavalry, Carrizozo Canyon, New Mexico, August 12, 1881. Jordan stubbornly held his ground in the face of a far superior number of the enemy, forcing them back again and again, and preventing them from surrounding and destroying the command.

Cpl. Isaiah Mays, Company B, Twenty-fourth U.S. Infantry, Arizona, May 11, 1889. Cited for gallantry in the fight between the paymaster's escort and robbers. Mays walked and crawled two miles to a ranch for help.

Sgt. William McBryan, Troop K, Tenth U.S. Cavalry, Arizona, March 7, 1890. McBryan was cited for conspicuous gallantry in action against the Apache Indians.

Pvt. Adam Paine, Indian Scout, Canyon Blanco Tributary, Red River, Texas, September 26-27, 1874. Paine rendered invaluable service to Col. R. S. Mackenzie, Fourth U.S. Cavalry, during this engagement.

Trumpeter Isaac Payne, Indian Scout, Pecos River, Texas, April 25, 1875. With three other men, he participated in a charge against twenty-five hostiles while on a scouting patrol.

Sgt. Thomas Shaw, Troop K, Ninth U.S. Cavalry, Carrizozo Canyon, New Mexico, August 12, 1881. Sergeant Shaw stubbornly held his ground in the face of a far superior number of the enemy, forcing them back again and again, and preventing them from surrounding and destroying the command.

Sgt. Emanuel Stance, Troop F, Ninth U.S. Cavalry, Kickapoo Springs, Texas, May 20, 1870. The sergeant was cited for conspicuous gallantry on a scouting mission against the Indians.

Pvt. Augustus Walley, Troop I, Ninth U.S. Cavalry, the Cuchillo Negro Mountains, New Mexico, August 16, 1881. Walley displayed extraordinary gallantry in action against the Apaches.

Sgt. John Ward, Twenty-fourth U.S. Infantry Indian Scouts at Pecos River, Texas, April 25, 1875. With three other men, he participated in a charge against twenty-five hostiles while on a scouting patrol.

1st Sgt. Moses Williams, Troop I, Ninth U.S. Cavalry, the Cuchillo Negro Mountains, New Mexico, August 16, 1881. Williams was cited for extraordinary coolness, bravery, and devotion to duty in standing by his commanding officer under heavy fire from a large group of Indians. Through his actions, Sergeant Williams saved the lives of at least three of his fellow soldiers.

Cpl. William O. Wilson, Troop I, Ninth U.S. Cavalry, the Cuchillo Negro Mountains, New Mexico, 1890. Cited for extraordinary gallantry against the Sioux Indians in the Campaign of 1890.

Sgt. Brent Woods, Troop B, Ninth U.S. Cavalry, Carrizozo Canyon, New Mexico, August 19, 1881. Through his gallantry in action, Sergeant Woods saved the lives of his fellow soldiers and the citizens of the detachment.

THE INTERIM PERIOD 1871-1901:

Seaman John Davis, USS *Trenton*, Toulon, France, February 1881. Jumping overboard, Davis rescued Coxswain Augustus Ohlensen from drowning.

Seaman Alphonse Girandy, USS *Petrel*, Manilla Bay, the Philippines, March 31, 1901. Girandy was cited for heroism and gallantry. He fearlessly exposed his own life in order to save others on the occasion of a fire on board his vessel.

Seaman John Johnson, USS *Kansas*, Greytown, Nicaragua, April 12, 1872. Johnson displayed great coolness and self-possession when Comdr. A. F. Crosman and others drowned, and, by extraordinary heroism and personal exertion, prevented greater loss of life.

Cooper William Johnson, USS *Adams*, Mare Island, California, November 14, 1879. Johnson rescued Daniel W. Kloppen, a workman, from drowning.

Seaman Joseph B. Neil, USS *Powhattan*, Norfolk, Virginia, December 26, 1873. Neil saved Boatswain J. G. Watson from drowning.

Seaman John Smith, USS *Shenandoah*, Rio de Janeiro, Brazil, September 19, 1880. Smith jumped overboard and rescued Fireman First Class James Grady from drowning.

Seaman Robert Sweeney, USS *Kearsarge*, Hampton Roads, Virginia, October 26, 1881. Sweeney jumped overboard and helped save a shipmate, who had fallen overboard into a strongly running tide, from drowning. Second award: USS *Jamestown*, Navy Yard, New York, New York, December 20, 1883. Sweeney rescued A. A. George, who had fallen overboard.

THE SPANISH-AMERICAN WAR 1898:

Ship's Cook Daniel Atkins, Torpedo Boat *Cushing*, February 1, 1898. Cited for heroism displayed in saving Lt. Joseph C. Breckenridge from drowning.

Sgt. Maj. Edward L. Baker, Tenth U.S. Cavalry, Santiago, Cuba, July 1, 1898. The sergeant was cited for extraordinary bravery displayed in rescuing a wounded comrade under heavy fire.

Pvt. Dennis Bell, Troop H, Tenth U.S. Cavalry, Tayabacoa, Cuba, June 30, 1898. After his comrades had been forced to withdraw to their landing craft, Bell went back ashore in the face of murderous fire laid down by the enemy to rescue his wounded comrades, who had fallen into the hands of the enemy and would have otherwise perished.

Pvt. Fitz Lee, Troop M, Tenth U.S. Cavalry, Tayabacoa, Cuba, June 30, 1898. After his comrades had been forced to withdraw to their landing craft, Lee went back ashore in the face of murderous fire laid down by the enemy to rescue his wounded comrades, who had fallen into the hands of the enemy and would have otherwise perished.

Fireman 1st Class Robert Penn, USS *Iowa*, Guantanamo Bay, Cuba, July 20, 1898. Although there was clear and eminent danger of an explosion, Penn displayed marked coolness and gallantry as he continued to fire two boilers while standing on a board one foot above boiling water blowing from the boiler under 120 pounds of pressure.

Pvt. William H. Thompkins, Troop M, Tenth U.S. Cavalry, Tayabacoa, Cuba, June 30, 1898. After his comrades had been forced to withdraw to their landing craft, Thompkins went back ashore in the face of murderous fire laid down by the enemy to rescue his wounded comrades, who had fallen into the hands of the enemy and would have otherwise perished.

Pvt. George Wanton, Troop M, Tenth U.S. Cavalry, Tayabacoa, Cuba, June 30, 1898. After his comrades had been forced to withdraw to their landing craft, Wanton went back ashore in the face of murderous fire laid down by the enemy to rescue his wounded comrades, who had fallen into the hands of the enemy and would have otherwise perished.

THE KOREAN WAR 1950-1953:

Sgt. Cornelius H. Charlton, Company C, Twenty-fourth Infantry, Chipo-Ri, Korea, June 2, 1951. The sergeant displayed conspicuous gallantry and intrepidity above and beyond the call of duty in action against the enemy. A grenade severely wounded Sergeant Charlton in the chest as he led his men up hill 542, but he kept coming. As he approached the enemy stronghold, another series exploded around him. With his dying strength, he fired a burst that eliminated the enemy, and his men were able to take hill 542.

Pvt. 1st Class William Thompson, Company M, Twenty-fourth Infantry, Haman, Korea, August 6, 1950. Private Thompson distinguished himself by conspicuous gallantry and intrepidity above and beyond the call of duty. He single-handedly held off a large attacking body of enemy, protecting his fellow soldiers, who were withdrawing.

THE VIETNAM WAR 1965-1973:

Pvt. 1st Class James Anderson, Jr., Company F, Second Battalion, Third Marine Division, Cam Lo, Vietnam, February 28, 1967. Private Anderson was cited for conspicuous gallantry and intrepidity above and beyond the call of duty in action. Anderson enclosed a live grenade with his own body and took the full impact of the blast, saving the lives of his fellow soldiers. He was killed instantly.

Sgt. 1st Class Webster Anderson, Battery A, Second Battalion, 320th Artillery, 101st Airborne Division, Tan Ky, Vietnam, October 15, 1967. The sergeant was cited for conspicuous gallantry and intrepidity above and beyond the call of duty in action against the enemy.

Sgt. 1st Class Eugene Ashley, Jr., Company C, Fifth Special Forces Group (Airborne), First Special Forces, Camp Lang Vei, Vietnam, October 12, 1971. Ashley was cited for conspicuous gallantry in action against the enemy. After leading his men in a successful assault on enemy forces that were dug in on a hill, Sergeant Ashley was killed by an exploding artillery shell.

Pvt. 1st Class Oscar P. Austin, Company E, Second Battalion, First Marine Division, Da Nang, Vietnam, February 23, 1969. With extraordinary courage and complete disregard for his own personal safety, Private Austin was killed when he exposed his body to enemy fire to prevent a wounded fellow soldier from being hit.

Sgt. Rodney M. Davis, Company C, Third Reconnaissance Battalion, Third Marine Division, Quang Nam Province, Vietnam, September 6, 1967. Cited for conspicuous gallantry and selfless devotion to duty. Sergeant Davis threw himself on a live grenade to save the lives of the men in his platoon.

Pvt. 1st Class Robert H. Jenkins, Company C, Third Reconnaissance Battalion, Third Marine Division, south of the Demilitarized Zone (DMZ), Vietnam, March 5, 1969. Displaying conspicuous gallantry and intrepidity with complete disregard for his own personal safety, Jenkins, while manning a machine gun, used his own body to shield a fellow soldier from the full impact of a grenade that exploded in their midst.

Spc. Lawrence Joel, Headquarters and Headquarters Company, First Battalion (Airborne), 503d Infantry, 173d Airborne Brigade, Phu Coung, Vietnam, November 8, 1956. Medical Aidman Joel, though seriously wounded himself and exposed to murderous enemy fire, continued to care for the wounded. Specialist Joel was cited for gallantry and intrepidity and risk of his own life above and beyond the call of duty.

Spc. Dwight H. Johnson, Company B, First Battalion, Sixty-ninth Armor, Fourth Infantry Division, Dak To Kontum Province, Vietnam, January 15, 1968. Johnson was cited for conspicuous gallantry and complete disregard for his personal safety. Armed with only a .45-caliber pistol, he climbed out of his tank and took on the enemy single-handedly, killing several. After emptying his pistol, he returned to his tank for a machine gun and ran back into a murderous barrage laid down by the enemy. Specialist Johnson coolly eliminated several more of the enemy and rescued several of his fellow soldiers.

Pvt. 1st Class Ralph H. Johnson, Company A, First Reconnaissance Battalion, First Marine Division, Ap Dong, Vietnam, March 5, 1968. Private Johnson was cited for conspicuous gallantry and selfless devotion to duty when, as part of a recon patrol inside enemy lines, he threw his body on a live grenade, saving the lives of two of his comrades.

Pvt. 1st Class Garfield M. Langhorn, Troop C, Seventh Squadron (Airmobile), Seventeenth Cavalry, First Aviation Brigade, Quang Nam Province, Vietnam, September 6, 1969. Risking his own life, Private Langhorn threw himself on a live grenade that was thrown in amongst a group of wounded comrades he was trying to rescue.

Sgt. Matthew Leonard, Company B, First Battalion, Sixteenth Infantry Division, Suoi Da, Vietnam, 1967. Sergeant Leonard was cited for conspicuous gallantry and selfless devotion to duty for withstanding numerous assaults by a superior force of enemy troops and, although wounded several times, exhibiting extraordinary courage and leadership under fire.

Sgt. Donald R. Long, Troop C, First Squadron, Fourth Cavalry, First Cavalry Division, Phu Coung, June 30, 1966. Under an intense barrage by the Vietcong, Long was aiding in the evacuation of the wounded by helicopter. When a live grenade was thrown into the midst of the wounded, Sergeant Long threw his own body on the grenade to save the lives of his fellow soldiers.

Pvt. 1st Class Milton L. Olive, III, Company B, 503d Infantry, 173d Airborne Brigade, Phu Coung, Vietnam, October 22, 1965. Olive was cited for conspicuous gallantry and intrepidity above and beyond the call of duty in action against the enemy. Private Olive saved the lives of his comrades by throwing himself on a live grenade and taking the full impact of the blast with his own body.

Capt. Riley L. Pitts, Company C, Second Battalion, Twenty-seventh Infantry, Twenty-fifth Infantry Division, Ap Dong, Vietnam, October 31, 1967. Pitts was cited for conspicuous gallantry and selfless devotion to duty. While leading an airmobile assault, Captain Pitts threw himself on a live grenade to save his men. Fortunately, it did not explode. He was later killed in a fire fight.

Lt. Col. Charles C. Rogers, First Battalion, Fifth Artillery, First Infantry Division, Fishook Province, Vietnam, November 1, 1968. Rogers was cited for conspicuous gallantry under fire. The colonel's display of fighting spirit, heroic leadership, and courage while under fire prevented his men from being overrun by a numerically superior enemy force.

1st Lt. Ruppert L. Sargent, Headquarters and Headquarters Company, Third Battalion, Sixtieth Infantry, Ninth Infantry Division, Hau Nghia Province, Vietnam, March 15, 1967. Lt. Ruppert Sargent was cited for conspicuous gallantry and selfless devotion to duty on the day he was killed in action.

Spc. Clarence E. Sasser, Headquarters and Headquarters Company, Third Battalion, Sixtieth Infantry, Ninth Infantry Division, Ding Tuong Province, Vietnam, January 10, 1968. Sasser was cited for conspicuous gallantry and intrepidity above and beyond the call of duty. Though severely wounded, Medical Aidman Sasser heroically tended to others for several hours, repeatedly refusing to leave his wounded comrades.

Sgt. Chester Sims, Company D, Second Battalion (Airborne), 501st Infantry, 101st Airborne Division, Hue Province, Vietnam, February 21, 1968. Sims was cited for conspicuous gallantry and selfless devotion to duty. While on a search and destroy mission, Sergeant Sims, a squad leader, threw himself on a booby trap and absorbed the explosion with his own body, saving the lives of his men.

1st Lt. John E. Warren, Jr., Company C, Second Battalion (Mechanized), Twenty-second Infantry, Twenty-fifth Infantry Division, Quang Nam, Vietnam, January 14, 1969. Lieutenant Warren was cited for gallantry and selfless devotion to duty. He and his platoon were ambushed by a well-dug-in enemy and a grenade was thrown into their midst. Lieutenant Warren threw his body on top of the grenade and saved the lives of several of his men.

CONGRESSIONAL MEDAL OF HONOR CITATION
LT. COL. CHARLES C. ROGERS
READS AS FOLLOWS:

Rank and organization: Lieutenant Colonel, U.S. Army, 1st Battalion, 5th Artillery, 1st Infantry Division. Place and Date: Fishook, near Cambodian border, Republic of Vietnam, 1 November 1968. Citation: For conspicuous gallantry and intrepidity in action at the risk of his life above and beyond the call of duty, Lt. Col. Rogers, Field Artillery, distinguished himself in action while serving as commanding officer, 1st Battalion, during the defense of a forward fire support base. In the early morning hours, the fire support base was subjected to a concentrated bombardment of heavy mortar, rocket and rocket-propelled grenade fire.

Simultaneously, the position was struck by a human wave ground assault, led by sappers who breached the defensive barriers with bangalore torpedoes and penetrated the defensive perimeter. Lt. Col. Rogers, with complete disregard for his safety, moved through the hail of fragments from bursting enemy rounds to the embattled area. He aggressively rallied the dazed artillery crewmen to their howitzers and he directed their fire on the assaulting enemy. Although knocked to the ground and wounded by an exploding round, Lt. Col. Rogers sprang to his feet and led a small counterattack force against the enemy element that had penetrated the howitzer position. Although painfully wounded a second time during the assault, Lt. Col. Rogers pressed the attack, killing several of the enemy and driving the remainder from their positions.

Refusing medical treatment, Lt. Col. Rogers re-established and reinforced the defensive positions. As a second human wave attack was launched against another sector of the perimeter, Lt. Col. Rogers directed artillery fire on the assaulting enemy and led a second counterattack against the charging forces. His valorous example rallied the beleaguered defenders to repulse and defeat the enemy onslaught. Lt. Col. Rogers moved from position to position through the heavy enemy fire, giving encouragement and direction to his men. At dawn, the determined enemy launched a third assault against the fire base in an attempt to overrun the position. Lt. Col. Rogers moved to the threatened area and directed lethal fire on the enemy forces.

Seeing a howitzer inoperative due to casualties, Lt. Col. Rogers joined the surviving members of the crew to return the howitzer into action. While directing the position defense, Lt. Col. Rogers was seriously wounded by fragments from a heavy mortar round which exploded on the parapet of the gun position. Although too severely wounded to physically lead the defenders, Lt. Col. Rogers continued to give encouragement and direction to his men in the defeating and repelling of the enemy attack. Lt. Col. Rogers' dauntless courage and heroism inspired the defenders of the fire support base to the heights of valor to defeat a determined and numerically superior enemy force.

His relentless spirit of aggressiveness in action are in the highest traditions of the military service and reflect great credit upon himself, his unit, and the U.S. Army.

CONGRESSIONAL MEDAL OF HONOR CITATION
SGT. 1ST CLASS WILLIAM M. BRYANT

READS AS FOLLOWS:

Rank and organization: Sergeant First Class, U.S. Army, Company A, 5th Special Forces Group, 1st Special Forces. Place and date: Long Khanh Province, Republic of Vietnam, 24 March 1969. Entered service at: Detroit, Michigan. Born: 16 February 1933, Cochran, Georgia. Citation: For conspicuous gallantry and intrepidity in action at the risk of his life above and beyond the call of duty. Sfc. Bryant, assigned to Company A, distinguished himself while serving as commanding officer of Civilian Irregular Defense Group Company 321, 2d Battalion, 3d Mobile Strike Force Command, during combat operations. The battalion came under heavy fire and became surrounded by the elements of three enemy regiments. Sfc. Bryant displayed extraordinary heroism throughout the succeeding 34 hours of incessant attack as he moved throughout the company position heedless of the intense hostile fire while establishing and improving the defensive perimeter, directing fire during critical phases of the battle, distributing ammunition, assisting the wounded, and providing the leadership and inspirational example of courage to his men. When a helicopter drop of ammunition was made to resupply the beleaguered force, Sfc. Bryant with complete disregard for his safety, ran through the heavy enemy fire to retrieve the scattered ammunition boxes and distributed needed ammunition to his men. During a lull in the intense fighting, Sfc. Bryant led a patrol outside the perimeter to obtain information on the enemy. The patrol came under intense automatic weapons fire and was pinned down. Sfc. Bryant singlehandedly repulsed one enemy attack on his small force and by his heroic action inspired his men to fight off other assaults. Seeing a wounded enemy soldier some distance from the patrol location, Sfc. Bryant crawled forward alone under heavy fire to retrieve the soldier for intelligence purposes. Finding that the enemy soldier had expired, Sfc. Bryant crawled back to his patrol and led his men back to the company position where he again took command of the defense. As the siege continued, Sfc. Bryant organized and led a patrol in a daring attempt to break through the enemy encirclement. The patrol had advanced some 200 meters by heavy fighting when it was pinned down by the intense automatic weapons fire from heavily fortified bunkers and Sfc. Bryant was severely wounded. Despite his wounds, he rallied his men, called for helicopter gunship support, and directed heavy suppressive fire upon the enemy positions. Following the last gunship attack, Sfc. Bryant fearlessly charged an enemy automatic weapons position, overrunning it, and singlehandedly destroying its three defenders. Inspired by his heroic example, his men renewed their attack on the entrenched enemy. While regrouping his small force for the final assault against the enemy, Sfc. Bryant fell mortally wounded by an enemy rocket. Sfc. Bryant's selfless concern for his comrades, at the cost of his life above and beyond the call of duty are in keeping with the highest traditions of the military service and reflect great credit upon himself, his unit, and the U.S. Army.

BIBLIOGRAPHY

Baker, G.P. *Hannibal.* New York: Dodd Mead & Company, 1929.

Bergerson, Louis. *France under Napoleon.* Princeton, New Jersey: Princeton University Press, 1981.

Bourrine, Louis. *Antoine de Fauvelet (Napoleon's private secretary) Memoirs of Napoleon Bonaparte.* Vol. II, Vol. II. New York: Charles Scribner & Son, 1906.

Bradford, Ernle. *Hannibal.* New York: McGraw Hill Brook Company, 1981.

Cashin, Herschel V., Charles Alexander, William T. Anderson, Arthur M. Brown, and Horace W. Bivins. *Under Fire with the Tenth U.S. Cavalry.* Chicago: American Publishing House, 1902.

Clift, Virgil A., and W.A. Low, eds. *Encyclopedia of Black America.* New York: McGraw-Hill Book Company, 1981.

Cole, Hubert. *The Betrayers, Joachim and Caroline Murat.* New York: Saturday Review Press, 1962.

Cromwell, John W. *The Negro in American History.* Washington, DC: The American Negro Academy, 1914.

DeBeer, Sir Gavin. *Hannibal, Challenging Rome's Supremacy.* New York: The Viking Press, 1969.

DeCaulaincourt, General Duke of Vicenza. *With Napoleon in Russia.* New York: William Morrow and Company, 1935.

Delderfield, R.F. *Napoleon's Marshals.* New York. Philadelphia: Chilton Books, 1962.

DuBois, W.E.B.. *Black Reconstruction.* New York: Harcourt, Brace and Company, 1935.

Franklin, John Hope. *From Slavery to Freedom.* New York: Alfred A. Knopf, 1964.

Franklin, John Hope, and Isadore Starr. *The Negro in Twentieth Century America.* New York: Vintage Books, 1967.

Garlan, Yvon. *War in the Ancient World.* New York: W.W. Norton & Company, 1975.

Gorman, Herbert. *The Incredible Marquis Alexander Dumas.* New York: Farrar & Rhinehart, Inc., 1926.

Gurney, Gene. *The United States Army in War and Peace, from Colonial Times to Vietnam.* New York: Crown Publishers, Inc., 1966.

Higginson, Thomas Wentworth. *Army Life in a Black Regiment.* Boston: Beacon Press, 1962.

Katz, William Loren. *Eyewitness, The Negro in American History*. New York: Pitman Publishing Corporation, 1967

Morris, Donald R. *The Washing on the Spears*. New York: Simon and Schuster, 1969.

Nelson, William H., and Harold T. Dunbar. *Journal of Negro History*. Vol. 2. Washington, DC: Associated Publishers, Inc., 1953.

Ploski, Harry A. and Roscoe C. Brown, Jr. *The Negro Almanac*. New York: Bellwether Publishing Company, Inc., 1967.

Ploski, Harry A. and James Williams. *The Negro Almanac, A Reference Work on the Afro-American*. 4th ed. New York: John Wiley & Sons, 1983.

Pratt, Fletcher. *Road to Empire, The Life and Times of Bonaparte the General*. New York: Doubleday, Doran & Company, Inc., 1939.

Quarles, Benjamin. *The Negro in the American Revolution*. Chapel Hill, North Carolina: The University of North Carolina Press, 1969.

_____. *The Negro in the Civil War*. Boston: Little, Brown and Company, 1953.

Rogers, J.A. *World's Great Men of Color*. Vol. I. New York: Futuro Press Inc., 1947.

Rose, Robert A. *Lonely Eagles*. Los Angeles: Tuskegee Airmen, Inc., Los Angeles Chapter, 1976.

Steward, T.G. *The Colored Regulars in the United States Army*. Philadelphia: A.M.E. Book Concern, 1904.

Wakin, Edward. *Black Fighting Men in U.S. History*. New York: Lothrop, Lee & Shepard Company, 1971.

Wesley, Charles H., and Patricia W. Romero. *Afro-Americans in the Civil War, from Slavery to Citizenship*, Pennsylvania: The Publishers Agency, Inc., 1978.

Webster's Biographical Dictionary. Massachusetts: G & C Merriam Company, 1970.

Wilson, Joseph T. *The Black Phalanx*. Hartford: 1882.

Woodson, Carter Godwin, and Charles H. Wesley. *The Negro in Our History*. Washington, DC: Associated Publishers, Inc., 1962.

Index

Greene, Rear Adm. Everett L., ix, 140-141
Green Mountain Boys, 195
Greer, Maj. Gen. Edward, 115-116
Gregg, Lt. Gen. Arthur, 104
Gregory, Maj. Fredrick D., 208, 210
Groton Heights, Battle of, 197
Guam, 148
    Agana, 144, 152
    Andersen Air Force Base, 156, 185

Hacker, Rear Adm. Benjamin T., 150
Haggard, Sir Henry Rider, xxiv
Haig, Douglas, xxiv
Haiti, xxi, xxiii, 18
Hall, Lt. Charles, 202, 203
Hall, Brig. Gen. David M., 183
Hall, Maj. Gen. Titus C., 177
Hamlet, Maj. Gen. James F., 116-117
Hammerhead, USS, 146
Hancock, John, 173, 182, 197
Hancock, USS, 152
Hannibal, xv-xxi
Hanno, xix
Hartford, USS, 212, 213
Hasdrubal, xix-xx
Harmon, Leonard Roy, 202
Harris, Sgt. James H., 212
Harris, Maj. Gen. Marcelite J., 162-163, 209
Hawaii, 42
    Camp H. M. Smith, 65, 102, 121, 185
    Fort Shafter, 86
    Hickam Air Force Base, 156, 186
    Pearl Harbor, 32, 146, 201, 203
    Schofield Barracks, 66-67, 83, 86, 103, 109
Hawkins, Sgt. Maj. Thomas, 212
Hayes, Lt. Marcella A., 208
Haynes, Lemuel, ix, 195
Hector, Edward, 196
Height, Dorothy I., 206
Hell Fighters, 5, 201
Hessian, 196
Hickerson, Col. R. P., 13
Higginson, Col. Thomas, ix, 198
Hilton, Sgt. Alfred B., 212
Holland, Sgt. Maj. Milton M., 199, 212
Holmes, Maj. Gen. Arthur, 117, 208
Honor, Brig. Gen. Edward, 104-105
Hopper, Brig. Gen. John D., Jr., 168-169
Hunter, Maj. Gen. David, 198
Hunter, Brig. Gen. Milton, 84-85
Hussein, Saddam, 49, 210
Hyksos, xv

Idaho, Idaho Falls, 149
Illinois, 73, 142, 173
    Camp Grant, 19
    Chanute Air Force Base, 162
    Chicago, 21, 126, 128, 146
    Fort Sheridan, 58, 126, 150
    Great Lakes, 30, 138, 203
    Rock Island, 60, 76
    Scott Air Force Base, 36, 168, 176-177, 183-185

Impervious, USS, 151
Indiana, 64, 123, 186
    Bloomington, 70
    Fort Benjamin Harrison, 62, 108
    Freeman Field, 23
    Gary, 183
    Indianapolis, 108, 124
    Seymour, 23, 187
Indian War, 195
Ingraham, USS, 151
Iowa, 198
    Des Moines, 201
    Iowa City, 186
Iowa, USS, 30, 200, 215
Iran, Doshan Tappeh Air Base, 164
Italy, xxiii, 88, 90
    Alps, xv-xviii, xxii, 27
    Anzio, 22
    Apulia, xv
    Arcadia, xvi
    Aulla, 27
    Bologna, 27
    Genoa, 27
    Ligurian Sea, 27
    Naples, xv, xxii, 150, 172
    Padua, xv
    Po Valley, 27
    Rome, xv-xviii, xx-xxi
    Samnium, xv
    Sicily, 22
    Taranto, 22
    Turin, 27
    Udine, 22

Jackson, Gen. Andrew, 2, 197
Jacksonville, USS, 146
James, Brig. Gen. Avon C., 184
James, General Daniel "Chappie," Jr., x, 12, 15, 34-37, 44, 207, 208
James, Cpl. Miles, 212
Jamestown, USS, 215
Japan, 6, 50, 80, 109
    Camp Zama, 38
    Johnson Air Base, 177, 187
    Kadena Air Base, 162
    Okinawa, 42-43
    Sarebo, 149
    Shiroi Air Base, 177
Jason, USS, 151
J. Douglass Blackwood, USS, 134
Jemison, Mae C., 209
Jenkins, Ensign Joseph C., 217
Jenkins, Pvt. 1st Class Robert H., 217
Jiggetts, Brig. Gen. Charles B., 185
Joel, Spc. Lawrence, 217
Johnson, President Andrew, 200
Johnson, Cooper William, 215
Johnson, Spc. Dwight H., 217
Johnson, Sgt. Maj. Gilbert H. "Hashmark," 207
Johnson, Brig. Gen. Hazel W., x, 12, 15, 38-40, 208
Johnson, Sgt. Henry, 201, 213
Johnson, Seaman John, 215
Johnson, Louis, 23

ABOUT THE AUTHOR

Henry Dabbs is a writer, film producer and director, painter, and designer. After graduating from the Pratt Institute, Dabbs became an advertising executive. In this role, he created the visual identity of numerous national accounts such as Procter and Gamble, General Mills, and General Motors, and launched an acclaimed minority recruitment program for the U.S. Navy.

During the turbulent 1960s, while others fought with didactic rhetoric, Mr. Dabbs spoke volumes with his paintbrush. Forty-eight of his paintings were in the Smithsonian Institution collection for more than twenty years. This series, entitled "Afro-American Panorama" depicts the history of Black achievement in this nation's history.

Dabbs is also the author of *Afro-American History Highlights*, a definitive survey of Black history—from the Olduvai Gorge to the Freedom Marches—and the Afro-American history section of the *New York Times Encyclopedic Almanac*. Dabbs also created the *Afro-American Fact Pak*, the first multimedia publication to deal with Black history, and a Black history video program of more than sixty-one volumes.

Mr. Dabbs retired from Madison Avenue several years ago to start Henry Dabbs Productions, a communications firm in Orlando, Florida.

Henry Dabbs and the Vice President of the United States, Hubert H. Humphrey, at the opening of a one-man show of Dabbs's African-American history paintings at the Frederick Douglass Museum in Washington, DC.